Television

A MEDIA STUDENT'S GUIDE

DAVID McQUEEN

A member of the Hodder Headline Group
LONDON • NEW YORK • SYDNEY • AUCKLAND

First published in Great Britain in 1998 by
Arnold, a member of the Hodder Headline Group,
338 Euston Road, London NW1 3BH

http://www.arnoldpublishers.com

Co-published in the United States of America by
Oxford University Press Inc.,
198 Madison Avenue, New York, NY 10016

British Library Cataloguing in Publication Data
A catalogue record for this book is available from the British Library

Library of Congress Cataloging-in-Publication Data
A catalog record for this book is available from the Library of Congress

Production Editor: Wendy Rooke
Production Controller: Priya Gohil
Cover Design: Stefan Brazzo

ISBN 0 340 70604 X (pb)
ISBN 0 340 71976 1 (hb)

Composition in 10/12½pt Sabon by
Phoenix Photosetting, Chatham, Kent
Printed and bound in Great Britain by
J W Arrowsmith Ltd, Bristol

For Sarah and Tom

Contents

Preface

This book is a comprehensive guide to the study of television that is designed to be read independently by students and also serve as a course book for use by teachers. It is intended to be an essential reader for 'A' level media students and an introductory text for degree students.

Each part offers a detailed introduction to the body of knowledge – theoretical, historical and practical – that is required for this important area of study at 'A' level and beyond. The major television genres are covered as well as those concepts and debates that relate specifically to the medium. The material is 'student friendly' to the extent that it aims to present complex debates, theories and histories in a thorough but concise and clear manner. Certain subjects lend themselves to be studied at the beginning or end of a course, depending on their intrinsic complexity. Hence more complex areas of study such as ideology or semiotics are placed at the end of the guide.

The material can be used in the classroom or for private study. Similarly, the Exercises and Essays section at the end of each chapter includes practical and theoretical group work (some of which will require access to technology and perhaps a tutor's assistance) as well as tasks for students to do individually. These tasks vary in level to reflect the broad spectrum of students at 'A' level and above who may be using this book. In either case this guide should be regarded as a necessary foundation for more detailed analysis and exploration of television texts.

Acknowledgements

I would like to express my appreciation to Tim Cooke for his help in shaping the outline and much of the contents of this book. His formidable grasp of every theoretical and practical aspect of media studies continues to astonish me. I would also like to thank the following people: my wife Sarah for her advice, support and constructive criticism; Leslie Riddle at Arnold, for her enthusiasm and encouragement for the project; Gerard Bryan, Kerry Jones, Andrew Devonshire and my mother for chasing up a long list of obscure requests; and all the authors contained in the bibliography who are the voices within this guide.

Finally, thank you to everyone at Pendleton College in Salford for making this book possible.

The author and the publisher would also like to thank the following for permission to use copyright material:

The BBC, Jennifer Saunders and Joanna Lumley for figure 6, from *Absolutely Fabulous*, and the BBC and Harry Enfield for figure 11, from *The Harry Enfield TV Show*; Stefan Brazzo for figure 1 and figure 4; The British Film Institute for figure 3, Logie Baird, and figure 12, cinema audience; Gerard Bryan for the photograph for figure 15; Carlton Television for figure 8, from *The Bill*; Channel Four for figure 5, from *Brookside*; DACS and the Estate of René Magritte for figure 17, 'Ceci n'est pas une pipe', 1929, by René Magritte (1898–1967); The Dying Rooms Trust for figure 10, from *The Dying Rooms*; Granada Television for the extract from a *Coronation Street* script; *The Guardian* for figure 14, 'Rupert Murdoch' by Frank Martin, and extracts from Andrew Cuef, 'Brookside Kiss' (7 January 1995); ITN for figure 9, from *News at Ten*; the Kobal Collection for figure 13, from *Teenage Mutant Ninja Turtles*, and figure 16, from *Brazil*; LWT for figure 7, from *Blind Date*; Random House UK Ltd for extracts from Francis Wheen, *Television: a history* (Ebury Press); Routledge Ltd for extracts from John Fiske, *Television culture*.

Every effort has been made to trace all copyright holders of material. Any rights not acknowledged here will be acknowledged in subsequent printings if notice is given to the publisher.

Part

I

Introduction to Television

1

Introduction to Television

TELEVISION IS A TWENTIETH-CENTURY PHENOMENON

Like most inventions, television was the combination of earlier technological developments and not the creation of a single 'creative genius'. Its history can be traced in the developments of radio, motion pictures, photography, the cathode ray and the electronic camera. Although much of this technology had existed for some time, experimental broadcasts did not take place until the mid-1920s. These broadcasts took place more or less simultaneously in Hungary, the Soviet Union, the USA and Germany.

Regular television transmissions began in 1936 in Britain, and in 1939 in the USA. Television was forced to close down completely in Britain throughout the Second World War and it was not until after the war that television was able to grow as a medium – partly thanks to military technology and expertise. It was during the 1950s that television overtook cinema as the most popular medium of entertainment for the majority of the population in Europe and North America, a phenomenon that has occurred, alongside industrialization and the resulting changes in living standards, virtually throughout the world.

Television viewing today is the most popular leisure activity in the world. In Britain around 94 per cent of all homes now have at least one colour television set, and 66 per cent a video cassette recorder. British people spend an average of over 25 hours watching television a week, with, on a typical day, 80 per cent of the population tuning into television (*Cultural Trends*, 1997, quoted in Glastier, 1997). In the USA it has been estimated that the average viewer watches more than five hours of television a day. The internationally televised funeral of Princess Diana in September 1997 from London was watched by an estimated two and a half billion people. Television's worldwide power and influence can be seen, most crudely, by the priority for capture that is given to television stations during army coups, or by the billions of pounds advertisers pay to television stations worldwide.

Marshall McLuhan writing in the 1950s and 1960s argued that all media were, in effect, extensions of the human body. Just as radio could be regarded as an extension of the ear, and a newspaper or book an extension of the eye, so television could be thought of as an extension of the human eye and ear, providing an enormous boost of information to the human central nervous system – connecting the viewer to a mass of information about the world previously unavailable. By providing such a boost television has transformed our lives unquantifiably. In the same way that electric light radically transformed our work and leisure, allowing, and in a sense creating, a society that can work, socialize, shop and 'play' 24 hours a day, so too has television shaped the way society operates in the modern world.

As the title of one of McLuhan's books famously suggested, *The medium is the message* (McLuhan and Fiore, 1967). By this phrase he meant that the technical form of the media determined the kind of messages and values that could be carried and was therefore vital in determining the 'experience' of the society using them. What then, are the messages carried by television and how are they made sense of by audiences? This book attempts to address that difficult question. McLuhan's writings are now considered dated and simplistic – he stands accused of 'technological determinism', a term suggesting that humans have little control over the technology they create. Nevertheless the ideas and questions McLuhan generated about the media are still widely debated.

The two positions most commonly occupied in arguments about television and the mass media can be crudely summarized as being broadly 'pessimistic' and 'optimistic'. The pessimists who are often associated with so-called 'mass culture theory' tend to stress the uniformity of media production and the role it plays in passifying and exploiting audiences. According to this view television is a kind of *opiate of the masses*, the phrase Marx used to describe religion. Cultural pessimists are concerned about the dominance and corrosive influence of US and transnational entertainment industries; about stereotypical representations of a range of social groups; the negative effects of television on audiences, particularly in relation to violent and sexual content; the commercialization of television and loss of 'public service' commitments; and the ideological role of television in 'controlling' the way we view the world.

The 'optimists', on the other hand, celebrate the diversity, complexity and equality which they see as a product of television. Television is considered to be as rich and subtle in its potential readings as Elizabethan theatre, and, like Elizabethan theatre, television is regarded as a familiar and popular experience for all sections of society. The optimists often accuse the pessimists of 'elitism', of denigrating popular culture. Optimists, like the pessimists, come in many guises. There are those who celebrate soap operas and other popular genres, respectfully stressing the pleasures and diverse readings of audiences; those who reject the view that television has harmful effects; those who welcome new technology and deregulation – the removal of the 'nanny state's' influence over broadcasting; and who argue that if television promotes any ideology, that ideology is the consensus of the wider society in which it is created and not a controlling mechanism of the dominant class.

I have drawn these complex arguments together in this introduction purely for convenience and brevity to illustrate that there is no critical agreement on the 'message' of the medium of television. The remaining chapters of part I will, I hope, begin to clarify and explore some of the approaches and perspectives offered on this relatively new, and vitally important, area of study. Television is so 'taken-for-granted', omnipresent and, in a sense, 'transparent' that the importance of understanding it in a critical sense has to be continuously asserted. However, rather than defensively arguing the need to study television, the question should be put the other way: how can we afford *not* to study something that has become so central to modern society?

Sources

Glastier, D. (1997): Live events thrive as TV viewing falls. *Guardian Weekly* 6 April.
McLuhan, M. and Fiore, Q. (1967): *The medium is the message*. Penguin Books.

Time for Teletubbies!

2

John Ellis and 'The Television Experience'

BROADCAST TELEVISION AS SOUND AND IMAGE

In *Visible fictions* (1982) John Ellis describes the fundamental characteristics of the 'experience' of television. He compares this experience with that of cinema and, by highlighting the differences, illustrates how the medium dictates the nature of the material made for it. The following account is a summary of some of the central points he makes.

Ellis uses three essential characteristics to distinguish television from cinema.

- *The quality and size of the image:* the television image is of a lower quality than the cinematic image in terms of its resolution of detail as it is composed of electronically produced lines and is rarely more than 30 inches in diameter. The viewer is physically larger than the image: the opposite of cinema. Television is also usually looked down on, rather than up at, as in cinema.
- *The environment in which the medium is experienced:* television is usually watched in domestic surroundings and is viewed in normal light conditions. Unlike cinema there is no surrounding darkness, no anonymity of the fellow viewer, no large image, no lack of movement amongst the spectators and far less 'rapt attention' to the screen.
- *The degree of concentration:* television has a lower degree of sustained concentration from its viewers (who are often doing other things, such as talking, while it is on) but it has a more extended period of watching and more frequent use than cinema (Chapter 12).

These characteristics help determine other key features of the television medium.

Television's Use of Sound

It is the relatively low level of concentration that viewers give to television that explains the importance of sound in the medium. By 'sound' Ellis refers to such elements as programme announcements, signature tunes, music in the various kinds of series which are used to ensure a certain level of attention and 'drag viewers back' to looking at the set.

Sound, he argues, holds attention more consistently than image. Many of television's characteristic broadcast forms rely upon sound as the major carrier of information and to ensure continuity of attention. The news broadcast, the documentary with voice-over commentary, the bulk of television comedy shows, all display a greater reliance on sound than cinema has developed itself. The image becomes illustration, and only occasionally provides material that is not covered by the sound track (e.g. comedy sight gags, news actuality footage). *Sound tends to anchor meaning on television, whereas the image tends to anchor it with cinema.*

Television's 'Stripped-down Image'

Television's lower level of sustained concentration on the image has had another effect upon television production. In contrast to cinema's profusion of detail, broadcast television's image is *stripped down, lacking in detail*. Ellis compares the fussy detail of a film shown on television with 'the visual bareness of a TV cop series, where cars chase each other through endless urban wastes of bare walls and near deserted streets'.

On television, then, background and context tend to be sketched rather than brought forward and subject to the 'fetishism' of details that often occurs in cinema, especially art cinema. The narratively important detail is stressed by this lack of other detail. Sometimes, it is also stressed by *music*, producing an emphasis that seems entirely acceptable on television, yet which would seem ludicrously heavy-handed in cinema. This is particularly so with US crime series, where speed of action and transition from one segment to another dictates the concentration of resources on to single meanings. Where detail and background *are* used in television programmes, for example BBC historical series, action tends to slow down as a result.

The 'stripped-down' image that broadcast television uses is, according to Ellis, a central feature of television production. Its most characteristic result is the emphasis on *close-ups* of people, which are finely graded into types. The dramatic close-up is of a face virtually filling the screen. The current affairs/news programme close-up is more distant (head and shoulders are shown) providing a certain distance, even reticence. Close-ups are regularly used in television, to a much greater extent than in cinema. The effect is very different from the cinema close-up. Whereas the cinema close-up accentuates the difference between screen-figure and any attainable human figure by drastically increasing its size, the broadcast television close-up produces a face that approximates to normal size. Instead of an effect of distance and unattainability, the television close-up generates an impression of equality and even intimacy.

The broadcast television image is 'gestural' rather than detailed; variety and interest are provided by the rapid changes of images rather than the richness within one image. Television compensates for the simplicity of its single images by the techniques of *rapid cutting*, and the organization of television studios is designed for this style of work. The use of several cameras and the possibility of alternation between them produces a style of shooting that is largely specific to television: the fragmentation of events that keeps strictly to the continuity of their performance. There is much less condensation of events in television than there is in cinema. Events are shown in *real time* from a *multiple of points of camera view*. Cinema events, by contrast, are shot already fragmented and are matched together in editing.

Television's Immediacy

Television, Ellis argues, often gives the *impression of being 'live'*. Although only news and sports coverage are routinely transmitted live, 'the notion that broadcast TV is live still haunts the medium; even more so does the sense of immediacy of the image'. This 'immediacy' Ellis describes as an affect of the 'directness' of the television image and is achieved by various means.

First, broadcast television very often uses forms of *direct address* – addressing its viewers as though holding a conversation with them. Announcers and newsreaders speak directly from the screen, simulating the eye contact of everyday conversation by looking directly out of the screen and occasionally looking down (a learned and constructed technique). Advertisements contain elements of direct address: questions, exhortations, warnings. Sometimes they go further, providing riddles and jokes that assume that their viewers share a common frame of reference with them (e.g. references to other advertising campaigns). This is also an operation of direct address – knowledge is assumed in the viewer who is addressed as an equal. The assumption made on behalf of the viewer in many advertisements is that 'we both know what we are talking about'.

The powerful effect of direct address in its most obvious form (speaker facing camera) is usually reserved for politically neutral figures (with the exception of party political broadcasts or an address by a head of state). Other strategies of direct address more commonly used by politicians include, for example, appealing to 'common sense' or, as with interviewers, asking questions on behalf of their viewers/constituents, 'what the ordinary people really want to know . . .'.

Second, broadcast television's own *perpetual presence* (there every night of the year), and its *series formats*, breed a sense of the perpetual present. The *tight scheduling* that is favoured by most large broadcast operations means that an audience wanting to see a particular programme has to be present at a very precise time, or they miss it. This increases the sense that broadcast television is of the present moment.

The forms which work best on television, Ellis suggests, are those which operate with this sense of immediacy. Soap opera, 'entirely cast in a continuous present', and the open-ended series formats of the situation comedy or the dramatic series create a sense of the immediate by being presented as ongoing, without the neat resolutions of cinema narrative, 'part of the texture of life'.

Immediacy and intimacy are also produced by television's constant use of 'the family'. This is particularly noticeable in dramas and soap operas, producing a 'bond between the viewers' conception of themselves (or how they ought to be) and the programmes' central concerns'. Thus broadcast television sets up a *community of address* – a 'them and us' complicity between broadcaster and viewer. The domestic place of the television set and its assumed audience (the family) become the norm against which any grouping outside can be measured. Certain attitudes are taken towards these outsiders – patronization, hate, wilful ignorance, pity, generalized concern, indifference. By defining those outside the consensus in this way, the consensus of television and family is further reinforced and confirmed.

EXERCISES AND ESSAYS

Exercise

Watch a popular television programme and note any ways in which it displays the characteristics of the 'experience' of television as outlined by Ellis.

Exercise and Essay

Show how any television text you have studied reflects the aesthetic procedures and constraints of the broadcast television medium.

Source

Ellis, J. (1982): *Visible fictions – cinema: television: video.* Routledge.

Logie Baird – 'the father of television'

3

History of Television

INTRODUCTION

The following account of the history of British television is largely based on more detailed histories provided by Wyver (1989) and Wheen (1985), amongst others (see other sources listed at the end of this chapter). It is provided to give a background to several key issues and debates that reoccur within this guide.

A Scottish engineer, John Logie Baird, is often credited with the invention of television. He had been experimenting with the problems of sending pictures from one place to another for a number of years and in 1926 he demonstrated a television by mechanically scanning a screen made up of 25 lines. His experiments continued for 10 years, but those who bought or built early receivers (at great cost) had to telephone him after transmission to check what they had been watching!

In fact, the race to build the first television had been going on around the world for some years. The idea of television had been in the minds of scientists since the 1880s. The invention of photosensitive selenium cells in 1873, the German Paul Nipkow's rotating scanning apparatus in 1884 and Karl Braun's cathode ray tube in 1897 were just some of the important developments that brought the possibility of what the British scientist Campbell Swinton described in 1908 as 'distant electric vision' a step closer.

At the same time that Logie Baird was transmitting rudimentary images in London the Hungarian D. Von Mihaly, a Japanese lecturer in engineering Kenjiro Takayanagi, Soviet inventor Boris Grabovsky and Russian exile Vladimir Zworykin, and an American, Charles Francis Jenkins, were independently giving *similar demonstrations of 'televised' images* of varying qualities at different locations *around the world*.

In April 1927 the American Telephone and Telegraph Company (AT&T) gave a public demonstration in which a speech by the US Secretary of Commerce, Herbert Hoover, was broadcast from Washington and watched in New York by an invited audience of business executives, bankers and newspaper editors. Hoover's appearance, the first by any politician on television, made front-page headlines in the next day's *New York Times*.

In May 1928 General Electric began making regular, thrice weekly, broadcasts from radio station WGY in New York. In August 1928 WGY transmitted Al Smith's speech accepting his nomination for the US Presidency, and in September 1928 it broadcast the first television drama – *The Queen's Messenger*. According to Wheen (1985):

> The play had only two characters in it, which was just as well, since anything with a large cast would have defeated General Electric's primitive equipment. Each camera could only scan an area twelve inches square – enough for a human head and not much else. Three cameras were used: one for the actress, one for the actor, and one for the two 'doubles'. These doubles had an essential part to play, as the main actress and actor could not move their heads without going out of focus. Whenever the script called for another shot – a hand holding a glass of wine, for instance, there was a switch to the third camera, where one of the doubles' hands would be seen.

In May 1927 John Logie Baird, aware of the competition from across the Atlantic, transmitted pictures of himself from London to Glasgow – more than twice the distance covered by AT&T's transmission of Hoover's speech the previous month. In February 1928 Baird gave a public demonstration of television transmissions from *London to New York* – an event described as of 'epochal importance' by the *New York Times*. In July 1928 he demonstrated *colour television* by using a spinning disc fitted with red, blue and green filters. However, 'the father of television', as he came to be known, was still unable to broadcast officially, until the Post Office's engineers were happy with the quality of his experimental transmissions. The British Broadcasting Corporation (BBC) was also unhappy about the quality of the transmissions and only reluctantly allowed him to use their transmitters from September 1929, when the radio was not on air – in the morning and late at night.

The first regular 'high-definition' television transmissions began from the BBC studios at Alexandra Palace, North London, in November 1936. ('High-definition' had been defined by Lord Selsdon's 1935 government report as a minimum of 240 lines.) Broadcasting was limited to a 25-mile radius from the transmitter. Initially the BBC used competing systems (EMI's electronic scanning system and Baird's mechanical system), requiring different televisions, on alternate weeks. Eventually, EMI's system was clearly shown to be more reliable and to have better picture quality than Baird's mechanical system. Because of such initial confusion and the high cost of television receivers, the earliest audiences tended to be both wealthy and few in number. The new medium was, at first, seen as an experimental 'poor relation' of radio.

Early television material, like early cinema, made use of sporting, political and social events such as the Derby, the coronation of George VI, classical concert performances and political speeches. These had the obvious attraction that they did not include any actual production costs other than the recording of the event. Early television also included forms from other media such as variety shows, plays and Hollywood-produced feature films and series.

The history of British television until the 1950s is dominated by the BBC, with radio and television policies and formats closely linked. It was decided at the outset of radio (and television) in Britain that strict control of broadcast transmissions was necessary, if only to avoid the early US experience of a free-for-all on the airwaves. The response was regarded by the popular press of the time as a draconian one, with only a single company, the British Broadcasting Company, granted a licence to transmit programmes. This programming was paid for not by advertising, which was explicitly forbidden, but by *licence fees* paid to the Post Office by wireless owners.

Early broadcasting committees described the wavebands available 'as a valuable form of public property' (Sykes, 1923) to be protected in the 'national interest'. How this national interest was to be determined, however, was never very clearly addressed. Following recommendations by the Sykes and Crawford Committees the British Broadcasting Company became a *nationalized Corporation* in 1926, continuing its monopoly of radio and television under 'indirect' control of the government. Unlike the press, the BBC was formally obliged to remain impartial. To maintain a degree of independence from the state the governing administration was to appoint a committee of 12 public figures ('the great and the good') on a five-yearly basis, who would, in turn, appoint a director general. The extent to which these committees were composed of 'political appointees' who could steer the BBC in directions favourable to the government has been a subject of controversy. So too has the BBC's real 'independence' in light of the government's power to set licence fees and thus apply financial pressure in the event of unfavourable or controversial political coverage (Chapter 14).

Under its first director general John Reith the BBC was given a mission to bring the 'best' of British culture to the nation, to enlighten, elevate and 'educate' wherever possible:

'The concept of public service, in Reith's mind, had, as a core element, an ideal of broadcasting's role in the formation of an informed and reasoned public opinion as an essential part of the political process in a mass democratic society' (Scannell, 1990).

In Germany and the Soviet Union state control of television was far greater, and the medium's potential for propaganda was exploited in a quite different way. Regular transmissions were being broadcast in the 1930s but the only sets built were designed for communal viewing. Berlin, for example, had 11 public viewing rooms, which were run by the German Post Office. Both Goebbels and Hitler took a close interest in the possibilities of television for broadcasting Nazi speeches, films and documentaries, as well as for morale-boosting entertainment. For example, the Berlin Olympics of 1936 were televised and audiences in the viewing rooms were said to be as high as 150,000. German television continued to broadcast in the evenings throughout the war (on the basis of 'forces' welfare) until the Berlin transmitter was destroyed by Allied bombers in November 1943.

British television broadcasts, by contrast, were stopped altogether during the war in case the transmissions aided enemy bombers. Marconi–EMI, whose television system had been selected in the trials against Baird's, built the Chain Home Radar system using much of the same equipment as was used for the television transmission. After 1945, however, Marconi UK, and other companies, were eager to capitalize on wartime developments in the electronics field and make use of existing assembly lines. The BBC resumed limited broadcasting in June 1946, when viewers were required to take out a 'combined sound and TV licence'. Nine months later it had an audience of less than 15,000, but by 1951 there were nearly 600,000 viewers. The new 'consumer society' was growing slowly in Britain compared with the USA. Nevertheless, by 1956 the total number of television receivers numbered six million, owing to increased wealth and new transmitters. This growth and the success of sponsorship on television in the USA led to pressure from manufacturers to break up the BBC's monopoly of the medium and allow advertising on British television.

TELEVISION IN THE 1950S

Television in the USA had stayed on throughout the war. By the 1950s big profits were being made in television, and advertising was being attracted away from radio. Variety and situation comedies (sitcoms) became the staple of the new medium. Advertisers could pay for complete programmes, so it was easy for sponsors to bring pressure to bear on programme makers. Lewis (1986) illustrates how much power these advertisers had:

> For example, you couldn't 'ford' a river in a Western sponsored by Chevrolet. And Ford are reported to have deleted a shot of the New York skyline because it showed the Chrysler building. In 1953, Kipling's 'The Light That Failed' had to be broadcast as 'The Gathering Night' because Westinghouse, who make light bulbs, was a sponsor. When the American Gas Association sponsored 'Judgement at Nuremburg' all references to gas chambers were eliminated from the account of the holocaust.

In Britain, increased affluence, pressure from advertisers and the electronics manufacturers and the BBC's only half-hearted commitment to the television medium led to growing demands for a commercial television channel funded not by the licence fee but by advertising. Following the recommendations of the Beveridge Committee (1950) the Conservative government introduced the Television Act in 1954 which enabled 'television broadcasting services additional to those of the BBC'. Although allowing advertising the Act also required commercial television to provide a 'public service' that would 'inform, educate and entertain' its audience.

Independent Television (ITV) – a group of independent regional television companies – began broadcasting in September 1955, initially to a fairly limited audience. Fear of financial collapse forced the networks to exchange their best programmes on a regular basis and schedule more popular items such as the US Western series *Gunsmoke* at peak viewing times. 'Spot' advertising breaks, limited to six or seven minutes per hour, were far less frequent and intrusive compared with US television, but with a high quota of US imports and cheaper production costs (e.g. cheaper prizes for quiz shows) ITV was soon making a profit. By 1956 it was clear that ITV was a success. The Canadian franchise holder Roy Thompson, first owner of Scottish TV, described commercial television as 'a licence to print your own money'. Opinions vary as to whether ITV represented a genuinely commercial alternative to public service broadcasting. According to Scannell (1990), the tight regulations and restriction placed on ITV meant that 'it was an extension of public service broadcasting not an alternative'.

While ITV grew, the BBC continued to build new transmitters so that by 1958 80 per cent of the population could receive BBC and ITV programmes. But the BBC's share of the audience was falling rapidly, reaching a low point of 28 per cent in 1957. While ITV set out to be popular with 'brash' new programmes seeking the mass audience, the BBC was still felt to be trying to 'improve' its audience, creating feelings of alienation with its upper-middle-class 'highbrow' approach. John Tulloch writes how

> The corporate bias in the management of the state, which the BBC exemplified, succeeded for forty years in playing down class conflict and creating a broad political consensus in economic and social policy. This consensus began to dissolve in the 1960s. Commercial television destroyed the BBC's monopoly and introduced new models of programming to the public, although it was itself established within a regulatory framework operated by the ITA that owed much to the corporate ideology of public service broadcasting.

TELEVISION IN THE 1960S

In the late 1950s the BBC began to challenge ITV's position with more popular, fast-moving programmes such as Jack Good's *6.5 Special* pop music show, the comedy series *Hancock's Half Hour* and the hugely popular *Grandstand*. This new more popular direction was further continued by the new Director General Hugh Greene who was appointed in 1960. Under Greene's control the BBC was given a younger and more contemporary image. Successful programmes included *That Was The Week That Was*, the gritty police series *Z Cars*, science fiction in the form of *Dr Who*, comedy such as *Steptoe and Son* and *Till Death Us Do Part* and controversial drama such as *Up the Junction* and *Cathy Come Home*. Tulloch (1990) suggests that

Competition forced the BBC into a high-risk strategy of dissent under the director-generalship of Sir Hugh Greene, who encouraged a vast expansion of broadcast journalism, 'kitchen sink' drama, and – most notoriously – political satire.

John Wyver also notes how this new, questioning attitude distinguished much of the Corporation's output in the 1960s, suggesting that it matched the political promise offered by a new Labour government and the broader social and cultural changes of the decade. But even in this new climate there were still limits, in television if not elsewhere, as when in 1965 the BBC stopped the transmission of *The War Game*, Peter Watkins's graphic account of a nuclear attack on Britain.

Part of the BBC's new-found confidence in the 1960s sprang from the findings of the Pilkington Committee, set up to advise the government on the future of broadcasting. The Committee's report published in 1962 praised the BBC's 'professionalism' and its commitment to public service broadcasting. It ruled out the need for advertising and accepted the BBC's bid to start a third channel (BBC2), which went on the air in 1964.

Its profile as an upmarket, special interest and cultural channel was successfully developed with series such as *The Forsyte Saga* and *Civilisation*, contrasting middle-class culture and popular presentation in ways which proved enormously popular and influential. Initially, at any rate, the transfer of more 'quality' programmes to the new channel meant that the BBC could put more 'popular' programmes on BBC1 and compete on a more equal footing with ITV.

In contrast to its praise for the BBC, the Pilkington Committee was widely *critical* of ITV which it effectively criticized for 'debauching' public taste. The Committee recommended that greater control be placed over its output via the Independent Television Authority (ITA) who were now in a position to condemn and where necessary punish 'triviality, lack of variety or innovation'.

The threat was clear to see. Since the mid-1950s new kinds of highly formulaic content were being produced specifically for the television medium, with the US market usually leading the way. These included game shows, talk shows, half-hour sitcoms and hour-long action drama series. Drama, like comedy, was constructed around a repeatable situation, often provided by a professional activity (e.g. legal or medical). A major limitation of the drama/comedy formula was that the central characters had to remain unchanged by the episode's events in order to be in their proper places by the following week's episode. The serial form provided the programming stability necessary to deliver viewers to advertisers on a regular basis.

ITV was in danger of moving towards the position of the networks in the USA of carrying their audiences from one show to the next using the principle of '*least objectionable programming*'. This meant that the majority of viewers who simply watched television, rather than selecting specific programmes, would watch whichever show they disliked least. The unit of television viewing was therefore not the individual programme but the daytime or evening schedule as a whole (Wyver, 1989).

In 1966 the ITA, spurred on by the Pilkington Committee report, asked each of the regional networks to look at the make-up of their prime-time schedules and to try 'to whet the appetites of the more intelligent viewers by providing more variation from the standard fare'. One indirect result was *News at Ten* – a half-hour news broadcast from ITN each weekday night. Another was an increasing public service commitment to cultural series such as *Tempo*, and a wide range of documentaries and dramas, notably *This Week* and Granada's *World in Action*.

Technical developments in the 1960s included the first transatlantic link with the relay of live pictures via the Telstar satellite in 1962, a worldwide satellite link-up with the Beatles singing 'All you need is love' in 1967 and the start of *colour transmissions* in the same year (Chapter 15).

TELEVISION IN THE 1970S AND 1980S

The difficult but apparently successful balancing act British television nego-tiated between public service and commercial pressures continued through much of the 1970s and 1980s, with Britain granted the dubious distinction of having 'the least worst television in the world'. The idea of 'competition for audiences but not for revenue' became accepted as the driving force of British television and the best means of ensuring a healthy public service commitment:

> The BBC knew that as its audience share fell, the case for a compulsory fee would become weaker and that getting the fee raised at the regular three yearly review would be trickier. . . . The popularity of programmes therefore did become a factor in BBC calculations in a qualitatively different way from previously (Seymour Ure, 1991).

Another sensitive factor in the BBC's and ITV's relationship with govern-ment was coverage of political issues. This was particularly the case under the Thatcher administration, with television scrutinized in its treatment of union disputes, the Falklands War and the ongoing conflict in Northern Ireland. It is claimed by some analysts that *Death on the Rock* – an ITV documentary on the shooting of suspected IRA (Irish Republican Army) terrorists by the SAS (Special Air Service), on Gibraltar – so enraged Prime Minister Thatcher that she began investigating means of breaking the BBC–ITV 'duopoly' at this point. It is these investigations which, it is said, led to the 1990 Broadcasting Act.

The Annan Committee (1977) proposed an open broadcasting authority, which would act as a publisher rather than as a production company for the proposed fourth television channel. In 1982 Channel 4 began broadcasting, except in Wales which was given a corresponding service – Sianel Pedwar Cymra (S4C). At the time, Channel 4 was a company wholly owned by the Independent Broadcasting Authority (IBA), with a brief to buy programmes from outside production companies, in the view that this would give the independent sector a much needed boost. Channel 4 was, and still is, required to present programmes that are complementary to those of ITV, appealing to tastes and interests not normally catered for by the original independent service. Initially this took the form of highly original 'offbeat' programming, much of which was aimed at cultural minorities. Arguably the Reithian notion of broadcasting for a national consensus had collapsed, and the new broadcasting environment was a pluralistic one; that is, it now tried to serve many audiences with different needs (Chapter 14).

In 1983 breakfast time television was launched, with the BBC beating TVam to the launch date with a populist blend of news, guest interviews, aerobics and weather forecasts all heavily influenced by US formats. TVam responded by ditching its four presenters – Anna Ford, Michael Jay, Michael Parkinson and David Frost – along with their 'mission to explain', and replaced them with *Good Morning Britain*, a far lighter, entertainment-led programme hosted by Anne Diamond and Richard Keys and supported by Roland Rat. The 1980s also saw definitions of late-night television extended as British television slowly moved towards the US model of 24-hour broadcasting.

TELEVISION IN THE 1990S

The 1990s have seen commercial pressures diluting much of Channel 4's original innovation and experimentation, with viewing figures being increasingly bolstered by US sitcoms and other more 'mainstream' fare. However, the greatest challenges to existing forms of television in Britain came in the aftermath of the 1990 Broadcasting Act. The Act overhauled the regulations of independent television, replacing the Independent Broadcasting Authority (IBA) with the Independent Television Commission (ITC) which implements new licensing arrangements. These are, in short, a blind auction, with the broadcasting franchise given for a particular region to any company making the highest bid (delivered to the ITC in sealed envelopes). Despite assurances of quality tests, early experiences have shown that commercial pressures drive programme makers inexorably downmarket to make financial savings and boost ratings.

Furthermore, mergers and takeovers by larger companies became commonplace following the Act, confirming fears of increased concentration of ownership (Carlton/Central, Meridian/Anglia, Yorkshire/Tyne Tees, Granada/LWT) and in June 1993 the ITV companies announced a desire to move *News at Ten* out of its prime 10 pm slot. The Campaign for Press and Broadcasting

Freedom (CPBF) predicts that in five years' time 'ITV will effectively be run by Carlton and one other company – possibly Granada – in the North' (Chapter 14).

Despite government's claims that it does not wish to reduce the role of public service broadcasting, the Broadcasting Act has had huge consequences for the BBC. One of many changes is their new obligation, along with the ITV network, to contract out 25 per cent of their output to independent companies. The CPBF also argue, in the publication *Selling the Beeb* (O'Malley and Treharne, 1993), that the current push towards market dominance in broadcasting 'would lead to the BBC being gradually dismantled'.

Granville Williams (1994) argues that, as a result of the 1990 Broadcasting Act, relatively secure public service broadcasting units committed to production values and often exploring issues and ideas in innovative ways have been replaced by small, freelance production companies that are highly vulnerable to business and political pressure:

> Broadcasting control, rather than being in the hands of regulatory bodies with the requirement to ensure high quality, balanced and universally accessible output, is now falling into the hands of major corporations and conglomerates, the likes of News Corporation, Finivest, Time Warner and Sony. Competition for advertising revenue has also cut into the editorial and creative independence of programme makers. Sponsorship, bartering and product placement by a small number of corporations are shaping the information and entertainment which audiences receive.

In April 1997 Channel 5 was finally launched after overcoming technical problems of retuning video recorders. The channel promised innovation in news and late-night talk shows, but faced its greatest challenge from shrinking terrestrial audiences and advertising revenues. Whereas television watching generally declined slightly between 1985 and 1995 the hours of terrestrial broadcasting transmitted every week grew from 471 in 1985 to 671 in 1995. If figures for satellite and cable are included, the total for a typical week in 1994 was 3701 hours. The 1980s and 1990s have been marked by growing cable and satellite markets since the establishment of the Cable Authority in 1984, Sky in 1989 and British Satellite Television in 1990 (which later merged, rather acrimoniously, in 1991 as BSkyB). Cable, satellite and, perhaps most importantly, digital television will, most critics agree, effect the greatest changes to the television we watch in Britain and around the world (Chapter 15).

EXERCISES AND ESSAYS

Task

Interview older relatives or friends and ask them what they consider to be the most important changes in television in their lifetime. Have these changes, in their opinion, been for the better or the worse?

Exercise

For each decade list some of the most important developments in television under the following headings:

	technology	institutions	content/representations
1920s			
1930s			
1940s			
1950s			
1960s			
1970s			
1980s			
1990s			

Essay

The changes in television over the twentieth century reflect, in a number of ways, the changing times. What are these changes?

Essay

What are the major forces that have helped shape contemporary British television?

Exercise

Research and prepare an essay plan for the following question with regard to the international history of the medium: 'In what sense can pre-war television be described as experimental?'

Sources

Broadcasting Act (1990): *Public general acts – Elizabeth II*, chapter 42. The Stationery Office.

Lewis, P. (1986): *Media and power: from Marconi to Murdoch*. Camden Press.

O'Malley, T. and Treharne, J. (1993): *Selling the Beeb*. Campaign for Press and Broadcasting Freedom (CPBF).

Scannell, P. (1990): Public service broadcasting: the history of a concept. In Goodwin, A. and Whannel, G. (eds), *Understanding television*. Routledge.

Seymour Ure, C. (1991): *The British press and broadcasting since 1945*. Basil Blackwell.

Sykes Committee (1923): Report, cmnd 1951. HMSO.

Television Act (1964): *Public general acts – Elizabeth II*, chapter 21. The Stationery Office.

Tulloch, J. (1990): Television and black Britons. In Goodwin, A. and Whannel, G. (eds), *Understanding television*. Routledge.

Wheen, F. (1985): *Television – a history*. Guild Publishing.

Williams, G. (1994): *Britain's media – how they are related*. Campaign for Press and Broadcasting Freedom (CPBF).

Wyver, J. (1989): *The moving image. An international history of film, television and video*. British Film Institute/Basil Blackwell.

Part

II

Introduction to Genre

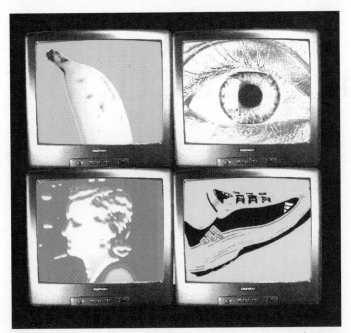

4

Introduction to Genre

BACKGROUND

Genre is a French word meaning *type* and refers to types or categories of media products. Soap operas, situation comedies, police series, quiz shows and news programmes are just some of the genres to be found in television. Television is a highly 'generic' medium with comparatively few one-off programmes falling outside established generic categories. Genres are identified by the particular *conventions* they use which we come to recognize through regular contact. Conventions are any elements which are repeated in such a way that they become familiar, predictable and associated in their use with a particular genre. Conventions include:

character
plot
setting
costumes and props
music
lighting
themes
dialogue
visual style

To take the example of news programmes – it is conventional to announce the beginning of the news with dramatic music, employ one or more newsreaders who are seated and are of 'smart' appearance and dress, neither too young nor too old (30–55 for men, 25–45 for women!) and not too 'obviously' from one region. The studio setting may include a desk, a computer terminal, a sheaf of papers and the illusion of a 'panel' behind and to the side of the newsreaders upon which images and motifs appear. The lighting will be high-key, without shadows. The visual style will usually include long shots at the beginning and end of sections with medium close-ups (head, shoulders and chest with some of the desk in shot) for the majority of the time. There will also be frequent use of computer graphics, where these are available, in addition to the footage recorded at the scene of the news event. The stories will be selected according to established news values (Chapter 9) and the dialogue will be written in a concise, formal style and may include stock words and phrases such as 'the full extent of the tragedy', 'news has just come in', and 'and finally'. These conventions make up the distinctive look and sound of television news.

How much we take these conventions for granted, how 'natural' they appear to us, only becomes really clear when we imagine, or witness, these conventions being broken. The temporary loss of studio lights has in the past resulted in a news bulletin being broadcast with shadows and unlit areas in the studio which appears odd and 'unsettling'. Imagine though, a news broadcast presented by a 16-year-old 'new age traveller' whispering in a thick West Country accent in extreme close-up. Furthermore, imagine the same news reader being without a desk, computer or earpiece, reciting the news facing away from camera in rhyming couplets scattered with slang and obscenities.

This example shows the *ideological significance of genres*. While the content, treatment and messages of genres are reinforced through repetition, those media forms which do not work within these formulas face a more difficult task in being accepted. The codes and conventions of genre, which are, incidentally, in a state of constant adaptation, tell us a great deal about the beliefs and values, at a particular time, of the society that produces them. From the example of the news broadcast we could suggest that our society tends to put more faith in the word of a smartly dressed, 'well-educated', middle-aged man or woman standing four or five feet away, looking us in the eye, than an unconventionally dressed teenager with a strong regional accent within one or two feet of us – a distance that normally signifies intimacy or aggression.

Genres then, reflect the dominant values of a society. Like these values, however, they are not fixed or uncontested. Thus, genres change, subgenres evolve and new genres emerge. What may seem 'normal', 'acceptable' and 'conventional' one year may be clichéd, outmoded and unacceptable several years later. Black or female newsreaders, for example, have been appearing more frequently in recent years owing to a variety of pressures both within and outside television institutions. Television representations of the police today are not always the gentle, uncorruptible father figures they appeared to be in police series of the 1950s such as *Dixon of Dock Green*.

For the television industry, such gradual shifts in the conventions of the various genres allows for creativity within the boundaries of tried and tested formulas. Successful formulas are only rejected after ratings begin to fall. Yet novelty is as important to the success of a genre as repetition or the use of conventional elements. Within the predictability of news presentation and dominant news values, there is unpredictability in the exact items that will be reported – where, how and to whom the conflict, accident, incident or disaster occurs. Within police series, new locations, characters, stories and styles of filming are constantly being tested. Changing too many elements, or not enough, may lead to confusion or disinterest in the audience. As Fiske (1987) notes:

Genre serves the dual needs of a commodity: on the one hand standard-isation and familiarity, and on the other, product differentiation.

EXERCISES AND ESSAYS

Exercise

Take a single page of a television guide. Identify as many genres and subgenres as possible from the page, listing the programmes under each category. List separately any programmes which do not seem to fit a pre-existing genre.

Look at one of the genres and compile a detailed written list of the dominant conventions (use the conventions suggested above to assist). Results can be written up as a page of a 'cookbook' of genres – listing 'ingredients' (conventions) and 'cooking instructions' (how they interact or develop) for a particular genre or subgenre (see Exercises and Essays in Chapter 6 for an example).

Exercise

Devise and outline a proposal for a police/detective *or* sitcom *or* game show programme. You should consider such aspects as plot, settings, characters, music, lighting and other generic conventions. There should also be an indication of choice of cast, approximate costs, advertising strategies and other production considerations. Your outline should be accompanied by a script/storyboard extract, video clip or trailer of the proposed product.

Essay

Conventions are the structural elements of genre that are shared between producers and audiences. They embody the crucial ideological concerns of the time in which they are popular and are central to the pleasures a genre offers an audience (Fiske, 1987).

Discuss with reference to any genre you have studied.

Source

Fiske, J. (1987): *Television culture*. Routledge.

Brookside lovers Viv and Beth

5

Soap Operas

SOAPS – AN HISTORICAL OVERVIEW

The term 'soap opera' was first used in the US Depression of the 1930s to describe radio serials sponsored by soap powder manufacturers such as Proctor and Gamble. These 15-minute serials, such as *Ma Perkins* and *Just Plain Jane*, were about women and concentrated on emotional dilemmas (the term 'opera' suggested the melodrama of the highbrow musical genre). It was hoped that by sponsoring radio programmes about women, their families and domestic affairs during the day, advertisers could reach an audience of housewives who would add soap powder to their shopping lists.

These 'never-ending' stories became very popular and the format switched successfully to television in the 1950s, expanding in length to 25 minutes then 60 minutes. *The Guiding Light*, which started on US radio in 1937, was the first to switch to television in 1952, and is still running. The term 'soap' in the USA still refers to daytime television dramas, which dominate the late-morning and early-afternoon slot (11 am–2 pm). Weekly higher-budget shows such as *Dallas*, *Dynasty*, *Knot's Landing* and *The Colbys* were known by Americans as prime-time serials (as they were screened between 6.30 pm and 10.30 pm).

Soap opera is an international phenomenon. Almost every country with a television station has its own soap opera, because they are cheap to produce and are popular with large audiences:

> The soap-opera formula – the serial drama with a small cast and limited studio sets – was an almost inevitable choice for any television service aiming to attract large audiences with low-cost programming. Latin American soap operas, called 'telenovelas', originated in Mexico and Cuba in the 1950s and were later also produced in Brazil and Puerto Rico. Daniel Filho, Brazil's most prolific maker of popular drama, suggested that under military rule in the 1970s, his soap operas provided, with football, the only permitted topics of conversation: 'In Brazil we believe in miracles, and all soap operas have a character who is going up in the world, making it.' Like their Indian and Chinese equivalents, these variation on the basic American formula could easily accommodate local cultural requirements. However, the telenovela formula was devised to fill time cheaply – and this need itself

arose from the adoption of the values of the multi-channel all-day commercial television, suitable for a rich country, by a much poorer one (Maltby, 1989).

In fact, locally produced soap operas are almost always more popular than even the most successful imports. Some countries other than the USA have tried, successfully, to export their home-grown soaps. These include Britain (*Coronation Street*), Australia (*The Sullivans, Neighbours*), Germany (*Schwarzwaldklinik*), France (*Châteauvallon*) and Brazil (*Malu Muher*). No country, however, has been as successful at exporting its serials as the USA (Alvarado, 1987).

In Britain, these US 'soaps' gained popularity in the 1980s and were partly responsible for renewed interest in the form by British producers. It is interesting to note that an obsession with ratings led these previously successful US programmes into increasingly sensationalist and far-fetched plot territory that eventually alienated their national and international audiences. It is a lesson that British producers should heed.

Currently, in Britain, the genre is enjoying an unprecedented combination of mass appeal, cult status and academic respectability. Britain's longest-running and most popular television soap is *Coronation Street*, which started in 1960. *Eastenders*, a close contender for highest ratings has, like its other rivals *Brookside*, and *Emmerdale Farm*, been running for well over a decade. Not all soaps, however, are without end. *Crossroads*, which ran from 1964 to 1988, was finally pulled from the screens despite high viewing figures and extremely low costs because the audience it drew was considered too old (and poor) to be of interest to advertisers (Chapter 12). *Eldorado* (1992–93), the BBC's soap set in Spain, is thought to have suffered from a poorly timed launch and was dumped despite widely acknowledged improvements and slowly rising audience figures.

The television industry is particularly keen on hooking younger audiences into their soaps. The remarkable popularity of Australian soaps such as *Neighbours* and *Home and Away* (originally imported as daytime fillers) with school ages led British soap producers to bring younger characters into their serials. As a result, a new generation of soap viewers with disposable income and undetermined buying patterns are delivered to advertisers on a regular basis. The 1950s vision of selling soap powder to housewives through continuous serials has extended to include a much wider range of products to men and women of various age-groups and status.

WHAT IS SOAP?

A soap opera is a serialized drama which runs for 52 weeks of the year with continuous storylines dealing with domestic themes, personal or family relationships and a limited number of running characters. Soap operas or serials are open-ended: several stories are interweaved over a sequence of episodes so that, unlike series, no single episode stands by itself. In serials, then, there is no point where all the elements of the story are neatly tied up, no 'moment of formal closure' as in traditional plays, novels and series. Soap operas are one of the few genres where weddings, for instance, are not a happy ending but the beginning of a marriage that may be troubled or even doomed to failure.

NARRATIVE ORGANIZATION IN THE SERIAL

In 'The continuous serial – a definition' Christine Geraghty (1981) suggests some other characteristics of the genre. Soaps begin with a *hook*, in which the threads of the storyline from the previous episode are taken up, but they also end with a *cliffhanger*, in which one or more dramatic situations are left in suspense, encouraging us to view the next episode to see what happens. These cliffhangers vary 'in intensity and importance. It is not necessary therefore to produce moments of high drama at the end of every episode, and a potentially rigid device is made more flexible by using it comically or for minor events.'

Use of the cliffhanger is balanced by moments of *temporary resolution* in the serial. These can occur, for example, at Christmas or at communal occasions such as weddings or funerals:

> Such moments are marked by the suppression of other stories, even though they will be picked up in the next episode. For once, the harmony within the group of characters will be stressed so that quarrels and differences which would threaten the equilibrium are temporarily suspended.

These occasions, however, are far less common than episodes which deal with several stories. Normally there are two or three stories which, within a single episode, are 'given approximately equal time . . . and very often reflect on and play off each other. As one story finishes, another is begun so that at least two stories are always in progress.'

Finally, the serial has a distinctive relationship to its own past. Although soaps can, and do, run for decades, accumulating complex storylines and histories for their characters, they must appeal to old and new viewers. 'Thus the past can be actively used within a story, be fleetingly referred to, or remain a potential resource for the audience', but 'the ability to "forget" what has happened in a serial's past is equally crucial' (Geraghty, 1981).

Flexibility and *variation*, then – characteristics which define a serial's relationship to its own past – are key terms that Gerraghty uses to distinguish the narrative strategies of soap opera. Thus the serial may break at a point of unfinished action or high tension, at moments of no particular dramatic importance or at moments of temporary resolution. These strategies prevent a sense of complete repetition and are backed up by similar variation at the level of characterization and plot.

SCHEDULING

Like series, serials are screened at *regular time slots* in the schedules. However, where successful series tend, in Britain, to be transmitted in 'blocks' of 13 episodes or so, with breaks inbetween blocks of weeks, or even months and years, soaps continue week in, week out, without a break, until the (very rare) time that the producers decide to discontinue them.

SERIALS V. SERIES

The major reason why even the most popular series eventually come to an end is that the scriptwriters simply run out of ideas. The demands of producing a continual stream of original, self-contained storylines eventually exhaust the imaginations of even the most talented writers. This is particularly true of British series which, unlike US series, are rarely written by large teams. John Cleese and Connie Booth, who created the classic comedy series *Fawlty Towers* (1975), recognized this fact when they turned down a lucrative offer to write 42 further episodes on top of the original 12. They knew only too well that they would never be able to maintain the inspired lunacy of the originals over such an extended period.

Soaps do not, by and large, suffer from this problem, for a number of reasons:

- The continuous, open-ended nature of the programmes (the serial form 'resists narrative closure') means that in any particular episode, *solutions do not have to be found for every situation.*
- Storylines tend to be developed by a group of *several writers*, who take it in turns to write the script for different episodes. This takes the creative pressure off the individual.
- Hence, the action of a particular storyline *does not have to conform to the demands of a rigid 30-, 40- or 50-minute time slot.*
- *Storylines can be developed slowly* over several hours of programme time, and can, if necessary, be *altered* as they go along.

THE IMPORTANCE OF SOAP

As Clarke (1987) notes, soap operas should not, as they often are, be dismissed as unimportant. They are important because of:

- the sheer *volume of output*;
- their *large audiences*;
- their importance as *revenue earners*.

THE ATTRACTION OF SOAP FOR TELEVISION INSTITUTIONS

The attraction of soap can be explained by the relative *cheapness of production budgets* compared with the substantial revenue soaps can generate because of their high ratings. Clarke (1987) explains how budgets are worked out according to 'above-the-line' (direct) and 'below-the-line' (indirect) costs. *Above-the-line costs* are those incurred directly by the programme or episode, including script, cast, set, costumes, travel and so on. *Below-the-line costs* cover everything which is there anyway such as studios, equipment, salaries of technicians and production staff.

In both these areas soap is cheap. Soap sets are reused week in and week out. They use everyday costumes and little or no location work. In terms of below-the-line costs, the routine of soap opera production is perfectly suited to the demands of the television industry.

Soap's large audiences enable lucrative rates to be charged for *advertising*. For non-commercial television the genre is now equally important. It is claimed that the large audiences that *Eastenders* guaranteed for the BBC saved it from privatization.

BRITISH SOAPS

It is interesting to note that US soaps tend to deal with the rich, Australian soaps concentrate on their middle class whereas British soaps have predominantly working-class characters (Alvarado, 1987). The first British television soap was *The Groves* (1954–57). Britain's longest-running and most popular television soap is *Coronation Street*, which started in 1960. There have been others along the way, including *Compact* (1962–65), *United* (1965–67), *The Newcomers* (1965–69), *Crossroads* (1964–88), *General Hospital* (1972–79) and *Eldorado* (1992–93).

British soaps tend to have a strong *regional identity* and are clearly located in a particular geographical area. The characters of US daytime soaps such as *The Bold and the Beautiful* are, by contrast, virtual prisoners of indoor sets – invariably darkened, claustrophobic rooms. Even in those US soaps that have a real location in their title such as *Santa Barbara*, we have no sense of a real place as a background to the emotional drama. No doubt the pressures of producing daily episodes on tiny budgets is largely responsible, and bigger-budget serials such as *Dallas* do include outdoor sequences shot on film.

British soaps until the 1980s, however, were largely produced by one of the regional ITV companies, part of whose remit was to reflect their regions and concerns to the rest of the country. Programmes such as *Coronation Street* set in Salford, *Crossroads* set in the Midlands and *Emmerdale Farm* set in Yorkshire allowed the companies concerned (Granada, Central and Yorkshire Television) to justify they were fulfilling their franchise obligations.

This tradition was continued by Phil Redmond's *Brookside*, set in Liverpool, which is produced for Channel 4, and the BBC soap opera *Eastenders* set in the East End of London. All these serials are filmed in the areas they refer to and attempt to *reflect something of the nature, accent and locations of their settings*. They are all, unlike US soap, committed to ideas of community – with regular public meeting points for all the characters such as in The Queen Vic in *Eastenders* or The Rover's Return in *Coronation Street*.

Finally, British soaps, particularly in recent years, can be distinguished from their US and Australian counterparts by a *willingness to engage in 'social issues'* such as unemployment, drugs, race and sexuality. This is not equally true of all British soap, but even *Coronation Street*, probably the most 'domestically centred' of the peak-time serials, deals with contentious issues, albeit solely in terms of their effects on the personal emotions of the characters involved.

CORONATION STREET

Coronation Street, Britain's longest-running soap opera, draws almost as much hyperbole as it does ratings for the ITV network. Britain's 'best-loved soap' is described by Roy Hattersley as a 'chronicle of our times' which 'now reflects the complicated class and racial structure that characterises British society'. A more sober analysis of the programme would admit that the serial is as much of a fairy-tale representation of Salford today as it was when it began in 1960. Massive unemployment, social deprivation and inequality, organized crime, drugs, alcoholism and violence are glossed over in favour of 'rose-tinted nostalgia' for a close-knit community of all ages meeting at the pub to discuss their problems. It is also difficult to see how a soap that managed, in over 35 years (until 1995), to avoid having a major black or Asian character could be said to be a fair racial representation of the North West or of Britain itself.

Many people enjoy the fictional drama and humour of stereotyped characters and sitcom scenarios as *escapist entertainment*. The quality of the acting, scriptwriting and production is usually high, and *Coronation Street* is rightly praised for these qualities. However, when a major politician claims it 'is the story . . . of the people who watch it' or that 'it deals with real characters and real emotions' the potential dangers of soap's realist *style* become apparent. Neither the producers, nor its audience, have been keen for the programme to stray into the territory of 'documentary'. The exception to this rule was Susi Hush, producer of the serial in the early 1970s, who was removed after two years because her policy of dealing with ' live' social issues such as drugs in the programme resulted in viewing figures dropping from between 16–20 million to below 10 million an episode.

Since that time, those involved in its production have never pretended that the serial is anything more than 'light entertainment'. Bill Podmore, who helped restore the programme to its number one position in the TV ratings, is quite explicit about his *distaste for controversy*: 'Although *Coronation Street* has touched on social comment, I never allowed the programme to become a platform for debate, moral or otherwise.' Furthermore, Podmore is critical of those soaps that do: '*EastEnders* took up the cudgels for just about every controversial issue, from homosexuality and AIDS to drug addiction. The series seems to plunge from one depression to the next' (Smith and Holland, 1987). *Coronation Street* remains the market leader of British soap owing to a skilful, if cosy, blend of *romance, drama* and *comedy*. It is this flexible combination that may yet see it outlive its rivals.

BROOKSIDE

Less than 50 miles away geographically, but a world away in terms of the picture it presents of modern life in Britain, is Phil Redmond's *Brookside*. His Liverpool-based soap opera, first screened in November 1982, positively relishes taking up issues, using the format unashamedly as a *'platform for debate'*. As with his earlier comprehensive school series, *Grange Hill*, Redmond uses the 'light-TV' formula to investigate serious, topical concerns: unemployment, industrial relations, drug misuse, the state of the National Health Service, child and wife abuse, rape, petty crime, homosexuality, incest. It is the reason, he claims, that he was drawn to the soap opera format: 'I always wanted to do contemporary drama that, while it would entertain, would raise people's awareness of contemporary issues' (*Independent on Sunday*, 1995).

It is a goal *Brookside*'s makers are proud to advertise. And, unlike *Coronation Street*, whose publicists refer to the serial as a 'folk opera', they do not fight shy of the term 'soap opera'. In the words of its own publicity, in *Brookside: the official companion* (Tibballs, 1994):

Pre-dating the BBC's *Eastenders* by more than two years, *Brookside* is frequently referred to alongside its rival as helping to create a new breed of British soap opera, shot with new technology in 'real' locations and with a 'new passion' which facilitates a more authentic and socially relevant representation of contemporary British life. But even as *Brookside* announces itself as unmistakably different, at the same time the programme offers the viewer more traditional pleasures, playing upon the idea of 'similarity' and 'familiarity' by willingly conforming to the recognizable conventions and characteristics of the established soap opera genre. For many viewers it is this co-presence of similarity and difference and the ongoing tension between these two elements which is the programme's greatest strength and which marks it out from other continuous television fictions.

The *stereotyped* view of Liverpool as a heavy-drinking, working-class city that laughs in the face of high unemployment, decay and deprivation has been *turned on its head*. The serial is set in a modern suburb without a 'pub', features successful yuppies as well as working-class characters and lacks the self-congratulatory tone of so much previous drama based in Liverpool. The danger for *Brookside* arises not so much from complacency as from charges of sensationalism. Three armed sieges, as many murders, rapes and car accidents, countless heterosexual and homosexual affairs, cases of drug addiction, AIDS, religious fundamentalism and domestic violence make Brookside look like the most dangerous close in Britain.

EASTENDERS

The same charges of *sensationalism* are often levelled at the BBC's *Eastenders*, first launched in February 1985. The decision to launch a soap opera was first taken by the BBC in 1981. Andy Medhurst (1994) argues that the hospital serial *Angels*, only broadcast for part of the year in the early 1980s,

> had not only shown a public appetite for BBC soap, but had demonstrated that the generic essentials of archetype, cliffhangers and vigorous emotionality could happily co-exist with an exploration of social issues and an unblinking vision of the complications of contemporary Britain.

Ironically, it was precisely this approach of gritty, 'realistic' portrayals of social problems tried out by Susi Hush 10 years earlier to such disastrous effect in *Coronation Street* which contributed to the success of *Brookside* and *Eastenders*. Clearly, what audiences found acceptable in the content of soap had changed significantly in that period, making it possible for producers of soap to be more *adventurous* and *controversial*.

At its launch *Eastenders* attracted 13 million viewers, but in the first summer this dropped to 7 million. Rescheduling at 7.30 to avoid a clash with *Emmerdale Farm*, meatier storylines and press attention drawn by Mary Whitehouse all contributed to the soap bouncing back to audiences of 20 million by its first anniversary. Putting the weekend omnibus aside, *Eastenders* has trailed just behind *Coronation Street* in the ratings ever since.

Tony McHale, a writer and director of *Eastenders*, sees the programme 'as heir to the radical values of the social-realism single drama of the Sixties'. He describes *Eastenders* as 'storytelling that engages on a social level'. He also recognizes the danger of writing for ratings:

> I've seen the show veer from sitcom to total melodrama. But it works best when it seems real. People can relate to stories about abortion, adultery, rape. What they can't relate to is the sensationalist elements. To me, it becomes a different programme when there's an armed siege in The Queen Vic. It should be about page ten news, not page one.

PRODUCTION

In a British soap such as *Brookside* or *Coronation Street* the production process begins between three and five months before screening. A team of about 12 writers, a story editor, storyline writers or script assistants and the producer plan a block of nine episodes at a story conference which can last up to two days. Initially, an agenda is distributed with questions about the characters for consideration. Gradually a rough storyline is agreed. There are usually around three stories in an episode which may include a balance of drama, romance and comedy.

After the conference the rough storylines are developed into detailed synopses by the storyline writers. Each of the 12 writers is then commissioned by the producer to turn synopses into a complete episode. After reading the synopses the writers attend a commissioning conference to discuss the finer details of plot and continuity. The writers then go away to work on their episodes alone, although they may call on the programme's researchers to make sure any factual information is correct.

When the script is delivered the producer and story editor or script assistant will read through them and discuss any changes necessary with the writer. Complete rewrites are rarely required, but if necessary the producer can commission another writer to do so. The producer will then hand the scripts over to the director.

A director will receive three scripts, a week's worth of episodes, and she or he will have a month to produce them. (There are up to four directors working on the serial in a four-week cycle.) In the first week the director will study the scripts and show them to other departments, such as casting, costume or design. With the production assistant she or he will discuss the administration for rehearsal and recording and mark up the hundreds of shots to be taken on a camera script. Scripts are then printed for cast and crew. The second week may involve rehearsals in addition to any of the preparations mentioned above. The third week is for rehearsing and recording.

Every minute of recording takes up to an hour to complete, which is in fact very fast for television. Detailed production techniques vary somewhat: *Brookside*, for instance, works with only one camera, whereas *Coronation*

Street has more than one camera filming each scene. Each episode is timed to last 24½ minutes approximately, and last-minute changes are sometimes necessary to fit this time slot. After a week's work the episode is 'in the can' and ready for editing.

In the fourth week the director and the production assistant move into the edit suite to produce a rough cut. This may be viewed by the producer before the director puts together a 'fine cut', the version which we see on our screens some months later.

CRITICISMS OF THE GENRE

In assessing soap it is important to remember its original (and continuing) function – *to deliver mass audiences to advertisers*, or, in the case of public service television, to justify continued public subsidy. In this sense, soap opera – a story without end, broadcast regularly (on a daily basis if possible) to large and loyal audiences – is the perfect television format.

'It helps me to relax'

The language of drug-abuse is often used to stigmatize the enjoyment of soap opera. Its appeal is frequently dismissed as 'escapist' and 'addictive'. Fans who spend hours each day watching serials are derided as 'soap fiends'. Cooperation between channels – for whom a ratings war on soaps would be self-destructive – allows viewers to get several uninterrupted 'fixes'. Effectively, such guaranteed, massive daily 'doses' offer an escape from the viewer's own life and worries through the problems and 'lives' of fictional characters, no matter how vacuous these may be. Fiske (1987) describes a typical criticism of the indefinitely deferred narrative structure:

> soap operas teach women by example to forgo the real, final satisfaction of desire in favour of a series of unreal, minor pleasures. These minor pleasures 'buy' the viewer, and win their apparently willing consent to the system that subordinates them. Women, this argument runs, harm themselves as a class by their pleasure as individuals.

There is no doubt that even the cheapest and 'trashiest' examples of the genre (*Prisoner Cell Block H*, *The Bold and the Beautiful* ?) draw large, regular audiences, many of whom claim a perverse pleasure in laughing at the inanity of a particular soap: 'I only watch it because it's so bad' is a common response to queries about soap's pleasures. It is often this *'ironic' enjoyment* of a (melo)drama and its crude emotionalism which can result in a more permanent commitment to a serial. The *predictable nature* of the genre offers security, even a sense of superiority, and this may be its greatest appeal.

Certainly, the task of bringing anything fresh to a product created under *assembly-line conditions* is exceptionally difficult, and it seems miraculous that many productions have, in fact, managed to do so. Frequently, however, the range and complexity of contemporary human experience is reduced to a series of clichés and stock scenarios. Television, as Graham Murdock (1991) argues, should 'engage with the greatest possible range of contemporary experience, both personal and collective, and interrogate the historical roots of present conditions. It must attack stereotypes and encourage viewers to make imaginative leaps into the world of the "other".' Soap's appeal to a mass audience is, its critics argue, too often maintained by insisting on the obvious, the bland, the grindingly unoriginal. At its worst, soap deadens the mind to any sense of possibility.

Another charge is that by picking up certain issues as dramatic or controversial storylines, soap opera can, in the process, *trivialize* these issues. British soap, in particular, adopts issues with political significance to generate storylines, and the 'realist' style of British productions lends even greater impact to the representation of these social ills. In 1995 the real-life wife of the then Leader of the Opposition, a practising magistrate, gave her support to a condemnatory statement attacking a judge's verdict on a case of murder in an episode of *Brookside*. Should it be a matter of concern that a fictional court case created far more press and public interest than any of the real cases of wife abuse and self-defence or murder that occur every year? Nevertheless, the writers and actors involved in this production felt responsible and concerned at the outcome of the case. What if this concern and responsibility were lacking? How do we react, for instance, to an unemployed Derek Wilton in *Coronation Street*? Does his irritating and idiotic characterization help shed any light on unemployment? To what extent did this storyline 'attack stereotypes'?

Finally, soap can also be accused of dividing people from each other for hours of viewing time, even in their own homes. By providing simple-minded, vicarious emotional experiences and the comfort of an ersatz community life soap, it is suggested, becomes less a communal talking point than the only common reference point in a lifestyle dominated by television. To use Richard Hoggart's phrase in relation to 'bad populist programmes' as opposed to 'good popular programmes', serial dramas often 'treat us like dimwits'. Writers such as Noam Chomsky would go so far as to claim that this is no accident but part of the 'military–industrial complex's' wider strategy of 'dumbing down', manipulating and pacifying national populations. As those who subscribe to the 'mass culture' debate argue, soap, as with other populist forms, 'is fabricated by technicians hired by businessmen; its audiences are passive consumers, their participation limited to the choice between buying and not buying' (MacDonald, quoted in Strinati, 1995).

A WOMAN'S GENRE? DEFENDING 'SOAP'

It has been argued that traditional narrative closure (as found in novels, plays, series and so on) places the viewer or reader in a position of omniscience. This reinforces the illusion of the individual as powerful and in control of events and stresses the role played by (usually) male heroes. Some feminist writers claim that the *open-endedness* of soap may be thought of as a *more feminine* type of narrative structure. A form in which things are never finally completed, where there are only moments of temporary resolution is seen as being closer to life, especially women's lives, which are dominated by tasks that are never-ending, such as housework and child rearing. Fiske (1987) also sees the 'endless deferment' of soap as 'an articulation of a specific feminine definition of desire and pleasure that is contrasted with the masculine pleasure of the final success'.

Geraghty (1981) notes an ambivalent attitude to gender representation in soap opera. A *range* of female types are presented in soap opera of various ages, classes and status:

> A progressive aspect of many soap operas is their sexualisation of older women. Soaps are almost the only television programmes which allow women who do not fit the stereotypes of slim, youthful beauty to have a romantic or sexual existence.

However, while for women over 40 having sex 'may be *thinkable* ... it is certainly not *watchable*' in soap, or on television generally, unlike physical relations involving younger women.

Almost uniquely on television, soap opera consistently includes *strong, independent* women, but Clarke (1987) asks, 'how rarely do such charismatic figures succeed in breaking out of their humdrum, frequently downtrodden situations?' To be fair, the same could also be argued for male characters and may be explained by the highly conventional and parochial 'world-view' that soap opera allows. Just as the pub's name The Rover's Return in *Coronation Street* suggests, all those who wander from the tight-knit, community of Weatherby are bound to return – soap demands its characters make the best of their *restrictingly small confines*.

In *On the Box*, Jane Root argues that the more traditional soap operas, such as *Crossroads*, portrayed 'a women's world, dealing almost exclusively with women's problems and women's stories. Most of the stories are about domestic life, families and unrequited female passion for unattainable (or impossibly flawed) men.' They had come to be marketed at, and associated with, women. As such, the genre 'suffered from the (low) status of its viewers' with the term 'soap' frequently used as a catch-all phrase for the 'worst' of television.

Soap opera's newfound respectability, Root suggests, came with *Brookside*'s widening of the format 'from its original, mainly domestic and female concerns'. *Brookside* broke new ground by including much stronger male characters and masculine stories. This *defeminization* of the genre, Root claims, may explain why *Eastenders* was given the status, facilities and massive backing of the BBC.

Brookside's regeneration of soap – particularly the sense of social awareness it encouraged – has forced a critical reconsideration of the genre. *Eastenders* and *Brookside* continue to raise issues and reflect something of the cultural and ethnic diversity of contemporary Britain. Neither is afraid of provoking a degree of controversy, whether it be stories of lesbianism, domestic violence, heroin addiction or AIDS. They address problems which other television forms ignore and they allow time and space to explore the complexities and repercussions that such problems can involve. Soap is, therefore, at least potentially, a *progressive* television form. It will be interesting to see if this recent tradition is continued (see also Chapter 12, pp. 164–8).

READING: '*BROOKSIDE* BACKS DOWN OVER LESBIAN KISS'

The following report by Andrew Culf, which appeared in the *Guardian* on 7 January 1995, is interesting as it relates to several issues explored in this chapter and in Chapters 11 and 12.

The producers of *Brookside* have dropped a lesbian kiss scene from tonight's omnibus edition of the Channel 4 soap, blaming salacious media coverage for the decision. The embrace was shown just before 9 pm last night, but has been cut from the tea-time repeat because it is screened at a time when more children are likely to be watching.

A spokeswoman for *Brookside*, which has more than five million viewers, said: 'the decision was made because inaccurate representations of the scene have appeared in newspapers prior to transmission without our knowledge, which we felt distracted from the original intent and thereby distorted the integrity of the storyline'. The scene featured a lingering kiss between medical student Beth Jordache, played by Anna Friel, and a new character, Viv, played by Kerrie Thomas, in the front seat of a car.

The spokeswoman said: '*Brookside* has previously screened three lesbian kisses and this particular kiss is no different.' The story, developed over the past 12 months, has given Beth two previous lesbian relationships. Philip Reevell, head of corporate affairs for programme makers Mersey Television, said: 'To talk about the storyline in a salacious way is to misrepresent it. *Brookside* has always reflected contemporary themes. The lesbian storyline is one, alongside domestic violence and a Down's syndrome baby.'

The decision to drop the scene was criticised by Peter Tatchell, of the homosexual pressure group OutRage. 'If Channel 4 is concerned about the way the scene has been misrepresented by the press, the best possible way to clear up any misunderstanding is to screen it in full and let viewers make up their own minds', said Mr Tatchell. 'Channel 4 yet again appear to be caving in to anti-gay prejudice. Kisses between men and women are not considered inappropriate at this time of day. Why should kisses between same sex partners be treated differently?'

The Independent Television Commission, which has received 14 complaints about the lesbian storyline in the past, has not upheld any of them. Its code makes no reference to lesbianism, although it covers taste and decency issues. However, the commission issued a formal warning to Channel 4 in October 1993, when *Brookside* showed a knife being used as a murder weapon in the omnibus edition. It said a large number of children were likely to be watching.

Brookside, which has recently screened its 1,500th episode, is Channel 4's most popular show. It is broadcast three nights a week, but there will be five episodes in the week beginning January 30, in a special one-off attempt to inflate its ratings. Trevor Jordache, murdered by his wife Mandy and daughter Beth, will be dug up from under the patio where his body is buried.

EXERCISES AND ESSAYS

Ways of Looking at Characters

Christine Geraghty (1981) suggests three ways of looking at characters:

- as individuated characters, based on the commonsense notion that characters should be seen as unique and distinct from other characters;
- as serial types, where a pattern seems to emerge in the kinds of characters found in soaps, for example J.R., 'Dirty Den', Grant Mitchell, Mike Baldwin (?); other characters may be defined as similar to, or different from, these types;
- as holders of status positions, for example grandmother figures, marriageable men and women, married couples, businessmen and women, and so on.

These concepts are useful if they help us to see some of the structural possibilities of a particular cast list. For example, if certain characters are written out they may have to be replaced by similar types.

Exercise

Find examples or arguments for *one* of the above ways of looking at character. For example draw up a list of 'serial types' or 'holders of status position', or examine why these categories can be seen to be inadequate on closer examination.

Exercise

A woman's sexuality does not, in soap opera, result in her objectification for the male. Rather it is a positive source of pleasure in a relationship, or a means of her empowerment in a patriarchal world. The woman's power to influence and control the male can never be finally achieved but is constantly in process. It is a form of power not legitimated by the dominant ideology, and can thus exist only in the continuous struggle to exercise it. A man's 'conquest' of a woman, his possession of her, may be said to have been achieved at the moment of sexual climax; a woman's control over a man, however, has no such final achievement. The emphasis on seduction and on its continuous pleasure and power is appropriate to a contemporary feminine subjectivity, for that subjectivity has necessarily been formed through a constant experience of powerlessness and subordination (Fiske, 1987).

From any of the soaps you have watched list any examples of

- a woman's sexuality being used as 'a means of empowerment';
- 'seduction and its continuous pleasure' being emphasized.

Group Exercise

▓ *Day 1*

Look at the following scene from an episode of *Coronation Street*. This is the script as the director and actors received it (including non-standard spelling). The space next to the script is for the director's notes – which detail how the scene will be shot; the result is a camera script. Prepare a camera script for the scene. (It will help if you look at how similar scenes are shot in a soap you are studying.) You have two cameras available. Mark each section of script indicating *shot number, camera 1 or 2, camera position* and *shot type* [long shot (LS), medium shot (MS), close-up (CU) and extremely close-up (ECU)]. Choose a location to film your script. Decide on props, costume, lighting (if available), actors, camera operators and director. Divide these tasks amongst you as a group. Draw up a floor plan and indicate the position of the cameras and any changes during the scene. You should plan for as few breaks in continuity as possible as this will make editing much easier. For the same reason the actors should rehearse and know their lines before the next session.

1. INT. WEBSTERS' LIVING
   ROOM, 9.45P.M.

   KEVIN, SALLY.

   MUCH AS THEY WERE AT THE END OF

THE LAST EP. IT'S CONTINUOUS
TIME MORE OR LESS.

KEVIN IS SITTING AT THE TABLE,
LOOKING AT SALLY.

KEVIN

How sure are you?

SALLY

Two tests. I did me own and had

one at Doctor's. It's definite,

Kev, I'm pregnant.

KEVIN

(BEAT) Why din't you tell me

before?

SALLY

I'd to wait to be sure. And

anyway, you wittered on about

this holiday and I never got a

chance.

KEVIN

(TWIGGING) That's why you

weren't keen?

SALLY

I din't want us spending money we

might not be able to afford.

Money we might need to set up for

the baby.

PAUSE

What're you thinking?

    <u>KEVIN</u>

(SHRUGS) Don't know to be

honest. I suppose I can't really

believe it. What about you?

    <u>SALLY</u>

Had to happen sooner or later,

din't it? I Mean, we always said

we would . . .

    <u>KEVIN</u>

Yeh, we did. (BEAT) It's

just . . . talking about it now, you

don't see it from the same angle, do

you. 'You'd make a lovely dad,

Kev'. 'We'll probably have at

least two, Kev . . .' Planning. That

feels different.

    <u>SALLY</u>

But we din't want to be old

parents, did we? Rate we were

going, we'd have been talking and

planning till we were fifty.

Then it'd have been too late.

(SITS OPPOSITE TO MONITOR HIS

FACE) What are you thinking?

> KEVIN

Bit frightened, that's all.

> SALLY

Whether you want it, or whether

we'll cope?

> KEVIN

Responsibility.

> SALLY

(INCREASINGLY UNCOMFORTABLE) But

you do want it?

HE STARES AT HER FOR A MOMENT.
HIS HAND SLIDES ACROSS THE TABLE,
TAKES HER'S, AND HIS FACE BREAKS
INTO A GRIN.

▥ *Day 2*

Film the scene. Remember that in the industry every minute of soap takes about an hour to complete. This is about how long you will have, so you will have to be well organized. The production assistant or director should log any problems.

▥ *Day 3*

Edit the sequence. Log and discuss any problems you had with meeting the deadlines – check the production assistant's notes from the previous lesson. These problems can be of many sorts (e.g. lack of experience with the technology, poor organization, unavailability of cast, crew, location, props, production facilities, and so on). Log what worked and what did not work. Note any suggestions for the next production to avoid the problems you experienced this time.

Group Exercise

Task: prepare three minutes of a soap opera. This could be made up of three scenes. Reread the section on production and work in groups of nine to write, act, produce and edit the sequence. A suggested scheme for production is outlined below.

▥ *Day 1*

Hold a story conference. It may be quicker to base your characters on types in the soaps you are studying. Outline the three scenes as a group of nine. Write a brief description of the characters and synopsis of one of these scenes in groups of three. The scenes should be simple and brief. All three people in the group should have their own copy of this work. The scenes may be, for example:

> Scene 1: a job offer.
> Scene 2: someone causes offence unintentionally (possibly humorous).
> Scene 3: a romantic proposal.

▥ *Day 2*

Hold a commissioning conference. Briefly discuss your three stories. If possible organize matching cuts from one scene to the next – these may be simple visual links such as a closing door at the end of one scene and an opening door at the beginning of another. They provide some form of continuity between scenes where there may be none.

Begin scriptwriting. In groups of three writeup your one-minute scene in full. Each scene should be no longer than the sample script from *Coronation Street*. Type the scene in the same format as the sample script. The same characters may appear in more than one scene, but this may cause continuity problems.

■ *Day 3*

Begin preproduction. Prepare a camera script for your scene. Discuss and organize all aspects of production.

■ *Day 4*

Rehearse and produce Scene 1.

■ *Day 5*

Rehearse and produce Scene 2; carry out post-production of Scene 1.

■ *Day 6*

Rehearse and produce Scene 3; carry out post-production of Scene 2.

■ *Day 7*

Carry out post-production of Scene 3. Edit the sequence together. Write up an assessment of the finished product.

Essay

Answer one of the following questions:

What are the major conventions of soap opera?
What are the distinctive narrative qualities of soap opera?

Essay

Discuss:

How is marriage represented in continuous serials?

Essay

The soap opera villainness is the negative image of the viewer's ideal self, which is constructed by the soaps as the ideal mother (Modleski).

Discuss this view with reference to soap operas you have watched.

Essay

Soaps are historically and culturally produced, which means that the feminine readings they offer are within and against patriarchy.

Illustrate this argument with examples you have studied.

Essay

A defining characteristic of soap opera is its denial of a unified reading position and of a coherent meaning of the text (Fiske).

Explain this position. Do you agree with it?

Sources

Alvarado, M. (1987): *Television and video.* Wayland.

Bazalgette, C., *et al.* (1983): *Teaching Coronation Street.* British Film Institute Education.

Beckett, A. (1995): Scouse Sultan of Soap: a profile of Phil Redmond. *The Independent on Sunday* May.

Clarke, M. (1987): *Teaching popular television.* Heinemann Educational in association with the British Film Institute.

Culf, A. (1995): *Brookside* backs down over lesbian kiss. *The Guardian* 7 January.

Dyer, R., *et al.* (1981): *Coronation Street.* British Film Institute.

Fiske, J. (1987): *Television culture.* Routledge.

Geraghty, C. (1981): The continuous serial – a definition. In R. Dyer, R. Geraghty, C. Jordan *et al.* (eds), *Coronation Street.* British Film Institute.

Hattersley, R. (1990): *Coronation Street* reviewed. *TV Quick.*

Little, D. (1995): *The Coronation Street Story.* Boxtree.

Maltby, R. (ed.) (1989): *Dreams for sale – popular culture in the 20th century.* Equinox.

Masterman, L. (1980): *Teaching about television.* Macmillan.

Medhurst, A. (1995): Risen from the east. *The Observer Review* February.

Medhurst, A. (1994): Letting them watch soap. *The Observer* April.

Murdock, G. (1991): Whose television is it anyway? *Sight and Sound* October.

Root, J. (1984): *Open the box.* Comedia.

Smith, J. and Holland, T. (1987): *Eastenders: the inside story.* BBC Books.

Strinati, D. (1995): *An introduction to the theories of popular culture.* Routledge.

Tibballs, G. (1994): *Brookside: the official companion.* Pan Books.

Absolutely Fabulous: Edina and Patsy

6

Situation Comedy

THE DEVELOPMENT OF BRITISH SITUATION COMEDY

The term *sitcom*, according to Neale and Krutnik (1990), describes a narrative series comedy, generally between 24 and 30 minutes long, with regular characters and settings. Like soap opera, situation comedy has its roots in *radio*. Live US performance humour, employing writers such as Mel Brooks and Woody Allen and stars such as Bob Hope and Jack Benny, had a strong influence on the development of zany broadcast comedy in Britain. This irreverent, working-class comedy was only given real expression for the first time on Forces Radio, during the Second World War. The 'vulgarity' of such material included lewd innuendo (honed to a fine art by, amongst others, Kenneth Williams) and caricatures of class and social types later taken to surreal extremes by Spike Milligan, Harry Secombe, Peter Sellers and Michael Bentine in *The Goons*.

Although most early comedy of this kind was in the form of sketches the sitcom format was being developed in the USA in the 1940s. A number of radio sitcoms in the USA transferred directly to the small screen in the late 1940s and early 1950s as did their stars, such as Lucille Ball. Her show *I Love Lucy* was one of several Hollywood television sitcoms imported to Britain. Until the 1960s the family depicted in US sitcoms tended to be husband and wife, without children – such as *Bewitched* or *The Dick Van Dyke Show*. These were known in the industry as 'Hi honey, I'm home' shows.

The influence of these shows in Britain can be seen in *Hancock's Half Hour*, where the use of reaction shots and the casting of straight actors for minor roles was developed. The 'naturalism' of *Hancock's Half Hour* – its grey bedsit setting, realistic if 'oddball' characters, low-key supporting performances, everyday plot developments and rambling cod-philosophical monologues set the tone for a distinctively 'British' brand of situation comedy. This comedy, grounded in aspirational frustrations, class antagonisms and a gloomy, mocking attitude to the mundane social realities of modern urban life was later exemplified by classic (and endlessly repeated) sitcoms such as *Steptoe and Son*, *The Likely Lads*, *Porridge*, *Fawlty Towers* and *Rising Damp*. The same vein of humour can still be found running through more recent popular sitcoms such as *One Foot in the Grave* and *Rab C. Nesbitt*.

ALTERNATIVE V. MAINSTREAM

In his book *Television Producers* Jeremy Tunstall shows how mainstream and alternative comedy are not discreet traditions but have tended, in their development, to inform and influence each other. The big successes of British comedy, Tunstall notes, have focused on 'working class loners, misfits and bigots. The archetypal British TV comedy was Steptoe and Son, about the embattled relationship between a rag-and-bone man and his eccentric and exasperating old father.'

Mainstream television comedy, Tunstall argues, incorporated the impact of US situation comedies, but was anchored to predominantly British working-class comic traditions. A comedy such as *Till Death Us Do Part*, when it began in 1964, was considered daring in its screen portrayal of a working-class bigot. For a time *Till Death Us Do Part* was the most popular programme in Britain, with audiences of 18 million. The series was attacked by Mary Whitehouse's 'Clean Up TV Campaign' for its disrespectful attitudes and strong language (the use of the word *bloody* was a cause for concern). According to Wheen (1985), the arrival of Lord Hill as a new governor at the BBC in 1967 saw the introduction of censorship to this programme which was resented so strongly by the writer that its production was suspended for four years. However, the series (or the Alf Garnett character) returned and ran on into the 1990s, by which time it had long since entered the mainstream.

Eccentric caricatures of English class and society were also to be found in *Dad's Army*, written by Jimmy Perry and David Croft (who went on to write other ensemble cast comedies: *It Ain't Half Hot Mum*, *'Allo 'Allo* and *Hi-De-Hi!*). The brilliantly cast types included a pompous bank manager, Captain Mainwaring (Arthur Lowe); a softly spoken and quietly exasperated second in command, Sergeant Wilson (John Le Mesurier); a spivvy black marketeer, Walker (James Beck); a doddery old-age pensioner (Arnold Ridley) whose only contribution to the platoon was to supply 'my sister Dolly's fairy cakes'; and the tight-fisted and manic Scot (John Laurie). *The Liver Birds* (started in 1969), *Man About the House* (1973), *Rising Damp* (1974) and *Last of the Summer Wine* (1974) were other eccentric but mainstream series located in typical everyday situations. These and other comedies appeared on the main channels (BBC1 and ITV) and attracted large audiences and considerable press attention, especially in the tabloid newspapers.

The 1960s and 1970s saw only a handful of variety shows and situation comedies aimed at *smaller, more adventurous* audiences. These included *That Was the Week That Was* (TW3), *Monty Python's Flying Circus*, Spike Milligan's *Q*, *Dave Allen* and *Not the Nine O'Clock News*. These programmes were generally shown on BBC2, whereas BBC1 and ITV aimed their shows at more general, mass audiences. By the end of the 1970s, however, none of the relatively daring or eccentric comic talent was shining as it had done in main-stream comedy for the previous two decades. Many of the great comedians such as Morecambe and Wise, Frankie Howerd, Ronnie Corbett and Ronnie Barker were ageing, and this showed in the tired material they produced, and inventive sitcoms such as *Dad's Army*, *The Liver Birds*, *Butterflies* and *The Rise and Fall of Reginald Perrin* were far outnumbered by banal comedies of social manners epitomized by *Terry and June*.

The creation of Channel 4 provided an opportunity to cater for more diverse tastes in comedy. Initially, little action was taken apart from the introduction of some new US sitcoms to the schedules. There were, however, some short films made by the Comic Strip Team, including *Five Go Mad in Dorset*, which received unexpected praise and attention. These films, which came out of the channel's youth programmes department run by Mike Bolland, introduced a more hip, sex-and-drugs-and-rock'n'roll edge to the kind of Eng. Lit. pastiches and media parodies pursued at the BBC by Oxbridge comedians since *The Frost Report* and *Not Only . . . But Also*.

The BBC was sufficiently anxious about Channel 4's success with the Comic Strip to allow producer Paul Jackson to assemble the same group of performers (plus Ben Elton, though minus the Strip's director and writer, Peter Richardson) to make *The Young Ones* for BBC2. The four students – a violent punk, a morose hippy, a wheeler dealer and a posturing 'anarchist' – live a monstrous parody of student life, destroying the house they share, viciously abusing each other, verbally and physically, eating stomach-turning food and turning to any substance or pathetic distraction (such as the white-dot signal on the television at the end of the evening) to avoid the boredom of doing nothing. Halfway through the episode a band would play on the set; there were incongruous interruptions such as puppet hamsters holding a conversation, a subliminal shot of a frog leaping, a ranting monologue by the deranged landlord as well as implausible jumps in time and violence taken to surreal excesses. As one television journalist has suggested, '*The Young Ones*, more so than the Comic Strip films, was a genuine alternative to all other television comedy. It demonstrated that you could break all the rules of narrative TV comedy and still hold a big (for BBC2) audience.'

BBC2 and Channel 4 now began to compete directly for the same young, 'smart' audience so beloved of advertisers. Paul Jackson's success with *The Young Ones* enabled him to launch the careers of Dawn French, Jennifer Saunders and Ruby Wax in *Girls on Top* and of Craig Charles and Chris Barrie in *Red Dwarf*. While on Channel 4, Mike Bolland, now head of entertainment, greatly increased original comedy output in the form of new sitcoms, sketch shows and stand-up comedy, including the highly influential *Saturday Night Live* (later *Friday Night Live*) where new names and careers were made.

As *experimental* comedy output increased massively in the early 1980s so did the rules by which it was judged. With multiplying hours of airtime and protected by youth television's 'public service' origins (where low ratings do not matter if the programme is deemed novel or daring enough) audiences of two million were now regarded as quite acceptable for a new show and new stars. Most of this alternative comedy did not aim for mass audiences. Many of the leading participants came from Cambridge University or (by the 1980s) Manchester University. These people lacked the typical mainstream comedian's lengthy apprenticeship in front of live audiences. Many had worked on the all-talk and fairly upmarket BBC Radio 4 and in London comedy venues and fringe theatres, as well as in West End commercial theatre.

Alternative comedy, as Tunstall suggests, is difficult to define, not least because it tends after an interval to join the mainstream. Nevertheless, a key difference from mainstream television comedy was that alternative comedians typically wrote their own material. They adopted deliberately non-commercial approaches; for example, the strong vein of *political satire* prevalent in 1960s shows such as *That Was the Week That Was* or much of the new comedy in the early 1980s which was not geared to massive ratings success. Indeed, several of these alternative shows included an element of topical references to recent events: *Spitting Image*, *The New Statesman* and *Drop the Dead Donkey*, were, by including topical political references, reducing the long-term, repeat-asset, value of their output.

However, the boundaries of mainstream and alternative comedy are continuously shifting. Not only are elements of the alternative always merging into the mainstream, but some comedians and comic styles, only recently regarded as too embarrassing to be still included in the mainstream, are soon dusted down and proclaimed to be classics. Benny Hill (who wrote his own scripts), after his dismissal by Thames Television apparently for being outdated and sexist, was being praised by Anthony Burgess in 1990 as 'one of the great artists of our age' and a genius of the 'comedy of sexual regret'. The BBC *Omnibus* arts programme also devoted an hour to Benny Hill in 1991, a year before his death (Tunstall, 1993).

As television critic David Housham suggests, the fact that Channel 4, of all channels, was prepared to screen repeats of Benny Hill, 'was a sign of the degree to which the cultural partitioning of British comedy, so energetically and noisily constructed in the early 1980s, has been steadily demolished in the 1990s'.

SITCOM NARRATIVE

The principal fundamental situation of the situation comedy is that things do not change (Grote, quoted in Neale and Krutnik, 1990).

The situation, to fill the demands of the time-slot, the demands of constant repetition of/in the series, needs to be one whose parameters are easily recognizable and which are returned to week after week. Nothing that has happened in the narrative of the previous week must destroy or even complicate the way the situation is grounded (Eaton, 1981).

Sitcoms, like all serials, employ a '*classical*' narrative structure that involves the disruption of a stable situation and its resolution within each episode. The reassertion of stability is different from that in feature films, however, where narrative closure establishes a new equilibrium. In sitcom, narrative closure is marked by a return to the original situation. The sitcom centres around the refamiliarization of a recurring situation, repeated and redefined in the face of various disruptions and transgressions.

Situation comedies, unlike sketch-based comedy series, have a clearly defined beginning, middle and end. The situation – the humorous development of the week – is usually based around a problem, the complication of this problem and its resolution within the half-hour episode. In her essay *Genre study and television* (1987) Jane Feuer quotes Horace Newcomb on this narrative strategy:

> Newcomb sees the sitcom as providing a simple and reassuring problem/ solution formula. The audience is reassured, not challenged by choice or ambiguity, nor are we forced to reexamine our values . . . Newcomb thus constructs the sit-com as the most 'basic' of the television genres in the sense that it is the furthest from the 'real world' problems such as are encountered in crime shows and from real world forms and value conflicts such as are encountered in soap operas.

Unlike soap, then, the basic 'situation' does not change but is subjected to a recurring process of destabilization–restabilization in each episode. The sitcom's process of narrative transformation relies, then, upon circularity. That is not to say that some modification of basic situation is impossible. Families may gain or lose children as they grow up (as in *Roseanne*), long-lost relatives are found, additional characters join series, old ones leave and background details change to keep the stories from becoming stale and repetitive. Nevertheless, the essential elements remain the same. Where there is a temptation to exploit a particular character in a new setting and with new characters a *spin-off* series may be the result. *Frasier* from *Cheers*, *Benson* from the anarchic *Soap* and *Going Straight* from *Porridge* are just three examples of this phenomenon.

The essential *circularity* and *ritualistic simplicity* of sitcom is illustrated by what Philip Drummond calls its 'synchronizing motifs'. These are repeated situations or catchphrases such as Victor Meldrew's exasperated, 'I don't believe it!' in *One Foot in the Grave* or the freewheeling downhill accidents of *Last of the Summer Wine*. These highly recognizable motifs are an important comic technique, as they are in sketch comedy where catchphrases such as Dick Emery's 'Oh, you are awful but I like you!', or Harry Enfield's 'Loadsamoney!' have entered the popular consciousness.

Situation comedy's 'simplicity' is also apparent in the choice of *themes* and *experiences* which the genre draws upon. Family and home, work and authority are the most commonly explored areas of sitcom. As Mick Eaton (1981) observes:

the two basic situations used continually over the years are 'home' and 'work' . . . these basic situations provide material for the constant repetition of character and theme, and fit the economic demands of the company's budget in allowing for the use of stock sets, and little or no filmed footage.

Home and work are common areas of experience and most people are able to recognize the humour that results in friction between people forced to live or work together. The *collision* of *values*, *identities* and *lifestyles* is at the heart of most comedy – and the harsher the collision, the louder the laughter. For this reason, most comedies involve characters confined by their circumstances, railing against each other or society. Taken to slapstick extremes the collision or conflict involves violent verbal and physical abuse, as can be found in *Fawlty Towers* or *The Young Ones*. The comedy 'situations' may also take the form of racial, sexual or class conflicts, for, as Mick Bowes (1990) notes, 'the genre is constantly having to handle areas of social unease'.

SITCOM AND REPRESENTATION

Situation comedies are frequently controversial in their representations. Sitcom, like so much television comedy, deals with *stereotypes* (simplified concepts of a social group) which can be offensive and can perpetuate myths that are damaging in their effect. They may also, through absence of certain representations, sustain deep-rooted inequalities and prejudices (Chapter 11).

Mick Bowes, in his essay 'Only when I laugh', illustrates the *ambiguous* role of stereotypes in situation comedy:

In a form which attempts to establish character and narrative and produce humour all in a half hour it is inevitable that characterisation will tend towards the stereotypical. In many senses stereotypes are both simple and complex – they are simplified ways of conveying distinct cultural images. In many senses what is important is to examine the place of the stereotype in the structure of the programme – is the stereotype the target of the humour or the producer of it? Are we laughing at the stereotyped group or with it? In this sense there is a considerable difference between the crude racist stereotype of Asian characters in *It Ain't Half Hot Mum*, who we are invited to laugh at, and the gay stereotypes of *Agony* who often function as a means of making the prejudices of 'straight' people seem odd and laughable.

The great tradition of British situation comedy has centred around *men*. *Steptoe and Son*, *Dad's Army*, *It Ain't Half Hot Mum* and *Only Fools and Horses* are just a few examples of sitcoms that are remarkable for having virtually no female roles. This is in contrast to US sitcoms where there is a long tradition of women having major characters: *I Love Lucy*, *Bewitched*, *The*

Mary Tyler Moore Show, Rhoda, The Golden Girls, Roseanne and *Grace Under Fire* are just a few examples.

In British sitcoms maleness becomes associated with 'dirt', 'disgustingness' and 'misbehaviour': only consider the roles in sitcoms such as *The Young Ones, Bottom, Men Behaving Badly* and *Red Dwarf*. Women are frequently absent or banished, as in 'Her indoors' from *Minder*, or Mainwaring's wife in *Dad's Army*. When women are there their relationship is usually as the mother figure to the inadequate men, as in *Terry and June* or *Some Mothers do 'Ave 'Em*. Much of the slapstick comes from the men being left in charge of domestic duties such as cooking or cleaning, with disastrous consequences.

In *Last of the Summer Wine* the old men are infantalized, and the women, for example Nora Batty, are powerful, domineering figures, akin to the northern seaside postcard representation of husbands and wives. Men and women in *Last of the Summer Wine*, as in so many other sitcoms, live in irreconcilably *polarized* worlds. The sexes only seem to mix at meal times – again suggesting a parent–child relationship operating at a deeper level within the representation.

The portrayal of men, like the portrayal of virtually any social group in sitcom, raises the question of whether it is possible to have comedy without stereotypes (see Chapter 11, pp. 154–7). British comedies are not socially engineered in the same way that some British soap operas are. This situation is the reverse of the case on US television where there are far more racial minorities shown in sitcom than there are in soap. The very rich backgrounds of the black characters in several shows such as *The Cosby Show* or *The Fresh Prince of Bel Air* may seem unrepresentative and at odds with our knowledge of wealth distribution in the USA, but, as Simon Hoggart has said on the subject,

> The charge of racism, or at least that *Cosby* is letting the side down by depicting a hopelessly glamorised black family, tends to come from whites. Alvin Pouissant, the black Harvard psychologist who advises *Cosby* on his scripts, argues that the Huxtables' success, as breadwinners and parents, helps to change whites' perception of blacks: 'It's doing far more to instal positive racial attitudes than if Bill came at the viewer with a sledgehammer or a sermon.'

What of the opposite charge that is sometimes levelled at the Scottish sitcom *Rab C. Nesbitt*, that the depiction of an unemployed, aggressive, drunken, work-shy Glaswegian slob in the central role does nothing but damage to the image of Scottish people? John Foster, a lecturer at the University of Paisley and a Govan resident for 18 years, defends the series on the grounds of its *oppositional humour*:

> In a sense, Rab represents the way Govanites would see Govan if they tried to make fun of themselves. It's a self-effacing humour – but it's also a kind

of oppositionalism, which says, 'This is us portraying us in terms of accepted values, in the worst possible light. It's a self-caricature launched against polite culture' (Kane, 1993).

The writer of the series, Ian Pattison, is blacker in his defence of the character:

> If you wanted to portray an accurate picture of Govan, you wouldn't have two parents living in that house. In terms of the social or family bond, the Nesbitts are like the Waltons, they're romanticised. There are whole blocks of kids in Moorepark, and not one has a father living in the house. So in that respect I think we're upholding the old values (Kane, 1993).

Sitcoms tend to provide familiar settings, situations and character types as a recognizable background to the comic excess of exaggerated plotting and performance. The use of stereotypes as a *negative* structural element in sitcom should, therefore, be set against the comic requirement of transgressing expectations that is fundamental to the success of the genre. This ambiguity lies at the heart of the character realism or shock value of 'quality' sitcoms.

THE BBC V. THE INDEPENDENT SECTOR

In his book *Television Producers* Jeremy Tunstall describes institutional differences between the production of comedy within the BBC and independent television. He suggests that the British style of situation comedy was largely developed at the BBC where it has always attracted high ratings and funding. In 1991, for example, situation comedies were ITV's fifth most popular genre, whereas on the BBC it was second after soap operas.

Tunstall's description is interesting because it clearly illustrates how the size and organizational structure of a media institution affects the type of material it produces. He compares the BBC's large output of situation comedies (about 25 a year on BBC1, of which 6 will be brand new) with that of a film studio, large magazine or book publisher where the risks of trying new things are hopefully offset by one or two big successes:

> Given the range and complexity of broadcast comedy – and its need for old mainstream favourites as well as radical new alternatives – the BBC has an advantage over ITV's single commercial network which schedules comedy in mid-evening and thus can only handle shows with high ratings. The BBC has continued to use radio as a training ground for writers, performers and producers. Moreover, with two TV networks, the BBC has been able to switch new radio talent to BBC2 before a final move to the showbusiness bigtime of BBC1. Of course, it seldom works that smoothly, but the BBC has a much wider range of possibilities than does ITV. The ITV cartel arrangement previous to 1993 in practice carved up the limited comedy time between the larger ITV companies; consequently, each of those ITV

companies aimed to have just one or two big comedy successes rather than to develop a comedy factory to rival the BBC.

Tunstall also shows how rival media organizations have a powerful influence on the choices made by their competitors. In the case of situation comedy, like soap opera, the creation of Channel 4 and its unique charter to cater for new audiences had a powerful impact on the programming policy of existing broadcasters. The fact that both ITV and BBC comedy efforts were shown up to be formulaic and out of step with the times was underlined by the alternative comedy successes of Channel 4 in the 1980s.

ITV's most original comedies of the 1980s owed much of their energy to the kind of comic talent and daring which had been the hallmark of Channel 4, where such qualities had been rewarded with younger (and therefore more commercially attractive) audiences. Tunstall picks out two comedy successes in particular – *Spitting Image* and *The New Statesman* by Central and Yorkshire Television, respectively:

> Both took political caricature to extremes not previously seen on British television. Both were popular with the young educated audiences; both required too much interest in politics to allow mainstream superpopularity. Both were expensive to make – especially *Spitting Image* whose original notion of presenting public figures as puppet-caricatures used many writers of separate sketches and required a small army of puppet artists, puppet-operators and voice-over artists. Both shows were unique and virtually impossible to copy. *Spitting Image* seemed to go far beyond the normal restraints of good taste and the libel law; it depended in part on the assumption that no politician – however grossly abused – would be so unwise as to try to sue a puppet. Both these shows were exceptions to the rules; they conformed only to the general rule that the British comedy system welcomed the zany, the unique, the eccentric and the lovingly written.

BRITISH PRODUCTION PRACTICES

It is commonly recognized that the success of a situation comedy lies in a strong sitcom character, well acted in a well written show. Whereas previously the roles of actor, director, producer and writer were traditionally quite separate in mainstream comedy, since the 1960s, particularly in the more adventurous or 'alternative' sitcoms, many of these roles have overlapped. Hence 'producer–directors' and 'writer–performers' are now common combinations in television comedy.

In Britain, writers have almost always been individuals or pairs, and until the 1980s were exclusively male. This situation may be contrasted to the US sitcom script-factory tradition. US production companies, such as the hugely successful Witt–Thomas Production set-up, favour a large team of regular house writers. They are far better paid than British sitcom writers, earning, according to Greg Brenman's documentary *Funny Business*, up to US$45,000 a week, but are expected to churn out a continuous stream of high-quality scripts (up to 52 per year) as opposed to the 6 or 12 demanded by British television companies. The burn-out rate for writers on shows with massive pressure ratings such as *Roseanne* is phenomenal, and the team working on scripts one year may be completely different from that working the following year.

The high-quality and export potential of so much US sitcom is forcing British production companies to consider team writing, perhaps suggesting a shift towards a more controllable, mass-production model. The journalist Geoff Deane, describing his experiences of writing a sitcom, is highly critical of the British comedy tradition and its writers:

> British humour is founded upon an array of peculiarly British foibles and preoccupations: our class system, our national reserve, our vulgarity and toilet fetishism, even our admirable intellectual quirkiness. These elements have long been the stock in trade of our comedy writers, and the harsh fact is that they mean nothing to anyone but the British. While the Yanks were making poignant and incisive comedies about the Vietnam war, we still had Terry Scott struggling to get his trousers on because the vicar had turned up for tea.

The producer's 'respect for the writer and the script' lies at the heart of British comedy, according to Jeremy Tunstall. No changes are made to the script without consultation with the writer(s). Once the script has arrived the producer or producer–director will cast the parts, organize a production–design team and begin rehearsal. The first readings are often nerve-wracking, because 'perhaps one million pounds rides on the success of the newly assembled group'.

Tunstall continues his description of the production process:

> All the outdoor filming (taping) may be done together in between one and several weeks; there are the usual problems of weather, transport and logistics. Next, the production returns to the studio for a succession of weeks; each week is spent rehearsing the actors, then come the camera rehearsals and finally, on the fifth or sixth evening, the show is taped in front of a studio audience. This recording is another anxious time for the producer, it is also difficult for actors confronted with an audience of 300 people, plus the probing attention of mobile studio cameras. A common practice is to use one 'slave' camera which only looks at the star. On the day following the recording the producer–director focuses on the relatively modest amount of editing involved in this type of studio-recorded production. Next day the weekly sequence begins again.

British television has operated on a tradition of a thirty minute comedy taking more than one week to tape, including the exterior filming which is inserted into the studio recording. Around 1990 there were pressures to make economies. In some comedy-sketch shows, for example, only 5 studio weeks would now be used to make enough sketches for 6 shows.

The comedy producer might make a total of 15 shows in one year. This might total between 17 and 22 weeks of combined outside filming and studio recording; for each of these weeks the producer would have spent at least another week on preliminary planning, including script supervision and casting non-continuous parts. In the remaining few non-holiday weeks of the year the producer might be working on a pilot for a new show, producing a one-off comedy special, and working on scripts submitted by independent producers.

EXERCISES AND ESSAYS

Exercise

List as many situation comedies as you can. Write a list of sitcom characters or character types under some or all of the following headings:

Other nationalities (e.g. Americans, Germans, French)
Old men: (e.g. Meldrew, Steptoe)
Young men:
Old women:
Young women:
Children:
Working-class characters:
Middle-class characters:
Upper-class characters:
Homosexual characters:
Any other group:

■ *Follow-on Task for Discussion or Notes*

How are the groups in these lists represented? What stereotypes exist? Do any comedies challenge stereotypes? How do they do this?

Essay

It's so bloody nice ... Felicity treacle Kendal and Richard sugar-flavoured snot Briers ... They're nothing but a couple of reactionary stereotypes confirming the myth that everyone in Britain is a loveable middle-class eccentric and I hate them [Vyvyan (referring to *The Good Life*) from *The Young Ones*, quoted by Bowes (1990)].

Either discuss what other 'reactionary stereotypes' can be found in British situation comedies *or* discuss the statement 'Comedy is not possible without stereotypes' with reference to British and US situation comedy.

Essay

The charges of conservatism, excessive stereotyping or racial, class, sexual and regional differences and so on, which are often levelled at the sit-com seem to pinpoint not so much the total imperviousness of the form but rather the particular way in which it operates as a site of negotiation of cultural change and difference.

Discuss the above statement.

Exercise

What are some common sitcom conventions? Try to think of any common characteristics; for example common settings include workplaces as in *On the Buses*, *Are you Being Served?*, *The Rag Trade*, *Drop the Dead Donkey* and so on. There are other common conventions. List some examples under the following headings:

Character
Plot
Setting
Costumes and props
Music
Lighting
Themes
Dialogue
Visual style

Exercise

Read the following 'recipe' for US sitcoms, written by David Bennum (1996).

1 female heroine
1 man-crazy best friend
1 oafish ex-husband or lover
2 or 3 dysfunctional buddies
children (optional)

Take the female heroine – preferably witty, attractive, neurotic in a cute sort of way and successful in creative occupation (actress, cartoonist, etc.) or – if these are out of season or otherwise unavailable – perpetually harried in a succession of low-paid jobs. Add the man-crazy best friend with reason to spend her entire life at the heroine's home. Add and subtract in quick and repeated succession one oafish ex-husband or lover. Sprinkle socially dysfunctional buddies on surface. Stir and half bake. Place crack team of gag writers in pressure cooker; remove immediately and replace with new team. Repeat process throughout every stage of the recipe. Stuff with one-liners about sex, relationships, work, relationships, sex, sex, and relationships. Garnish with children (optional) gifted with precocious line in quips. Five minutes before the dish is complete, add weepy moment, swiftly followed by this week's moral (careful; ratings will not rise unless this is timed just so). For larger servings (if entertaining *Friends*, for instance) multiply ingredients proportionally. Do not use this recipe for highbrow sitcom – consult the *Woody Allen Cookbook*.

Write a recipe for British sitcoms.

Essay

Discuss the statement 'Comedy is really about conflict' with reference to British and/or US situation comedy, *or* illustrate the statement 'The necessity for the continuity of characters and situations from week to week allows for the possibility of comedy being generated by the fact that the characters are somehow stuck with each other' (Eaton, 1981) with reference to British and/or US situation comedies.

Sources

Bennum, D. (1996): US sitcoms. *The Guardian Friday Review* 13 September.

Bowes, M. (1990): Only When I Laugh. In Goodwin, A. and Whannel, G. (eds), *Understanding television*. Routledge.

Deane, G. (Date unknown): Only fools and authors. *Arena* (magazine).

Eaton, M. (1981): *Television situation comedy*. In Bennett, T., Boyd-Bowman, S., Mercer, C. and Woollacott, J. (eds), *Popular television and film*. British Film Institute Publishing and Open University.

Feuer, J. (1987): Genre study and television. In Allen, R. (ed.), *Channels of discourse: television and contemporary criticism*. University of North Carolina Press.

Hoggart, S. (1988): Black gold. *The Listener* 31 March.

Kane, P. (1993): Class act. *The Guardian Weekend* 20 November.

Neale, S. and Krutnik, F. (1990): *Popular film and television comedy*. Routledge.

Salisbury, L. (1992): We're America's worst nightmare. *Radio Times* 12 December.

Tunstall, J. (1993): *Television producers*. Routledge.

Wheen, F. (1985): *Television – a history*. Guild Publishing.

© LWT

Cilla Black and the *Blind Date* contestants

7

Game Shows

GAME SHOWS – AN HISTORICAL OVERVIEW

The following outline of the history of British game shows is based on David Mason's more detailed *A brief history of game shows*, to be found in Mason's *Gameshow handbook* (1991), Francis Wheen's *Television – a history* (1985) and Garry Whannel's essay 'Winner takes all: competition' in Goodwin and Whannel (eds), *Understanding television* (1990).

The simple spelling quiz *Spelling Bee*, transmitted live from the BBC's Alexandra Palace on 31 May 1938, was the very first television game show. In this show contestants simply tried to spell words correctly and, predictably, the show was not a great success. One immensely important discovery by the early programme planners was that quite trivial parlour games, if skilfully and entertainingly presented, were enormously popular with the television audience. The first regular television game show of this kind, and the longest running one, was *What's My Line?* (which began in the USA in 1950 and in Britain in 1951) where celebrity panellists guessed the occupation of a contestant. In the USA in the 1950s big prizes were introduced to the format. One of the most famous was CBS's *The $64,000 Question* which began in 1955. This was based on a radio show called *Take It or Leave It* which had a top prize of just $64. The contestants in *The $64,000 Question* were put in 'isolation booths', the questions protected by 'security officers' and the rewards so high that even the losers were given a Cadillac. Within three months of its launch *The $64,000 Question* was being watched by 85 per cent of the television audience and many imitations were being spawned.

By 1957 half of the network's top-10 programmes were quizzes, including *The $64,000 Question, The $64,000 Challenge* and NBC's *Twenty-One*. An English professor, Charles Van Doren, who won US$129,000 on *Twenty-One*, was the first 'celebrity' to be launched by these shows and was even invited to be a guest presenter on the *Today* show. The quiz-show bubble was about to burst, however, as it was revealed that winners were being selected by the networks and the advertisers:

In 1958, publicity was given to rumours that the quiz shows were 'fixed' – that favoured contestants were being told the answers in advance. The following year, Charles van Doren confessed to a congressional sub-committee that his appearance on *Twenty-One* had all been rigged. Before his show he had been taken aside by the producer and given the answers, with instructions that he should arrange to 'tie' with the current champion that week, to build up tension. The next week he was allowed to win, and he continued to win for several months. He told the committee that when he learned that he was finally going to be allowed to lose, he was relieved.

Dozens of similar revelations were made after Van Doren testified. President Eisenhower said that the fixing had been 'a terrible thing to do to the American people'. All the high stakes quiz shows were hastily removed from the schedules (Wheen, 1985).

[Incidentally, the Van Doren/*Twenty-One* scandal which rocked America's trust in the television networks was the subject of the feature film *Quiz Show* (1995) directed by Robert Redford.]

Double Your Money and *Take Your Pick* were the first game shows on British television to offer cash prizes and were both launched on the new ITV commercial network. However, the IBA set limits on the prizes available and there was generally more emphasis on the enjoyment of competition rather than material rewards.

In the 1960s game shows developed alongside advances in the nation's 'white heat' of technology. *The Golden Shot* (1967), for example, used a miniature camera lens attached to a crossbow held by a blindfolded archer who contestants directed over the phone to hit targets.

In the 1970s the personality of the host and the contestant became at least as important as their ability to win prizes. *The Generation Game* was typical of a show where to be seen to be 'having fun' was central to the show's success. The surprise success of the decade was *Mastermind*, where the only prize was a glass bowl, and the questions were very difficult. The success was probably a result of its format – inspired by Nazi interrogation techniques. The contestant was isolated in a pool of light on a black leather seat and subject to rapid-fire questioning by the Icelandic quizmaster Magnus Magnusson. Instead of name, rank and number contestants had only to reveal their 'name, occupation and subject'.

Memory-based 'factual' knowledge was being disrupted by the end of the 1970s by the rise of the populist 'we asked one hundred people . . .' form of game show such as *Family Fortunes* or *Play Your Cards Right* where public opinion and 'common sense' were more highly valued. Whannel (in Goodwin and Whannel (eds), 1990) draws parallels here with broader political and ideological shifts:

Many of the traditional assumptions and certainties of post-war Britain were being dismantled by the rise of Thatcherism. In its early populist phase, Thatcherism challenged established political knowledge by reference, mediated through the tabloid press, to the 'common sense' of ordinary people. During the same period, game shows shifted from a dependence on the traditional empirical/factual model of knowledge, towards a celebration of the views of ordinary people as a source of understanding.

However, Whannel notes a return to fact-based quiz shows in the 1980s. The likes of *Fifteen to One*, whose model seemed to be the Victorian classroom, reflected a return to 'Victorian values', including notions of competition in schools. Whannel, again, suggests the historical and ideological dimension to the trend:

> by the late 1980s, Thatcherism has consolidated its power, and having successfully dismantled the old Butskellite welfare state consensual politics, is in the midst of an active reconstruction of major social institutions. As the project of imposing a new educational orthodoxy gets under way there are signs of a regeneration of the knowledge-as-fact school of quiz.

Nevertheless, the hit show of the 1980s and one of the most successful game show formats on television today is the ultimate personality quiz show *Blind Date*. Although the responses of the contestants have become increasingly scripted there is still, it is suggested, voyeuristic pleasure in watching the selection of an anonymous, 'no strings attached' sexual liaison (with Cilla Black as the procuress) and the ritual trading of highly personal insults which follows it. The success of *Blind Date* may, like many game shows, lie in 'the audience's sadistic pleasure in watching other people being humiliated in public' (Wheen, 1985).

In the 1990s game shows developed and mutated further both at the fringes and in the mainstream of the genre. The generic fluidity of *Strike It Lucky* hosted by the frenetic Michael Barrymore – a combination of quiz show, talent contest, variety and chat show – attracted a large mainstream audience. At the 'fringe' Julian Clary's *Sticky Moments* shown on Channel 4 offered a camp version of *Blind Date*'s grating innuendos draped over the comfortingly recognizable and predictable frame of the game show. Clary combined the deadpan humour of a Larry Grayson with the exotic, glamorous appeal usually reserved for the female assistant. The use of obviously straight contestants heightened the comic impact of his homosexual *double entendres*. Channel 4's *Don't Forget Your Toothbrush* also parodied many of the conventions of game shows yet successfully harnessed the 'vulgar' 'showbiz' energy of US-style entertainment (exploited earlier and with less irony) in ITV's *The Price is Right*.

THE POPULARITY OF GAME SHOWS

Clarke (1987) identifies four types of game and quiz shows – specialist, intellectual, celebrity and populist shows. Each type has its own appeal. *Specialist* shows such as *Film Buff of the Year*, for instance, may target those with a keen interest in film, but may also have a general appeal beyond the 'buff' who is able to answer even a handful of the obscure questions. The same is also true of *intellectual* shows such as *University Challenge* or *Mastermind*. The appeal of *celebrity* shows (which employ at least vaguely recognizable personalities) lies not with prizes or meeting a difficult challenge but with the ability of the celebrities to provide amusing conversation and anecdotes. Shows such as *Have I Got News For You* are clearly structured by a quiz show format but are quite open about how unimportant and frequently arbitrary the scoring is. In this sense they are closer to chat shows in their essential appeal.

The fun and excitement of contests, both mental and physical, is given an added showbiz spin in *populist* game shows. The lure of large prizes and how contestants perform under the stress of trying to win them is one common appeal. As Clarke notes, in those programmes where the prizes are largest the content is virtually irrelevant: questions involve commonplace general know-ledge, or absurd guesswork. The contests, in this sense, are more a test of character – how participants respond to the possibility of winning or losing a valuable prize, for example. Populist game shows also exhibit the charac-teristics of popular entertainment as identified by Richard Dyer, offering 'abundance, energy, and community, in contrast to the scarcity, exhaustion, and isolation more common to lived reality' (quoted by Whannel, 1990).

Where prizes are less important there may be a stronger 'educational' appeal as in intellectual shows such as *Mastermind*. An audience that finds populist shows loud and vulgar will often prefer their entertainment disguised as self-improvement. The recitation of obscure facts learnt parrot form, usually with a 'classical' emphasis will have greater status than, for example, estimating the price of a consumer product. The deliberately low-key prizes for such quizzes – dictionaries, glass bowls, book tokens, and so on, set aside their competitors from those of more populist shows: knowledge on 'intellectual' shows has its own reward.

A powerful appeal of all game and quiz shows is the strong element of *audience participation*. For the populist shows this will involve cheering, clapping, whooping and general high spirits – an atmosphere essential to the success of the programme and insisted on in the studio. This is achieved through warm-up comedians, free wine, cues to begin and end noise and frantic arm-waving by the floor manager if the volume is not sufficient. The audience in the studio and at home are encouraged to consider the show as a great night out (or in!) to celebrate, in Bruce Forsyth's words, 'a bit o' fun' in a warm, communal atmosphere. It is generally accepted by contestants and audience alike that such celebrations are rigorously stage managed.

The widely recognized and highly paid talents of hosts such as Barrymore and Forsyth is their ability to let audiences and contestants surrender total control to them. They wield this power with the confidence and flair of the music hall impresario or the variety artiste. Fiske (1987) suggests that in populist game shows there are elements of carnival where 'the constraints of the everyday are evaded and its power relations temporarily reversed'. As such, the game show host's role is that of Carnival King, whose rules and decrees, though temporary, are absolute.

The fact that such shows are presented as if live – when, in fact, they are taped in batches of at least three or four, helps the viewer identify and feel as if she or he is there. Furthermore, the mystery of who will win creates *suspense* in the narrative similar to that in crime and detective stories. The contestants and winner are practically the only variable amongst the other elements of setting, story structure, events, atmosphere, and so on which change from week to week.

Another form of audience participation which is common to virtually all quiz and game shows is the degree to which viewers can participate *actively* by trying to answer the questions themselves. There is an opportunity to compete at your own level and award yourself a 'self rating' against the competitors. The purely physical competition of *Gladiators* sets it apart from game shows with physical elements such as *The Krypton Factor* or *The Crystal Maze* for this very reason. Although *Gladiators* employs virtually all the conventions of a populist game show – it has a live audience, presenters, competition, excitement, glamour, competitors who are members of the public, points and prizes – the lack of opportunity for audience 'self rating' makes its status as a 'game show' problematic.

The fact that quiz and game shows are one of the very few television genres to feature 'ordinary people' is a frequently overlooked appeal. They may be young, physically attractive, talkative, extrovert and even exhibitionist (as seen frequently on *Blind Date*) or shy, unglamorous or of any age, class and race (*Countdown*, *Fifteen to One*). As such these shows have an *egalitarian* appeal. The fact that a taxi driver should be the 'Mastermind' of the nation, for example, helps promote a myth of social and educational equality which Masterman (1985) (amongst others) has explored in more detail.

GAME SHOWS – 'RITUAL, GAME, RITUAL'

The following account of the role of 'ritual and game' in game shows provides a summary of some of the points made by John Fiske in *Television culture* (1987).

In his book *Television culture* John Fiske examines the elements of 'ritual and game' in quiz and game shows. He traces the ancestry of such programmes back through radio to party and community games which were used to pass the time, keep warm, distract from hunger and boredom and bind a community together. Fiske defines *ritual* as something which brings people from different ages, backgrounds and status together to share in a *common experience* to create *shared meaning* and *unified identities*. A church service, for example, is a ritual where all are equal and all are treated equally.

Elements of ritual can be found especially at the beginning and end of game shows. At these points the contestants are given equal time and space within the privileged areas of the studio and share an understanding of the conventions and rules with the host and 'participating' audience. The standardized introductions, endings, physical placements and glamorized lecterns or desks, catchphrases and audience responses are all suggestive of a religious ceremony.

Whereas, as Lévi-Strauss suggests, rituals move from difference to equality, games move in the opposite direction. Most sports, for instance, are games, with the 'competitors' starting out equal and finishing as winners or losers. This *philosophy* of competition is also present in game shows. There is a strong emphasis on individual skill and ability and prizes for the winners. After the ritualized beginnings of the game show, the same each week, the game itself takes over. All the contestants start equal and have equal opportunities – but they are not all of equal ability and this rapidly becomes clear. The game is usually structured so that contestants are progressively eliminated until there is only one winner.

The end of the show moves back to the ritual of the opening with the host taking the winner, usually by the hand, to a hallowed part of the set, where no one has yet set foot, the 'altar' upon which the prizes are displayed. The losing contestants are then asked to join the winner where they celebrate the end of the game together with the audience.

Why Should These Elements of Ritual and Game be Pleasurable?

The following reasons have been suggested:

- Social cohesion and escapism: people need and enjoy a certain amount of ritual in their lives. Work, education, area, accent, experiences all tend to divide us from each other. Rituals bring us together and, for a time, distract us from the differences – which, for many, feel very unfair.
- Identification: by identifying with the winner we can share the sensation of winning – but we can also share the sadness and disappointment of the losers which, perhaps, makes it easier to bear our own disappointments. The prime qualification for being on most quiz shows is to look and sound 'ordinary' so that the mass audience can identify with the contestant.
- Comfort and reinforcement: these shows are highly conservative and conformist – they are based, fundamentally, on rules. At the heart of the ideology of quiz and game shows are a set of beliefs which reflect those at the heart of our society. These include the myths that all start equal regardless of race, colour, gender, region and class; that it is not who you know (the old school-tie network, and so on) but what you know that is important, and that if you do not succeed it is because you did not try hard enough, or acquire sufficient knowledge or have a lucky break.

Why Quiz and Game Shows are Popular with the Television Industry

Quiz and game shows are popular with the industry because they are cheap, easy to produce and they attract large audiences. 'The great appeal to a controller is that they're unbelievably cheap', says BBC's entertainment development head Keith Lygo. 'They shoot six "Blockbusters" shows in a day.' They are cheap and easy to produce for much the same reason that soap opera is cheap – the above-the-line costs are a reusable set, a presenter and perhaps an assistant and a few prizes, which are often of little value or are donated by a firm looking for publicity. Below-the-line costs are kept low because they can be filmed quickly in a studio space with a small crew on a regular basis.

CRITICISMS OF THE GENRE

Quiz and game shows have very low status in television's 'pecking order'. Reasons for this include: their origins in oral culture and 'popular' forms of entertainment; their audiences (in daytime housewives, retired people and the unemployed, and in the evenings the working and lower middle class); and their cheapness, throwaway nature and tendency to be 'bland and repetitive', or 'greedy and aggressive'. Quiz shows, in fact, stand opposite to 'high culture' in all their distinguishing traits:

> The 1962 Pilkington report into television singled out quizzes as the medium at its most trivial and socially harmful. Critical attitudes to quiz shows echoed attitudes to gambling – winning required no merit; prizes were too much for people to cope with (Beckett, 1995).

Criticisms of quiz and game shows are not, however, confined to the disapproval of 'establishment' figures out of touch with 'popular culture'. Such shows are also attacked generally for 'selling' dominant ideology through their competitive narrative structure and by perpetuating myths of equal opportunity (see above). At an individual level they reaffirm heterosexist attitudes through the widespread use of decorative assistants (for instance, *Don't Forget Your Toothbrush*) and by the assumption that heterosexual relationships are the only possibility (*Blind Date*). They promote crass materialism through the fetishistic concern with prizes and 'screaming, dancing, arm-waving' consumerism (*The Price is Right, Supermarket Sweep*). Furthermore, they frequently (as with *Mastermind*) reassert a view of education that is mechanistic (the rote learning of facts), 'unpleasant', 'dehumanizing' and 'closely associated with humiliation and failure' (Masterman, 1985). The journalist and travel writer Bill Bryson (1995) mocks the pretensions of British 'educational' quiz shows:

I remember once years ago watching a special international edition of *University Challenge* between a team of British scholars and a team of American scholars. The British team won so handily that they and Bamber Gascoigne and the studio audience were deeply, palpably embarrassed. It really was the most dazzling display of intellectual superiority. The final was something like 12,000 to 2. But here's the thing. I am certain beyond the tiniest measure of doubt that if you tracked down the competitors to see what has become of them since, you would find that every one of the Americans is pulling down $350,000 a year trading bonds or running corporations while the British are studying the tonal qualities of sixteenth-century choral music in Lower Silesia and wearing jumpers with holes in them.

Quiz and game shows, ultimately, are ambiguous in that, with their roots deep in egalitarian rituals they offer some of the utopian aspects of popular culture whilst embodying several dystopian values and assumptions of contemporary society.

EXERCISES AND ESSAYS

Exercise

Watch an episode of a quiz show and try to answer as many of the following questions in as much detail as possible:

- On what channel and at what time is the show scheduled? Is it produced by an independent production company, or is it made by the BBC or one of the ITV networks?
- Describe the title sequence and introductory music.
- What is the set like? What colours or shapes are common? Is there more than one area? Why do you think the set was designed the way it is?
- Comment on the presenter's manner, dress, relationship with the contestants and audience and role throughout the show.
- Describe the contestants.
- What kind of knowledge or skill is being tested? How important is scoring, if there is any at all? How important is competition?
- What role does the studio audience play? How can audiences at home join in?
- What is the target audience of the show? How successful do you think it is? Why is it so successful or unsuccessful?

Exercise

Devise a quiz or game show for a target audience not currently well catered for in the schedules. Research the following headings to plan your work:

- current choice of game shows and their likely target audience (use a weekly television guide to help draw up a list);
- target audience not well catered for currently (think of a particular age-group and/or interest group, for example teenage football fans);
- other programmes that are popular with this audience (use a television guide to help draw up a list);
- programme elements that are popular with this audience (what makes them appealing to this group?).

The Game or Quiz Show – Format

Use your research to help you plan a new quiz or game show. Agree on the broad shape of the show – originality is what is being looked for; the show should ideally be ground-breaking in some way. Are there different parts to it? What sort of atmosphere will the programme be looking for – serious, light-hearted, riotous? Once you have a sense of what the show is about plan the following in more detail (individuals, pairs, and so on may take one task each):

- Devise ideas for the title sequence and introductory music.
- Design a set, in three-dimensions if possible.
- Describe the presenter's manner, dress, relationship with the contestants and audience and role throughout the show.
- Describe the contestants.
- What kind of knowledge or skill will be tested? How important is scoring, if there is any at all? How important is competition?
- What role does the studio audience play? How can audiences at home join in?
- What is the target audience of the show? How successful do you think it will be? Why?
- On what channel and at what time will the show be scheduled? Will it be produced by an independent production company or is it made by the BBC or one of the ITV networks?

Practical Production

This will take good organization, division of labour and some effective leadership within the group. Carry out the following tasks:

- Script the questions (not the answers).
- Cast the quiz host, assistant (if any) and contestants. Appoint a director, camera operators, a floor manager, and so on.
- Organize costumes, painting of set, props, and so on.
- Rehearse an episode – organize the positions of cameras (more than one if possible, three ideally).
- Carry out a camera rehearsal – camera operators know what to expect and what to film. Suggest one camera on host (close-up), one on contestant answering question (close-up) and one (long shot) of both.

- Film uninterrupted wherever possible. Try to get audience and audience involvement – applause, and so on. Run three cameras simultaneously without cutting or pausing. It is then possible to edit sequence afterwards fairly smoothly.

Essay

Why are quiz and game shows so popular with television companies and audiences?

Essay

What can an analysis of contemporary game shows tell us about the society in which we live?

Essay

How are quiz and game shows unique as a television genre?

Essay

Provide a detailed analysis of any one quiz or game show currently on television.

Sources

Alvarado, M. (1987): *Television and video.* Wayland.
Beckett, A. (1995): A question of thought. *The Independent on Sunday* February.
Bryson, B. (1995): *Notes from a small island.* Black Swan.
Clarke, M. (1987): *Teaching popular television.* Heinemann Educational in association with the British Film Institute.
Cooke, T. (1993): Case study game and quiz shows. Oldham Sixth Form College (unpublished).
Fiske, J. (1987): *Television culture.* Routledge.
Goodwin, A. and Whannel, G. (eds) (1990): *Understanding television.* Routledge.
Mason, D. (1991): *Gameshow handbook.* Random Century.
Masterman, L. (1985): *Teaching the media.* Routledge.
Wheen, F. (1985): *Television – a history.* Guild Publishing.

The Bill

8

Police Series

INTRODUCTION TO THE GENRE

Series are those programmes which have the same stars and the same locations every week but which have different stories each episode. These stories are self-contained, unlike serials whose stories continue from one episode to the next. In the early days of television the most popular series were westerns, but since the 1950s the police series has taken its place as the most successful series genre. Furthermore, unlike the western it is a genre that has been easily adapted by many countries worldwide (Alvarado, 1987).

The two genres, both in television and film, have several parallels. Thematically they are concerned with 'justice' versus savagery or 'the frontier'. They feature lone, rogue males (consider Clint Eastwood's highly influential roles in both genres); duos with an element of comedy (*Butch Cassidy and the Sundance Kid*, *Alias Smith and Jones*, *Starsky and Hutch*, Regan and Carter from *The Sweeney*, Morse and Lewis in *Inspector Morse*) or teams (*The Magnificent Seven*, *Hill Street Blues*, *The Bill* and so on). They also feature powerful individual villains and their sidekicks or anonymous groups ('Indians', gangs) who are dehumanized by the lack of development of any kind of character.

Furthermore, much of the action and pace of police series ('tracking', chasing and fighting) is borrowed from the western as are many characteristic camera techniques such as the use of close-ups, high and low angle shots, fast intercutting, in addition to all the visual clichés of hide outs, shoot outs and death scenes. Therefore, although westerns were not the only influence on police series they were important because they anticipated several key features and developments in the genre.

A CONCISE HISTORY OF POLICE SERIES

The following account of the evolution of television police series covers some of the major developments in the USA – where the genre originated, and in Britain. It concentrates on key moments in the history of television representations of the police and examines some of the ideological background to the debate. Many of the points which follow illustrate several issues raised in Chapters 11 and 16.

The 1950s

Television westerns such as *Wanted – Dead or Alive* and *Rawhide* were filmed for the US television networks by major studios such as Warner from the mid-1950s, often using a combination of stock film and cheap, reprocessed studio sets, props and costumes. Because they were filmed rather than broadcast live, these popular and seemingly endless number of made-for-television series were both relatively cheap and highly exportable. From 1954 the major studios were also filming crime series for television. When the popularity of the rather simple-minded westerns with their cold-war morality began to fade in the 1960s, the studios and television companies simply stepped up their production of police series. These were equally suited to the conveyor-belt production techniques and resources of film and television studios. They also presented a similar black-and-white morality but tended, in US series at least, to avoid the kind of moralistic monologues that concluded many westerns.

Dragnet, which had been on film since it began in 1951, was the first US 'cop show' to be shown on British television. It was supposedly based on real-life crimes found in the files of the Los Angeles Police Department. It ran for 300 episodes from 1951 to 1958 and was only the first in a flood of US police series that, along with the western, began America's long colonization of the world's television screens. As Francis Wheen (1985) notes:

> The foreign earnings from these sales represented pure profit to the film companies, who could therefore afford to charge ridiculously low prices – as little as $1,000 for a one hour episode. In countries such as Canada and Australia, indigenous programmes all but disappeared from view: why bother to spend large sums of money on a home produced drama when an American telefilm could be had for a tenth of the cost?

The popularity of US police series on British screens led to Britain's first detective series, *Fabian of the Yard* (first broadcast in 1954). Robert Fabian, a well-dressed, pipe-smoking North American (his nationality was aimed at the larger television audience across the Atlantic) assisted Scotland Yard in catching the (frequently foreign) criminals. Police techniques were often explained and the cases pieced together in a routine, logical manner so that it seemed only a matter of time before the suspect was apprehended. Dispassionate, professional dialogue added to the sense of 'docudrama' that this and other early police series encouraged. The lesson that crime did not pay was spliced into the implacable nature of police procedure and the police's role, represented as one of 'noble defenders of the public'.

Perhaps the most famous and longest running series from this period is *Dixon of Dock Green* (1955–76) based on the British film *The Blue Lamp*

(1949). The series revolved around George Dixon, a bobby on the beat. His reassuring presence emerged at the beginning of each show from the darkness of a London night, whistling 'Maybe It's Because I'm a Londoner', to address the viewers directly: 'Evenin' All . . .'. Each case was a foregone conclusion, with Dixon introducing the story to camera – a technique common to police series of the time. For two decades the series maintained a highly idealized view of the police, as represented by Dixon. He combined authority and gentleness, bravery and common sense, dedication and humanity. His private life was shown to be as caring, upright and fatherly as his public role as guardian, neighbour and friend of the community. The series has been attacked as a 'drama of reassurance', 'sanctimonious' and 'divorced from reality' and it certainly appeared dated, despite various changes, by the time it was pulled from the BBC schedules in 1976.

The 1960s

By contrast, *Z Cars* shocked its first viewers by the grittiness of its character-ization. It was also highly popular with 14 million people watching the first series in 1962. The series, at first, was live – but pre-recorded scenes were filmed 'on location' outside the studios and the programme strove for a 'documentary look'. The programme initially encountered fierce opposition from many senior policemen (the Chief Constable of Lancashire was one of the first to withdraw his support) for its depiction of a force that could be rude, aggressive and unpleasant. The setting was Kirkby, a neglected inner-city district in Merseyside with a real-life 'wild-west' reputation. The series' writer John Hopkins was interested in the effects of crime and criminality on the police. His policemen drank, swore, got things wrong, even beat up their wives. Yet despite brutish characters such as Barlow, the policemen, as in virtually every series since, were essentially good men who cared about the lives and crimes they were involved in. David Buxton (1990) observes:

> the police series proudly waved the banner of realism throughout the 1960s, integrating some of the formal properties of the soap opera construction of an in-depth personality by focusing on the continuing dramas of everyday life within what was presented as an accurately rendered description of police routine work. One of the practical difficulties of this format was that realism required a large number of regular characters and therefore complex plotting and writing as in a theatrical piece: the British police series was something of a cross between soap opera and drama. This formal solution was not taken up on American television until the 1980s, when *Hill Street Blues* episodes were farmed out to different writers in fifteen-minute segments. Realism demanded that stories be sometimes left with threads dangling, sometimes even with police failure: this was not yet acceptable for many American viewers, for whom the presence of violent crime was justifiable only by its eventual punishment.

Police series such as *Softly, Softly* and *Z Cars* emphasized the 'human dimension' of police work. The social democratic consensus of Britain in the 1960s was reflected in the representations of the police who understood and related to the human qualities of the criminals they dealt with. The authoritarian and repressive view of law and order as personified by Inspector Barlow in *Z Cars* (at times unsympathetically portrayed as a bully) was a minority tendency for the most part held in check.

In the 1960s in the USA, political and public concerns were being expressed about the rising levels of screen violence in police series such as *The Untouchables* – set in the 1920s. (Interestingly, the 1920s, like the 1960s, were a time when the USA was violently divided, although the issues were apparently different: prohibition rather than civil rights.) Newton Minow of the Federal Communications Commission (FCC) described television in this period as a 'vast wasteland' of 'game shows, violence, audience participation shows, formula comedies about totally unbelievable families, blood and thunder, mayhem, violence, sadism, murder, western bad-men, western good-men, private eyes, gangsters, more violence and cartoons' (Wheen, 1985). His threat to remove the networks' licences was taken, at least partly, seriously. Similarly, whenever there was enough public clamour to reduce screen violence – as there was following the assassinations of Jack and Bobby Kennedy and of Martin Luther King – the networks toned down the levels of brutality until the issue was out of the public eye. They also increased the use of car chases and explosions to compensate, particularly following the success of *Bullitt* (1968) and *The French Connection* (1971) at the cinema.

The 1970s

Towards the end of the 1960s, as the continuing racial crisis grew, and the generation gap widened through opposition to the Vietnam War, television executives witnessed a widespread rejection of commercial television programming – particularly by 'important' (i.e. soon-to-be-wealthy) college-educated consumers who dismissed it as 'mass intoxication' of conservative values. As Buxton (1990) argues:

> A new type of hero was needed to breach the divide between young and old, between civil society and the 'Establishment'. This was to be a new breed of policeman, an individualist who worked within the system in his own, unorthodox manner, upholding the social order but fighting injustice from above as well as below and protecting the citizens from a psychopathic criminal class by virtue of his superior personality. The private detective of the Chandler type, a romantic individualist who is 'anti-establishment' because of his special sensibility and cynical knowingness (rather than any political conviction), was collapsed and remodelled into an offbeat representative of authority and the existing order.

In the world of cinema – a medium in crisis in the 1970s and hunting for an audience, any audience – such figures were occasionally forced to reject the police establishment they had joined [*Serpico* (1973) is the classic example]. Such wholesale rejection never occurred in television. In vaguely liberal and multiracial shows such as *Ironside*, *Mod Squad* and *Hawaii Five-O* the police officers often behaved more like tolerant social workers than tough lawmen. By the early 1970s, however, the streetwise, 'cool' elements of mythical 'hippie' police were being combined with a drive for violent, conclusive resolutions to escalating crime. US economic crisis, unleashed in part by the oil crisis and the ideological insecurity posed by Vietnam and Watergate, led to shows set against a background of endemic urban crime in which neither liberal nor conservative crime-solving methods could be wholly endorsed. The success of police detectives such as those found in *Kojak* and *Starsky and Hutch* lay in their ethnic street connections and exploitation of underworld networks combined with a willingness to engage violently with organized criminals and deranged killers.

Many of these elements were copied directly in Britain where such US shows were equally popular. Violent was certainly at the core of *The Sweeney* (1975–78). This programme marked a watershed in representations of the police showing its heroes Regan and Carter from the Flying Squad as rough, boozing cockneys who got things done by breaking the rules. When they were not jumping out of vans with pickaxe handles they were in confrontation with their superior officers for whom they showed absolute contempt. Far from the family man ideals of *Dixon of Dock Green*, Regan was a divorcee who drank on and off duty in dingy pubs and strip joints and discussed 'pulling birds' with his partner. Regan and Carter consorted with criminals for information and threatened and intimidated suspects in interrogation. Although most senior officers were appalled by this representation of their force, it was, according to serving officers, very popular and influential with police trainees and officers at the time and in several respects true to life. A line from the series, 'You're not going to hit me, my sergeant is going to hit me', was, apparently, taken from an actual case (Sweeting, 1993).

Another British series that owed much to the formula established by *Starsky and Hutch* was *The Professionals* (1977–83). Unlike so many of the somewhat camp spy pop series of the 1960s such as *The Man from Uncle*, *Mission: Impossible* and the British series *The Avengers*, *The Professionals* took itself, and its portrayal of violence, more seriously. Bodie and Doyle, agents of CI5 – a quasi-military crime-breaking and anti-terrorist unit – operated, like James Bond, with a 'licence to kill'. Doyle, like Ken Hutchinson, played the sensitive, educated, humanist half – more likely to drink wine or herbal tea at home, a martial arts expert who could be found meditating or pursuing other 'feminine' arts such as cooking. The dark-haired Doyle, like Dave Starsky, was a macho braggart, who drank pints and boxed and had a wolfish grin and an eye for women. Their Capri was Britain's answer to Starsky's Ford Torino and there was an equal amount of running around buildings, fighting and shooting. Like *Starsky and Hutch*, *The Professionals* reconciled a tolerant, jokey veneer with authoritarian methods at a time of widening racial, industrial and class divisions in Britain (see quotes from Stuart Hall in Chapter 16). The shadowy nature of CI5, its often strikingly similar techniques to the SAS, MI5 and other British secret services and its glamorization of violence left the series open to charges of incipient fascism.

Gordon Newman's brief but highly controversial *Law and Order* series was perhaps the first and only attempt on British television to show the police in a highly unsympathetic light. Newman's thesis – that the police service does not contain the odd bad apple, but that, 'because of the pathology of the people who go in there, the whole barrel is unsound' was reflected in the corrupt, violent and ultimately disinterested characterization of officers such as Pile. The programme was described as 'outrageous' by Metropolitan Police Commissioner Paul London, and the Prison Officer's Association banned the BBC from filming inside its establishments for a year (Kerr, 1990). Nevertheless, police officers were on the set for every shot advising the programme makers and the result had a disturbing authenticity that contributed to the furore it created. The immoral relationship between police and criminal and the suggestion in *Law and Order* that the police were part of the problem, not the solution, was to be a powerful conclusion to a trend in police series that had developed since *Z Cars*.

The 1980s and 1990s

The development of the police genre in Britain is, however, far from being only one of growing cynicism with the police. In the mid-1990s sceptical portrayals of police corruption such as *Between the Lines* have run at the same time as the simple-minded, anodyne innocence of *Heartbeat*. Even, as Thomas Sutcliffe points out, '*Dixon of Dock Green*, the epitome of consolatory police drama, actually overlapped for a time with *The Sweeney*, a conjunction that now seems unthinkable.'

The 1980s and early 1990s saw several British series with women cast in the leading roles. *The Gentle Touch*, *C.A.T.S. Eyes*, *Juliet Bravo* and *Prime Suspect* can be seen as a British response to the popularity of earlier US series such as *Policewoman*, *Charlie's Angels* and *Cagney and Lacey*. The focus of these programmes often shifts away from the process of catching criminals and 'action' to issues such as the pressures of police work on personal relationships. 'Women's' issues relating to the workplace such as sexism and frustrated promotion are examined as are crimes related to sex (e.g. domestic violence, rape, child abuse). It is interesting to note that the masculinity of male characters in series such as *The Bill* is an integral part of the characterization but is seldom explored as an issue, whereas in police dramas which have women as their central characters such gender issues are frequently central and explicit.

Another highly influential US police series was *Miami Vice* (1985–90). Described by some commentators as 'MTV Cops', *Miami Vice* flaunted an overt concern with style, visuals and imagery, frequently interrupting the narrative continuity with rock music sequences. When the series was not in upbeat celebration of the affluence and tropical bounty of Miami (sports cars, beaches, bikini-clad women, palatial mansions) it seemed to plunge into extended scenes of noirish 'atmosphere' and unease. According to Buxton (1990):

> *Miami Vice* was the first series to make use of neurophysiological research on the viewing process: research carried out in the Communication Technology Laboratory of the University of Michigan has shown that (American) viewers tend to become impatient with overly elaborate stories or characterisations. In an attempt to maintain constant visual and sound excitement, the series uses aesthetic devices from the clip (aggressive camera movements, 'unnatural' colour schemes and mood music) to fill out the story rather than resorting to 'irrelevant' complications of plot and dialogue, both reduced to a minimum. Executive producer Michael Mann's motto was said to be 'no earth tones': sienna, ochre, red and brown were eliminated in favour of rose, lemon, aquamarine, turquoise and peach, the sensuous feel of pastel and fluorescent colours.

The series employed the same *Starsky and Hutch* formula of chalk-and-cheese buddies: Sonny Crockett – tough, white, straight-talking, small-town Vietnam Vet – against Ricardo Tubbs – sensitive, black-Hispanic, New York sophisticate. Both seemed perilously close to the world of easy money and drugs that they investigated. As Fiske (1987) observes, 'Crockett and Tubbs are close to voicing the underworld they are meant to control': Crockett drives a Ferrari, they wear designer clothes, they become involved with women associated with the gangs they are investigating, they act the parts and seemed to flirt with the roles of cocaine dealers or users (in Tubbs's case mirroring the stereotypically Latino drug dealer and literally speaking 'their' language – Spanish), and all this set against a backdrop of images and music that seems at once to celebrate and condemn Miami's vice.

Strinati (1995) sees *Miami Vice* as an interesting example of postmodernism – its insistence on surface and style and self-conscious references to popular culture. Fiske (1987) goes further by praising the 'liberating', 'disruptive' pleasures and possibility of 'evading' ideology that *Miami Vice*'s postmodern assemblage allows. Buxton (1990) rejects 'the pretence that postmodern style is somehow beyond ideology' and places *Miami Vice* in a firmly supportive position between the two major pillars of Reaganite free-market ideology: 'law and order and conspicuous consumption'. The degree of critical debate that the series provoked was certainly an indication of its significance in the enormous canon of US police series.

The long-running British series *The Bill* gained recognition for quite different qualities from *Miami Vice*. Originally an hour-long series made using lightweight, hand-held video cameras, *The Bill* was first transmitted in 1984 and was relaunched in 1988 as a half-hour biweekly with audiences at around 12 million. The programme mimicked the 'fly-on-the-wall' style of Roger Graef's mould-breaking series about the Thames Valley force, *Police*. Former executive producer of *The Bill*, Peter Cregeen, described the 'philosophy' of the series as 'an attempt to reflect current society and make it documentarily accurate – which was very much the philosophy that lay behind *Z Cars*'.

The Metropolitan Police are happy to cooperate with the makers of *The Bill*, based at the mythical Sun Hill station, via the ex-police officers who act as the programme's advisers. Nurturing better relations with the media, and, by extension, promoting more positive images of the police, has been a prime objective of senior policemen as far back as Scotland Yard Commissioner Harold Scott in the 1960s who encouraged the making of *Dixon of Dock Green*. Surveys have shown that the public gets most of its information about the police from the series. Alec Marnoch, a senior officer in the Metropolitan Police tasked with driving through an improved image of the force with the public, admits to using the series to spread the message of a new 'customer-oriented service', 'I could get it (the message) to a wider audience through putting it over *The Bill* than sometimes through sending out police orders or written instructions' (Sweeting, 1993).

This suggests that police series can play an ideological role in legitimizing the police and the powers they are given. With several elements of society at odds with these powers – miners, printers and racial minorities in the 1980s; travellers, poll tax demonstrators and road protesters in the 1990s, just to take a few examples – representations of the police play a critical role in maintaining a public concept of 'order' and the police's 'duty' in maintaining it.

The large number of police series on television today is an indication of the continuing popularity of the genre. Establishing the star status of the performers is a crucial factor in a programme's ratings. Actors such as Jimmy Nail in *Spender*, John Thaw in *Inspector Morse* and Robbie Coltrane in *Cracker* are seen as key factors in those series' success. The genre has, nevertheless, been popular for at least a hundred years in novels, short stories and the cinema. Crime fiction offers a narrative puzzle that can involve the audience or reader. Television continues the tradition of Hollywood and fiction writers such as Agatha Christie and Raymond Chandler by adapting many of their stories and characters. Another reason for its popularity may be that it allows us to bear witness to violence and taboo acts, to consider the unthinkable, with the reassuring knowledge that order will be restored at the close. Furthermore, they provide an escape from the routine of our work and lives: 'Modern police heroes work by inspiration, hunch and decisive action, not by boring attention to repetitive detail and cautious, modest advances' (Clarke, 1987).

However, the sheer number and bewildering variety of crime series may also reflect a lack of public confidence or consensus about the police and how they should be represented. With modern society increasingly fragmented, representations of the police, like the police themselves, have to be all things to all people. Low public confidence in the police or its ability to deal with a rising wave of crime appears to be matched by a need for *fictional* heroes and resolutions. These may be historical or escapist fantasies with little bearing on modern reality or they may be apparently 'realistic', 'gritty' and often gruesome depictions of police work. But they are fictional no matter how authentic in detail they appear and should be judged quite separately as such.

EXERCISES AND ESSAYS

Exercise

Analyse an episode of two contrasting police series. Make careful notes of the names of the central characters (police and criminals) – their costumes, rank, speech, mannerisms and character, methods of dealing with investigation, type of crimes, sets and settings, 'atmosphere' of the series, viewing time and probable audience.

Use these notes to write the following essay. (You may want to use the headings suggested above as guidelines for the paragraphs that make up the essay.)

Essay

Compare the representation of police and criminals in two (or more) contrasting police series of your choice. Are there any marked similarities or differences? What generalizations could be made about the representation of police and criminals in police series as a whole?

Exercise

Examine the representation of women in police series. Are they represented at all, and if so what roles are they given? What sorts of crimes are they usually involved in – either as criminals or as police officers? Are women defined differently by the kind of 'issues' they deal with?

Essay

Examine the evidence for or against the assertion that 'Women, or their lives, are often constructed in crime series as damaged, scarred or lacking in some way', *or* discuss whether you agree with the statement that in *Cagney and Lacey* and other police series featuring major female characters the treatment of crime in terms of 'women's problems' and the foregrounding of domestic issues is merely 'the reconstruction and representation of feminism and feminist issues within a patriarchal discourse' (Baehr and Dyer, 1987).

Exercise

Analyse the opening credits for two or more contrasting police series. What do these sequences tell us about the programmes that they introduce? Consider elements such as music, settings, action, reoccuring motifs, title and fonts, special effects, pace of editing, lighting, use of colour, costumes and appearance of characters.

Essay

Do you agree with the statement 'Police series reinforce a conventional, class and property based morality and pander to the lowest tastes in society'?

Exercise

The crime thriller conventionally features a number of enigmas – some based on characters, others on events. The central enigma may be about an event such as murder or robbery. Character based enigmas (a series of suspects) will work towards the resolution of that central enigma (Adrian Tilley, in Lusted, 1991).

Summarize, in no more than two paragraphs, how this feature is shown in a single episode of a crime series you have watched.

Essay

Genre spells out to the audience the range of pleasures it might expect and thus regulates and activates memory of similar texts and the expectations of this one (Fiske, 1987).

What 'pleasures' can an audience expect from a police series?

Exercise

Devise your own police series. Describe:

- the central characters
- the setting
- the types of crimes investigated
- the mood of the series – upbeat, uncritical (e.g. *Heartbeat*), darker, more ambiguous (e.g. *Cracker*)?

Practical Production

Use the ideas devised in the previous exercise to storyboard and/or film the opening titles for the new series.

Sources

Alvarado, M. (1987): *Television and video.* Wayland.

Baehr, H. and Dyer, G. (eds) (1987): *Boxed in: women and television.* Pandora.

BBC2 (1993): *Barlow, Regan, Pile and Fancy* (documentary).

Buxton, D. (1990): *From the Avengers to Miami Vice: form and ideology in television series.* Manchester University Press.

Clarke, M. (1987): *Teaching popular television.* Heinemann Educational in association with the British Film Institute.

Cooke, T. (1993): Police and crime. Oldham Sixth Form College (unpublished).

Fiske, J. (1987): *Television culture.* Routledge.

Hall, S. *et al.* (1982): *Politics, ideology and popular culture 2.* Open University Press.

Kerr, P. (1990): F for fake? Friction over faction. In Goodwin, A. and Whannel, G. (eds), *Understanding television.* Routledge.

Lusted, D. (ed.) (1991): *The media studies book.* Routledge.

Strinati, D. (1995): *An introduction to theories of popular culture.* Routledge.

Sutcliffe, T. (1995): New idea for a cop show? No, it's been nicked. *The Independent* April.

Sweeting, A. (1993): A fair cop, guv? *The Guardian* May.

Wheen, F. (1985): *Television – a history.* Guild Publishing.

Trevor McDonald at ITN's *News at Ten* desk

9

Television News

WHAT IS NEWS?

An unimaginably vast number of events happen in the world every day. A handful of these events, considered by news institutions to be 'important' or 'interesting' are selected and represented to audiences. These audiences may be local, regional, national or international and each is targeted by television, radio and press news media in different ways.

Definitions of news are constantly shifting: much that is regarded as news in television newsrooms today would have been rejected without hesitation 30 years ago, and vice versa. Not only has the criteria by which what is regarded as 'important and interesting' changed dramatically but also the way such information is packaged has evolved over the years into the format we recognize today. The dictionary defines news as *a recent event*: a newcast takes such events and forms them into narrative by using 'live' footage, journalists' reports, the opinions of different people and 'unbiased' comment. News events cover a wide range of situations, involving people, animals and things; some marvellous, some mundane, but all of which only become 'newsworthy' because of their being positioned in newscasts or newspapers.

It is important to remember that news material is *bought* and *sold* like any other product. British television news is not subject to direct commercial pressure as it is in the USA because ITN and Channel 4 News receive their income directly from the ITV network or Channel 4 and not from advertising revenue. Nevertheless, high costs or low ratings spell trouble for any news organization. ITN, for example, has to show value for money to the independent networks it serves because SKY news offers a cheaper, populist alternative.

Television news organizations may be in competition, but they buy and sell stories from each other and are linked by their dependency on regular news *sources* such as the large news agencies, governments, political parties, the police and any number of official, 'recognized' institutions. The similarity of major stories, their treatment and even running order far outweigh the differences to be found in television news programmes in Britain. This suggests that television news has a fairly uniform 'agenda' of what its editors regard as interesting or uninteresting, important or unimportant.

What makes news on television, therefore, will be determined by this *agenda*. Who sets this agenda is a complex and controversial question. What is described as 'traditional practices' suggests the selection of stories is simply a matter of journalistic skill. The clichéd notion of a 'nose for news' is something which television journalists and editors have to develop. In practice it means trainees must work with 'experienced' journalists or editors until they recognize the type of stories that are acceptable and are capable of packaging the items in ways that the news organization approves of. The concept of 'traditional practices' helps partly to obscure the question of who is setting the agenda. This question is examined in more detail on pp. 109–13 below.

NEWS – AN HISTORICAL OVERVIEW

The coronation of George VI was one of the first events to be recorded by the fledgling BBC shortly after its launch in 1936 and one which helped boost early sales of television sets. Before the war there was no news service as such, although the BBC screened Movietone and Gaumont newsreels on a weekly basis. The BBC television closed down for the duration of the war and the service only resumed with a broadcast of the Victory Parade in June 1946.

The BBC's newsreel division was producing its own footage by 1948 supplemented by 'live sound' recorded on the spot – although difficult to synchronize at this stage. They recorded dramatic scenes such as accidents, storms, fires and floods with the emphasis very much on what made exciting images. Elizabeth II's coronation in 1953 gave a huge boost to television sales, with the BBC broadcasting the ceremony live. By the mid-1950s television news was overtaking British cinema newsreels in importance. Traditionally, the five major newsreel companies had been the only source of images of world news events that people may have heard about on the radio.

In 1954 the Newsreel Division of the BBC came under the control of News Division which until that time had only produced radio reports. The *News and Newsreel* service ran news items in the same running order as Broadcasting House, with no allowance given for the quality of footage that might accompany it. Frequently, there was no footage at all, only photographic stills clumsily rotated by hand on a revolving apparatus before a camera lens.

The style of *News and Newsreel* has been described as 'impersonal', 'sober', 'self-conscious' and the content as 'hard', 'heavy' and with an obsession for accuracy or official confirmation even if it meant the loss of a scoop. On one occasion a BBC reporter's eye-witness account of the death of a speedboat racer on a Scottish loch sent just before a news bulletin was not used because no agency had yet confirmed it.

In *Putting reality together*, Schlesinger quotes observations on the content of BBC broadcasts as devoted to international and foreign events – including much news from the United States, especially if it relates to the United Kingdom; news of the British Commonwealth; home, political and industrial events; significant developments in literature, the arts, science, and other fields of learning; and the activities of the royal family [and] . . . a tendency to eschew the reporting of crimes and accidents, a lack of humorous or light stories, and an absence of colourful adjectives.

The difference between the media had been appreciated up to 20 years earlier. W.A. Pullan writes in *Picturegoer* in 1935,

Newsreel commenting is vastly different from [radio] broadcasting as has been proved on more than one occasion . . . A newsreel commentary must be all-embracing, conclusive, pithy, full of punch, dramatic, compact (quoted in Momi, undated).

All the things, in fact, that the daily 20 minute *News and Newsreel* was not. Stuffy, untelegenic newsreaders, dull, wordy, primitive, distanced and confused production and 'hopelessly upmarket' news values meant that many viewers thought the programme inferior to the pre-1954 BBC Newsreel.

What changed the BBC's approach to news, it is widely recognized, was the growing threat of ITN, the news service of ITV which was launched in 1955. Only weeks before ITN's first transmission the BBC was still not showing its newsreaders' faces on the screen, for fear that this would jeopardize the bulletin's impartiality. By contrast, the commercial pressures driving ITV meant that ITN was encouraged to reach a wider audience by promoting the personalities of its newsreaders. Schlesinger (1987) quotes Robin Day on his role as one of the original ITN newscasters:

as the newscaster became known to viewers, his professional grasp of his material, and his lively interest in it would make the news more authoritative and *entertaining*.

Drawing extensively on the model of ABC and CBS journalism in the USA ITN allowed the news values of television to emerge and embraced more populist elements such as human-interest stories, vivid action film, the use of reporters on the spot, 'vox pop' location interviews with members of the public, humour and a more combative interviewing style. Wheen (1985) describes how in contrast to the 'deferential' interviewing style of the BBC, ITN's reporters were unafraid to tackle senior politicians and statesmen:

During the Suez crisis . . . it was ITN that broadcast the first pictures of British and French troops landing at Port Said. ITN followed this success with another world exclusive in 1957, when Robin Day interviewed President Nasser in Cairo. Since diplomatic relations between Britain and Egypt were still severed, Nasser's comments generated enormous interest, especially as he expressed his willingness to resume Egypt's 'friendship' with

Britain. For Day, too, the interview was a triumph, proving that the ITN style would be applied even to heads of state. When Day asked whether Nasser accepted Israel's right to exist, the President accused him of 'jumping to conclusions'. 'No,' Day replied, 'I am asking a question.'

ITN exploited the celebrity status of its early presenters – Robin Day, Ludovic Kennedy, Christopher Chataway, Reginald Bosanquet – to compensate for the fact that many news stories took place without cameras being present, and other stories – a fall in the balance of payments or a rise in inflation – were not particularly 'visual' in any case.

A major problem of news at this time was its refusal to deal with any given subject for more than about a minute. The main fear was that audiences would be bored by anything longer. The resulting lack of depth given to any television news report created a vacuum in news presentation that led to the development of the current affairs programme – a kind of offshoot of television news. *Panorama*, *Tonight*, *Searchlight*, *World in Action* and *Sixty Minutes* followed in the footsteps of the US *See It Now* whose creator Edward R. Murrow dared to challenge such orthodoxies as Joseph McCarthy's Communist blacklist and the US involvement in Vietnam. These programmes sought out and found controversy on a range of 'sensitive' issues such as Northern Ireland, defence spending, homelessness, political corruption, the dangers of smoking, road accidents and spying scandals. Clashes with television's governing bodies and the government of the day were frequent, usually centring on problems of 'national security' or 'impartiality'. Francis Wheen (1985) describes a typical argument in his history of television:

In September 1963 *World in Action* revealed the appalling living conditions of black people in South Africa and Angola (which was then a Portuguese colony), causing an inevitable protest from the ambassadors of the two countries. The ITA agreed that the programme had not been impartial, and decreed that in future all Granada's current affairs programmes should be vetted before transmission by the Authority's staff.

The insistence on 'impartiality' and 'balance' led to such absurd situations as films promoting holidays in the Republic of South Africa being shown alongside documentaries and current affairs programme condemning apartheid.

The political power of television images, combined with the increasing use of television satellite transmission around the world (after 1962) gave the medium even greater importance. Coverage of the civil rights campaigns in the USA in the late 1950s and early 1960s was widely seen as making possible the passage of the Civil Rights Act of 1964 and the Voting Rights of 1965. Following broadcast footage in 1965 of marines razing to the ground the Vietnamese village of Cam Ne, burning alive some of its inhabitants in the process, President Lyndon Johnson famously rang the President of CBS shouting: 'Frank, are you trying to fuck me?', adding that, 'yesterday your boys shat on the American flag'. In 1968, protesters outside the Democratic Convention in Chicago chanted 'The whole world is watching' while police beat them in front of the news cameras.

This awareness of the potency of television images was not confined to the USA. One of the causes of the Soviet invasion of Czechoslovakia in 1968 was the ending of television news censorship under Alexander Dubcek's liberal regime. During student riots in France in 1968 the government intervened to prevent television journalists giving airtime to student leaders. The resulting strike by television journalists meant that during five violent weeks of social unrest that brought the country close to revolution, French television (ORTF), controlled by the Ministry of Information, had only brief news bulletins produced by a skeleton staff. Following De Gaulle's defeat of the students the striking journalists lost their jobs and the state's monopoly of broadcasting continued.

Controversy has also dogged British news broadcasts. The 1980s and 1990s provided challenges for ITV and, particularly, the BBC to provide 'balance' and 'impartiality' in periods of political and economic crisis, when the country was (at times violently) divided. The miners' strike, the 'Falklands War', welfare cuts, coverage of Northern Ireland, party politics, the Campaign for Nuclear Disarmament were just some areas where broadcasters found themselves under fire from more than one direction for their coverage. In fact, Britain was totally divided on most of these issues – there was no 'consensus', and as such consensus or even 'balanced' reporting was an impossibility. As Andrew Goodwin (1990) notes

> As the social and political consensus has broken down in postwar Britain, so television has encountered more and more problems in knowing how to represent that world.

Television news found itself under attack from radical Tories in the government such as Norman Tebbit, those on the left of the Labour Party such as Tony Benn, and from the centre, with the Social Democratic Party claiming it was receiving insufficient coverage. Throughout the Conservative government in the 1980s and early 1990s the threat of removing the BBC's public sector broadcasting status was a real possibility and one which critics on the left feel neutered news and current affairs coverage.

Broadcasters looked across the Atlantic to see what kind of news US stations, responsible only to their advertisers, were offering. Whereas news had been regarded as something of a public duty in the 1950s and 1960s, by the early 1970s it had become a 'profit centre', as important a weapon in the ratings battle as a soap opera or game show. According to Francis Wheen (1985):

> The trend setter was *Eye Witness News*, a local programme put out by stations owned and operated by ABC. It used a simple formula: plenty of sports reports; even more weather forecasts; a little news, kept as 'soft' and

'visual' as possible; and interminable jokey banter between the anchor-people and the weather-man ... This kind of inanity became known as 'Happy Talk' news, and stations around the country hired 'news consultants' to come in and convert their programmes to Happy Talk.

Such 'news consultants' – often the same US ones – are still being used around the world and in Britain. Frank N. Magid Associates from Marion, Iowa, worked on the ITN revamp in 1992, researching viewers' attitudes, refreshing the 'writing techniques' and 'picture packaging'. The results, as the journalist Rosie Millard (1993) notes, are that, internationally, news programmes have a certain similarity:

From Sweden to Greece, Liverpool to America, we see the same bright set; the jaunty electronic theme tune; the branding of packages within the programme ('Focus on Britain' ... 'And Finally') and the emphasis on live, 'happening events' (witness the increased use of live links by News at Ten).

Commercial pressures on British television news production have been growing since the late 1980s when competition from satellite broadcasting started to take a share of the British audience – ending the BBC–ITN duopoly of television news. This development was also regarded, by many who opposed the government, as a move to undermine public broadcasting and with it any potential opposition to Conservative Party policy. Conservatism, it was felt, was clearly best supported by a commercial broadcasting sector under the control of large (private sector) commercial interests that government policy supported. In fact, transnational corporations such as Ted Turner's CNN or Rupert Murdoch's SKY were capable of operating with or without national government backing. Government legislation, which resulted in limiting the BBC's ability to defend its interests in a variety of ways, only marginally hastened their success.

NEWS VALUES

Although the day-to-day agenda of news items may appear to change, the *underlying principles* of *selection* and *presentation* of news are more constant. These principles are often described as 'news values' and include some of the following characteristics.

Personalization

The social power of elite persons is underscored by the narrative power that familiarity confers (Fiske, 1987).

'Personalization' (i.e. events seen as the actions of individuals rather than of forces), Brian Dutton suggests, is one of the most important news values held by journalists. In the historical context of violent racial attacks or changes in legislation affecting thousands of asylum seekers extensive television news coverage of a libel action by two individuals against another for describing them as 'racists' would seem wholly disproportionate. When those individuals are well-known media and sports personalities, however (Ian Botham, Alan Lamb, Imran Khan in July 1996), then the widespread coverage seems completely 'natural'. According to Pilger (1992):

> On the day Robert Maxwell died, an estimated 6000 people were killed in a typhoon in the Philippines, most of them in one town. .... On the BBC's *Nine O'Clock News* Maxwell was the first item; the disaster in the Philippines was one of the last in a round-up of fillers.

Political or industrial disputes are frequently reported in terms of personalities. Scargill v. Thatcher, Major v. Blair. The *human interest angle* of the story of an individual or small group can graphically illustrate the effects of any news item. The horror of war, for instance, is brought home most powerfully by showing its effect on one family or child (a technique ITN employed in Bosnia). Used excessively, though, as many critics suggest British television does, the personalization of issues in this way fails even to attempt to unravel the causes of the wars, famines, industrial or political disputes and other conflicts:

> Clearly the news is peopled by real individuals, but in representing events through people the news is following the conventions of classic realism, for it assumes that the way to construct an understandable and authentic version of the real is through the actions, words and reactions of the individuals involved. Social and political issues are only reported if they can be embodied in an individual, and thus social conflict of interest is personalized into conflicts between individuals. The effect of this is that the social origins of events are lost, and individual motivation is assumed to be the origin of all action (Fiske, 1987).

Negativity

> The bigger the tragedy, the greater the images of the disaster, the more prominence it acquires (BBC news presenter, Martyn Lewis, 1993).

Hard news: serious, 'important', dramatic events – wars, disasters, terrorism, political and economic crises, crime, the deaths of famous persons – have traditionally dominated television news. *Soft news*: consumer features, entertainment, human-interest stories, bizarre or amusing tales, experiences recounted in the first person, personality gossip have, until recently, remained in the province of magazine and tabloid journalism. Martyn Lewis, writing for the *Daily Mail* in April 1993, sparked a fierce debate by publicly calling for more *good news* on television. Viewers, he claimed, were sick of television's 'remorseless emphasis on disaster, conflict and failure'. He put forward an argument for more positive hard news such as the increase in productivity of miners through the late 1980s because it was 'part of the fabric of understanding of what is now happening in the mining industry'. That Lewis, writing for the loyally Conservative *Daily Mail*, chose the 'mining industry' – if it could still be called that – to support his case, exposes the ideological dimension of such arguments. Certainly, ex-miners and unionists complain that the destruction of mining communities, closure of profitable mines and decline in safety standards and working conditions for the few remaining miners under privatized companies did not get enough coverage on television news.

In fact, Lewis's suggestions, based on developments at ABC in the USA, where a segment of the main evening news called 'American Agenda' explored solutions to what seem intractable problems, had already been taken up by ITN. Their thrice-weekly feature package 'Focus on Britain' launched in November 1992 was exactly the type of feature he was calling for.

The issue of soft news was only briefly addressed in the debate. Lewis criticized the '"And finally . . ." tailpiece, the frivolous, often funny story, which, on a rationale assessment of what is important in the world that day, would never make it into a properly packed news bulletin'. Market pressures which shifted the press towards soft news, lifestyle features and entertainment in the late 1980s and early 1990s were slowly being felt in television newsrooms. The *tabloidization* of news – already experienced in the USA and graphically illustrated on satellite 'infotainment' shows such as *Hard Copy* – was felt to be a growing threat in Britain. ITN's 1992 revamp – a response to such commercial pressures – was criticized by those in the industry as 'a Las Vegas floorshow', 'stylish but not informative', encouraging 'downmarket news values' and 'formulaic' presentation. Lewis's coverage of a delivery of Christmas presents from British schoolchildren to children in war-torn Armenia on 19 December 1996 is, perhaps, typical of the kind of good news story he was pressing for. Reporting from the Armenian capital, Yerevan, on 'a story which touched a nation's heart', Lewis interviewed grateful parents and children as they opened the 'personally wrapped gifts'. The report is symptomatic of a shift towards sentimental 'human-interest' stories that do little, or nothing, to explain distant conflicts and reinforce a smugly paternalistic view of Britain's role in world affairs.

The journalist John Cole, amongst others, argued that news values should not be set by public opinion: 'News', he wrote, 'must be judged by whether it is right, interesting and significant' (Bromley, 1994). Less subjective and more useful definitions of news are given by Corner (1995) as 'part of general citizenship rights, "to provide knowledge and understanding about circumstances of consequence to readers, listeners and viewers, to contribute not only to their understanding but also to their capacities for judgement and action"', or by Fiske (1987) as 'factual information that its viewers need in order to be able to participate in their society'. Defined by its function in this way, news remains a highly controversial form but one more easily distinguished from various types of 'infotainment' that adopt the conventions of news. However, the fact remains that when people talk about 'the news' they generally refer to the particular events which have been reported in news output. As such, functional definitions such as those quoted above may be no more than altruistic ideals against which we can measure the reality of news production.

Locality

Regional television news covers news from that region, or how *national* news affects the *region*. National news, such as the BBC's six o'clock bulletin, tend to concentrate on developments close to home. It is often remarked that a news event in London will take precedent over an identical event in Glasgow. A plane crash in France will be considered more important than a similar crash in Russia. News from Africa or India usually has to involve a major catastrophe before it is covered, reinforcing a view of developing countries as places of natural and political disaster and not much else. Such catastrophes are also usually covered in relation to how British people are affected.

News for international audiences such as CNN or BBC World News are also accused of being top-heavy in terms of 'Western' news. This is owing to the reliance of such organizations on the larger news agencies such as Reuters (British), AFP (French), AP and UPI (USA). Being based in 'the developed world' and having most of their journalists employed there means that the transborder data flow works to the disadvantage of Third World countries. According to Unesco in its report *Many voices, one world*:

> Associated Press sends 90,000 words daily from New York to Asia on its world wire service. In return Asia flies a mere 19,000 words for worldwide distribution [and] A study of one particular day's news in Venezuela in 1977 showed that for every 100 items received from the USA, Venezuelan sources dispatched only 7 – and these via AP or UPI, both US agencies (quoted in Lewis and Pearlman, 1986).

This *disparity* in news material is reflected in, for example, CNN's coverage of elections in the USA, Russia (as a former superpower) and Europe compared with other regions. It is also reflected in the Western 'perspectives' of the so-called 'Third World'. As the journalist John Pilger (1992) remarks:

> The fact that Africa's recurring famines and extreme poverty – a poverty whose rapid increase is a feature of the 'new age' – have political causes rooted in the West is not regarded as news. How many of us were aware during 1985 – the year of the Ethiopian famine and of 'Live Aid' – that the hungriest countries in Africa gave twice as much money to *us* in the West as we gave to them: billions of dollars just in interest payments.

We were shown terrible pictures of children dying and we were not told of the part our financial institutions had played in their deaths. This also was not news. The camera was allowed to dictate a false neutrality, as is often the case, with the reporter playing the role of the concerned innocent bystander and caption writer. Public attitudes flow from both perspective and omissions. Unless prejudice is countered, it is reinforced. Unless misconceptions are corrected, they become received truth. This 'neutrality' is commonly known, with unintended irony, as 'objectivity'.

Timing

Hand in glove with objectivity go authenticity and immediacy. Both these link news values in particular with qualities of television in general. For authenticity links with realisticness, and immediacy with 'nowness' or 'liveness', both of which are central to the experience of television. In news, both work to promote the transparency fallacy and to mask the extent of the construction or interpretation that news involves (Fiske, 1987).

The more recent the events, the more newsworthy they are. Television's main advantage over the press is that it can deal with today's news, or even news as it breaks, unlike most daily papers which can report only yesterday's events. During the Gulf War CNN's reputation as a news channel soared throughout the world because it reported events as they happened. John Eldridge in his book *Getting the message* (1993) comments:

These CNN reports had a raw quality about them. They were unfiltered happenings. We see one reporter knock over another as the sirens wail out in Dhahran and they instinctively duck to avoid the anticipated missile. At times, because of the noise or because their voices are muffled by gas masks we can scarcely hear what they say. But what kind of knowledge is this? It was fairly described by one critic on BBC2's *Late Show* as 'immediacy without understanding, drama without information' (22 January 1991).

There are many occasions when the 'live' nature of television news reports is employed only for *effect*. Live links to an empty Downing Street, or outside talks where nobody has emerged, are a common sight. In the same article on the Gulf War, John Eldridge quotes an ITN reporter, Alex Thomson:

One of the standard devices is the live two-way . . . you go to your man on the spot . . . Bill, what's the latest? That's fine. In Dhahran you didn't know what the latest was because the latest was 150–200 miles away, or in Riyadh. So what was a perfectly respectable journalistic device – asking someone who was there – actually became completely downgraded and abused in that situation . . . I'm informed that such and such is going on. The only reason they knew was that they phoned their office (the London newsroom) just before going on air and the office had read over to them the latest wire copy. I know. I did that (*Tales From the Gulf*, BBC2, 19 July 1991).

A story such as the Gulf War is extremely attractive to television news because, although the details of the conflict and its outcome were difficult to predict, the story had 'legs' and would run for weeks if not months. To this extent it was *predictable* as a news event. 'Day 13 of Desert Storm' was the screen caption behind the newsreader, while expertise, 'three-dimensional' maps, satellite links, Middle East specialists and army experts could be called in, safe in the knowledge that the story was not going to disappear tomorrow. News stories such as this develop the narrative qualities of soap opera or epic sagas with easily recognized characters (mad dictators, determined generals, brave soldiers); cliffhangers (will Iraq use chemical weapons?), twists in the plot (the capture of air force pilots) and reversals of fortune (Iraqi soldiers chased out of Kuwait).

For a story to run and maintain a high priority on the news agenda there must be a daily supply of fresh, dramatic or unexpected developments. The war in Bosnia floated out of the headlines once the reports of Serb concentration camps and mass murder had been aired. Only major military advances, the death of UN soldiers or the final US brokered peace deal could push the first war on European soil since the Second World War back into the headlines. For similar reasons the Dunblane massacre of schoolchildren remained the lead item for many days, whereas the drawn-out government inquiry on possession of handguns – an inquiry that, in the opinion of the police federation, could end similar atrocities – was barely mentioned either on television or in the press for several months until their conclusions were made public. In this way the 'public inquiry' is a well-known government stalling device that allows 'tempers to cool' or tragedies to be forgotten.

Pictures

Television news is generally given greater credence by the public than either newspapers or radio; probably because it is perceived to be less partisan than the press, and because it offers the 'evidence' of pictures that isn't available on the radio (Goodwin, 1990).

We quickly learned how television affects the selection and arrangement of news. The fact of yesterday's air disaster may no longer be top news tonight – but the *first* film of the scene may well merit first place in this evening's television news (Robin Day, quoted in Schlesinger, 1987).

The emergence of ITN witnessed a rediscovery of the importance of 'picture value' in British television news – a concept already clearly grasped in US news bulletins and, previously, by British newsreel. Today, 'picture value' has very high importance – too high according to many critics. A common complaint is that television news's reliance on dramatic, visual events reinforces the lack of coverage given to long-term developments which may be far more 'important' in terms of their effects. Floods, for instance, affect many people and make dramatic footage. The destruction of forests, however, which in many instances causes such floods and displaces as many people, is a daily reality and therefore makes far less dramatic footage for a news report. Unemployment, pollution, malnutrition, disease and political oppression are also slow-acting, if far-reaching, developments, but lack the visual punch of an earthquake or a rocket exploding and so tend to have a lower priority on television bulletins.

Short-term, immediate and easily explained filmed news items will generally take precedence on television bulletins. For example, minor outbreaks of violence amongst Hong Kong citizens queuing for documentation at the British consulate found its way into British news reports because a camera crew were present at the incident. Had the crew arrived five minutes later it is highly unlikely the item would have been covered at all.

In fact the majority of film on news items shows places and persons connected to a story *after* the event. The principal action is over and news teams resort to a repertoire of visual prompts around which the spoken narrative can be organized. These include shots of the location, library film, 'stagings', photographs of individuals or families, or footage from related stories. As John Corner (1995) suggests, when cameras are present at the news event the effect can be very powerful:

> such picturing may serve to crystallise the whole report and to enter public circulation with a force no other form of contemporary journalism could possess. The examples of the first pictures of the mid-1970s Ethiopian famine, broadcast all over the world, are often cited here. Other, more recent, examples having international significance would be the scenes of the Baghdad shelter following the Allied bombing in 1991 and the scenes of the Serbian-run internment camps in Bosnia, shown by television in 1992. In both cases, and in many others, the television pictures attain a 'nodal' status for subsequent public debate about the circumstances depicted, and often for political responses to them too.

Simplicity

Related to all the points above is television news's preference for *simple* stories over *complex* ones. This is hardly surprising given the constraints of time and the medium. A typical news programme attempts to pick out what it considers will be of interest to its viewers from thousands of news reports and reduce all that information into the same number of words as can be put on one page of a broadsheet newspaper. Furthermore, the *speed* of electronic news-gathering and the pressure for television stations to be first with the news has 'turned newspapers into magazines' according to Peter Ibbotson, former editor of *Panorama*:

> Being unable to compete on news, they put their resources into features. As a result of this same process, however, TV itself has become less interesting. The immediacy has meant that pictures are thrown onto the screen straight away and the painstaking TV journalism has been pushed aside (quoted in Woffinden, 1996).

It is relatively easy, for example, to focus on the images of suffering caused by 'war' – such as civilians whose legs have been blown off by mines. It is more difficult, however, to investigate the more complex causes of such atrocities such as Western 'aid' in the form of weapons, government subsidies to arms manufacturers or the reluctance of Western powers to sign international treaties outlawing mines. In this sense television news tends to be *reactive*, rather than *investigative*. John Birt's reform of news coverage at the BBC was partly a response to this criticism. The 'mission to explain' – providing 'focus, context and background' to news bulletins – is, however, undermined by the medium's reactive news values. According to Bob Woffinden in his article 'Fast and loose' this is true of the media in general at the moment:

> Immediacy is all . . . . Opportunities for mature reflection have evaporated. The media seem to be lurching from crisis to crisis with little in between – certainly none of the painstaking monitoring that might help prevent disaster occurring. News events are regularly conveyed as a series of news dramas; covering non-emergency (but serious enough) stories becomes difficult.

In his book *Television culture* Fiske illustrates how these deadline pressures and news conventions mean that television news stories are effectively pre-written; they 'write' the journalists:

> For news is as conventional as any other form of television, its conventions are so powerful and so uninspected because the tyranny of the deadline requires the speed and efficiency that only conventions make possible. The type of stories, the forms that they will take, and the programme structure into which they will be inserted are all determined long before any of the events of the day occur. During the forced withdrawal of Belgium from the (then) Belgian Congo, an American journalist landed at Lusaka airport and, on seeing a group of white women waiting for evacuation, rushed over to them with the classic question, 'Has anyone here been raped, and speaks English?' His story had been 'written' before landing, all he needed was a few local details.

ACCURACY, OBJECTIVITY AND BALANCE IN TELEVISION NEWS

It is quite plausible to believe that all media images are constructed and still maintain that some constructions are more truthful than others (Goodwin, 1990).

In his book *Television form and public address*, John Corner makes distinctions between the journalistic principle of 'impartiality' and the 'regularly associated and often confused' notions of 'accuracy', 'objectivity' and 'balance'. *Accuracy* he takes to mean the correctness of facts – names, dates, quotes, and so on. This is not always as straightforward as it sounds. In the early 1980s news reports of marches by the Campaign for Nuclear Disarmament often gave both CND organizers' and police estimates of the numbers attending as they varied so enormously. Clearly, the dividing line between facts and opinion is sometimes a blurred one but, as Corner notes,

no one doubts the possibility of a journalist being 'accurate' about a lot of things for a lot of the time as agreed by the very widest spectrum of political and social opinion and very few people doubt the desirability of them being so.

Objectivity as defined in *The Concise Oxford Dictionary* as 'that which is external to the mind' and 'that which is unaffected by subjective mental operations' is clearly, Corner observes, philosophically and practically as impossible for journalists as for anyone else. To say 'objectivity' is possible is to assume that an unarguable interpretation of an event exists. In fact, all reporting implies a point of view – in the selection or non-selection of stories (thereby setting a value upon them), the placement and angle of the cameras (behind police lines or demonstrators, for example), the selection of interviewees and relevant questions, and the language and tone adopted by reporters and presenters. Ironically, as Fiske (1987) points out, despite unanimous critical agreement that no communication can be totally 'neutral' or 'objective', 'The idea that television is a window on the world, now known as the "transparency fallacy", still survives, if anywhere, in TV newsrooms.'

Balance is also a notion presenting problems, according to Corner. It usually implies the idea of equal time given to 'defined positions'. As such, the act of nominating the 'positions' and allocating them airtime becomes an institutional responsibility fraught with controversy. The timing of broadcast material presenting opposing views according to a sliding scale reflecting electoral popularity occurs both in the studio and at the headquarters of the major political parties, particularly around elections. The 'stopwatch', in this way, can become the arbiter of 'balance' both figuratively and literally – with the main political parties dominating the debate and exercising enormous pressure and influence on television news production. Such reductive 'stopwatch' practices are further complicated when there are more than two positions or parties. Where the point of 'balance' for the presentation of different views would seem to be between two parties – the 'middle ground' – a further problem occurs when this position is occupied by a centrist party, in which case the slant of reports would tend to be 'biased' in favour of that party above others.

Bias, 'the term applied to the media when they give an "unfair" advantage to one side in a dispute, either by misrepresenting, underplaying or ignoring alternative points of view' (Gill and Adams, 1988) is an accusation which television news must be careful to avoid. In various studies, about 70 per cent of people asked trusted television news to be unbiased: only 8 per cent trusted newspapers (Bromley, 1994). Broadcasting organizations are legally obliged to show 'due impartiality'. *Due impartiality*, as defined by the BBC charter and the various acts of parliament covering independent broadcasting, means taking into account a full range of views and opinions but also giving prominence to mainstream opinions, whilst recognizing shifts in public opinion. Where 'points of view' are given they must be clearly signalled as such and immediately matched by an opposing view. For ITV and the BBC this principle is supposed to operate *within* any programme; on Channel 4 impartiality is required only *across* the range of programming shown. News broadcast on *all* channels, however, must be 'fair' and free of bias in respect of all legally expressable political and social viewpoints (blatantly racist opinions, for example, should not be given airtime as a result of UK race-relation legislation).

The problems associated with such terms as accuracy, objectivity and balance, notwithstanding, few critics would argue that 'impartiality' in the sense of 'equity of representation' was not a principle worth defending in television news. According to Andrew Goodwin (1990), bias is not the opposite of truth:

> The real issue is whether the range of biases represented is fair. In other words, does it adequately reveal the range of points of view held by the public?

Corner (1995) concludes his investigation of the issue by defining 'impartiality' simply as that which is 'not partial, not prejudiced', and 'bias', in the negative sense, as a 'significant departure from fairness'. Thus,

> it is not necessary to have uncompromised access to the 'truth' of circumstances in order to advance a reasonable and cogent case for a report being biased in a way which is detrimental to journalism's public function. Here an uncompromising philosophical scepticism does not make a helpful guide, since it is that which is realisable *in practice* which requires attention. The omission of *arguably* significant details, perhaps ones published in other national news sources, the treating of an interviewee to hostile

questioning in a way which prejudices their expression of opinion, the suggestion of causality which is not substantiated, the use of certain labels to define groups in a pejorative way, these are all grounds for a claim of bias.

Bias in the News

Evidence of bias (as defined above) in television news comes in several forms. Andrew Goodwin (1990) illustrates how bias emerges from the news values that shape what broadcasters consider to be newsworthy. The following examples illustrate only one aspect of what he calls *unconscious bias* in news production:

> One of the classic values employed in selecting news is 'negativity', and when this is combined with 'frequency' (news has to be as new as the publication or broadcast presenting it) the effect is often of a barrage of bad things in the world which seem to have no rhyme or reason. One of the Conservative Party's complaints has been that when they close a hospital ward, that is news; but when they build a new hospital, that isn't news. Hence broadcasting creates an image of a heartless, uncaring Conservative government, through the bias of news selection. This is exactly the argument that trade unionists have been making for years about strikes. When we go to work, they say, that isn't news. When we go on strike, that is news. Hence broadcasting creates an image of a lazy workforce willing to strike at the drop of a shop steward's hat. Here, bias in news values themselves creates the problem.

In a peculiar way, television's obligation to select the news under 'opinion-free' conditions makes true investigative journalism – usually fuelled by a strong sense of commitment or (in)justice – almost impossible. As a result, television has a frequently noted tendency to respond to a news agenda set by the press – which *is* unapologetically partial and biased in its news coverage. A huge majority of national papers have traditionally taken a Tory 'line', a position changed only by the Labour landslide of 1997 (which, many critics suggest, was a result of Labour's Thatcherite policies). It therefore seems hardly surprising that the most consistent and thoroughly documented claims of bias in the selection and construction of news on television have come from the trade union movement and the left in British politics.

THE GLASGOW UNIVERSITY MEDIA GROUP AND BIAS

The Glasgow University Media Group (GUMG), who produced a series of seminal studies on television news during the 1970s and early 1980s, have produced some of the most heavily researched accusations of bias. In what became known as the 'Bad News' books they tested their hypothesis that television news systematically *favoured* dominant groups by investigating its coverage of a whole range of different stories. Through extensive videotaped evidence they argued that the news reproduced a coherent middle-class ideology. The news, therefore, did not show 'due impartiality' but relied upon certain class-related presuppositions or 'points of view'.

These 'points of view' could, GUMG argued, be found in television news's choice of topics and favoured interpretations (a right-wing 'agenda'); in the language employed by reporters and presenters; in interviewing styles and the choice of interviewees; and in the placing of oppositional views within a framework of debate set out by the establishment.

Three types of bias were picked out in their study of industrial relations in the late 1970s. First, the GUMG found, the media was biased by its *mis-representation* of social 'reality', overemphasizing the contribution of strikes to the poor economic performance of Britain. As a part of this misrepresentation certain workplaces, such as the car industry, were given excessive coverage. Second, the media worked *within* a *dominant ideological consensus* – which suggested that strikes are never justified and are always the fault of the workers. Third, it argued that working-class voices were *excluded* from the production of news. The occupational culture of television, GUMG claimed, was dominated by people from middle-class backgrounds. Television workers were separated both materially and symbolically from the working class. Information that contradicted the dominant middle-class world-view was either excluded or existed only in fragments. These three notions of bias combined to produce a powerful ideology that distorted reality, reaffirmed dominant relations and excluded contradictory perspectives.

Contradictory perspectives were also markedly absent during coverage of the Falklands War in 1983 which was, in the view of GUMG, overdetermined by direct forms of control imposed by the Minister of Defence, the lobby system and the journalists' own judgement of public opinion. In his book *Understanding media cultures* (1995), Nick Stevenson deftly summarizes how the symbolic production of good news necessitated by the need to cement together military, state and public concern was highlighted by GUMG's discussion of task-force families:

> Much of the coverage of the families of those soldiers involved in the Falklands war was focused on women. According to the Glasgow group, the lives of the women only became newsworthy as a result of the absence of the men who were making the news. News journalists, in this context, represented women relatives in terms of their traditional roles as carers and emotional supports for men. This not only misrepresents the real, given the decline of traditional family patterns and women's increasing engagement in the economy, but ideologically positions women as 'vessels of emotion'. The women interviewed were unlikely to be asked to reflect critically upon state

policy, and were much more likely to be asked how they felt. This discursive strategy trades upon an unspoken division between a rational male public sphere and an effective feminine private realm. Further the heavily gendered search for good news creates the notion of family and community solidarity centred around the visible private suffering of women.

Official sources were also heavily relied on by news journalists in the 1984–85 miners' strike. Coal-board press releases were often quoted verbatim, as with the highly charged phrase 'the drift back to work' which was used frequently. Violence on the picket lines was, in the view of GUMG, over-emphasized – with miners rather than the police invariably held to be responsible. With events at the Orgreave colliery, for instance, it was claimed news footage was played out of sequence to code the miners rather than the police as violent. Miners' leader Arthur Scargill was found to be subject to far more aggressive interviews than were Coal Board officials or the government. Furthermore, there was virtually no discussion of the so-called 'Ridley plan' – a Conservative Party strategy developed years in advance of the strike that suggested stockpiling coal and boosting gas and nuclear power in order to defeat the National Union of Miners (NUM), close mines and weaken trade unionism generally.

GUMG's (1982) conclusion to their detailed content analysis of news broadcasts was that:

> television is biased to the extent that it violates its formal obligations to give a balanced account. Our research also led us to discover that the broadcast institutions are extremely hierarchical, that close links exist between them and a range of 'official' and 'accepted' sources. The result of this is that the news gives preferential treatment to some ways of seeing the world.

As Stevenson (1995) notes, however, the GUMG were not proposing a conspiracy thesis in which broadcasters and the powerful were plotting to brainwash the public. They regarded much of this bias to be the result of *unconscious* professional practices and the *class background* of television journalists, editors and producers.

The arguments of the GUMG have been countered by various critics. Martyn Harrison (1985) suggested that the GUMG's self-confessed Marxist stance negated their research because their prejudices would interfere with their judgements. Casting doubt on the supposedly 'objective' content analysis of GUMG in this way, however, only goes to highlight the problems of 'objectivity' that this debate throws up. If Harrison is correct, how can individual 'subjects' – with viewpoints, opinions, biases – 'objectively' judge anything? To admit as much is to make Harrison's and all other researchers' work effectively meaningless. Putting this objection to one side, contrary to the GUMG's (more heavily documented) findings, Harrison's (1985) and Alastair Hetherington's (1985) studies found that television news coverage of the miners' strike was generally impartial (quoted in Branston and Stafford, 1996; Goodwin, 1990). As Branston and Stafford (1996) note, 'Arthur Scargill, for example, was argued to have been given many more hours coverage in interviews than were government representatives.'

Further objections to the GUMG's findings were provided by Guy Cumberbatch's Broadcast Research Unit Report (1986) on audience response to coverage of the strike. This study admitted that one of the problems with measuring bias was in gaining access to a reliable account of the real that was independent of the media of mass communication. The Broadcast Research Unit's conclusion about audience response to news coverage over the period of a year indicated that the general public were satisfied by the balance provided in the reports of the dispute. Stevenson's (1995) response to this study is simple:

> Cumberbatch's retreat into the audience makes it impossible to make objective truth claims about television content ... I would argue that whether audiences perceive bias is a different order of analysis to whether bias exists.

WHO CONTROLS NEWS? THE IDEOLOGY OF NEWS PRODUCTION

The state in every country uses various means to control or restrict broadcasting, and Britain is no exception to this rule. Although direct censorship of television output is rare, though not unknown, *indirect* controls of various types are operating constantly. The most obvious form of control comes from the power governments have to grant broadcasting franchises and (in the case of the BBC) funding. In addition, the government-appointed BBC Board of Governors is composed, according to Stewart Hood (1994), of establishment figures and political 'placemen' who can, to some extent, steer the Corporation in directions favoured by the party in power:

> It has been composed traditionally of members of the establishment who have 'sensible' views on political and social matters, on taste, decency, etc. It has been interesting to discover that one member in recent times had been an employee of MI6. The Board is drawn from 'the great and the good' and is therefore thoroughly unrepresentative. Its members have no identifiable constituencies. Their interests are undeclared. During the General Strike of 1926, Baldwin took the view that there was no need to commandeer the BBC because it would know what was expected of it. Today's government can be equally easy in its mind about the Board of Governors.

Whereas the press are hampered by very few legal restrictions regarding what may be printed, broadcasting is subject to legislation which effectively outlaws views that radically threaten the *status quo*. The points of view allowed on television in any debate are carefully framed by notions of 'impartiality' (see above) and the limits of parliamentary consensus. The influence of the major political parties is, therefore, powerful in establishing limits to 'acceptable' political debate, definitions of what count as political problems, and their potential solutions:

> There are of course many political groups who hold competing explanations of the social and economic world who receive little or no sympathetic coverage on television news broadcasts – terrorists, fascists, anarchists, and revolutionary socialists are generally excluded by virtue of their lack of support and/or their rejection of the rules of the game of political life in a parliamentary democracy (Goodwin, 1990).

In addition to legal restrictions and government-appointed overseers, the BBC is subject to political leverage, particularly in the run up to the periodic setting of the licence-fee level. During the 1980s and early 1990s the Conservative Party under Mrs Thatcher proved ideologically hostile to the liberal sense of social responsibility historically associated with public service broadcasting. The traditional 'fit' between the values of British politicians and broadcasters was, therefore, disturbed and the BBC found itself under concerted attack from the government. This was exemplified by coverage of the Falklands War where the BBC's supposed stance of neutrality in its reporting of the conflict was condemned as 'unpatriotic'.

Fear of licence-fee cuts, running disputes over coverage of Northern Ireland, the controversial appointment of Director General John Birt (seen by many as a move to prepare the BBC for privatization in some form), the 1990 Broadcasting Act, staffing and training cuts, de-unionization and 'producer choice' (Chapter 14) have combined to reduce the BBC's editorial independence and strategic public service role. The result, according to Brian Winston, amongst others, is that the BBC is in danger of being little more than a service business monopoly as it moves into the twenty-first century. He calls for a constitution that could protect the public service responsibilities of the BBC from government interference of various kinds, including the appointment of its governors, and asks:

> what business does the state have, in a modern democracy, claiming 'responsibility' for organs of expression beyond its own information and publicity apparatuses? (quoted in Hood, 1994).

However, powerful ideological pressures exist within, as well as outside, broadcasting institutions. *Recruitment criteria* operating in broadcasting institutions and particularly in the prestige area of news journalism tend to favour middle-class applicants from 'public', private or grammar schools who are university educated (frequently Oxford or Cambridge). Various 'equal opportunity' measures are slowly changing the traditional white, male image of the newsroom, but change has not as yet reached into senior management positions. The result is, as the GUMG and others have suggested, a 'world-view' that remains, essentially, white, male and middle-class.

Self-censorship also contributes to the process of creating a 'univocal' position in the news. Journalists will be unwilling to waste time on stories or angles that they know are divergent from the 'norm' because they will be rejected by more 'experienced' senior journalists. News, being so tightly controlled by ideological conventions and deep-rooted traditions, is difficult to change quickly and radically, even by those in a position to do so, because any violation of these 'rules' would disrupt the expectations of the regular news viewer, who might change channels. These conventions include, for example, describing the actions of management in the passive voice – a technique Fiske calls *exnomination*. Thus, management never appears as an agent in the conflict:

> Geoff Duke, whose dismissal at Port Hedland, for alleged misconduct, triggered the strike (Fiske, 1987),

whereas the *nomination* of union action through the active voice discredits its status:

> the Rail union failed to come to an agreement with management (ITN, 22 August 1996).

To rewrite basic conventions such as these requires a huge ideological leap. As the GUMG point out, the verbs 'reject', 'demand' and 'threaten' are used when referring to unions and workers, but more positive terms such as 'offer' or 'promise' are used where employers are concerned. Therefore a phrase such as 'Management rejected the unions offer to work for a 4% pay rise' jars because it appears within a *framework of debate* set out by the unions and not, as would normally be the case, the management.

The high production standards of television news is another factor excluding groups outside the dominant consensus from news bulletins. Whereas a major political party or a large corporation such as BSkyB are in a position to at least partially 'manage news' through the use of expensive press briefings, glossy press releases and promotional material, less-well-funded organizations have fewer opportunities to appear in the public forum of television news. As news production grows in technical complexity whilst attempting to be 'stylishly perfect' television's journalistic values become increasingly passive.

A related point to production standards is the use of 'experts' and 'official sources'. To ensure a steady flow of news that can be easily packaged, news organizations have an elaborate system to 'control, process and routinize' the production of news. According to Ralph Negrine (1989) journalists rely heavily on institutions such as parliament, the courts, the army and the emergency services to guarantee a regular supply of news. The use of set events and 'the diary' – including anniversaries, birthdays, celebrations and 'pseudo-events' of various kinds – took up almost 70 per cent of BBC news bulletins according to one study. The use of specialists and news categories also ensures a regular supply of news. These categories include: home affairs, the economy, parliament, foreign affairs, crime, science, education and sport. As Fiske (1987) notes:

> The semiotic and political practice of categorizing social life into neat compartments – the economy, education, crime, industry, etc. – is an essentially reactionary one, because it implies that a 'problem' can be understood and solved within its own category: localizing the definition of problems encourages local 'solutions' and discourages any critical interrogation of the larger social structure.

A greater danger, as Negrine (1989) argues, is that dependence on 'legitimate' sources ensures that the television news (and the media in general) 'reproduce the definitions of the powerful, without being, in a simple sense, in their pay'. Journalists compromise their independence by becoming overly dependent for information on, and building too close a relationship with, their sources. In this way they gradually *absorb source values and perspectives*. It is well known, for example, that the Watergate scandal was uncovered by general reporters and not political correspondents. They were not dependent for their livelihood on a close relationship with political sources.

More recently the reliance on US and British military sources during the Gulf War has been the subject of controversy. Noam Chomsky and Edward Said are two intellectuals who have questioned the absence of debate and the orchestrated drive for war in the media:

> Americans watched the war on television with a relatively unquestioned certainty that they were seeing the reality, whereas what they saw was the most covered and the least reported war in history. The images and the prints were controlled by the government, and the major American media copied one another, and were in turn copied or shown (like CNN) all over the world (Said, 1993).

Negrine suggests that the analysis of source journalist domination and collaboration contains within it a suggestion that public opinion is 'orchestrated' by the powerful for political and social purposes. He makes use of Stuart Hall, and his Birmingham-based colleagues, to make the distinction between '*primary*' and '*secondary*' definers. Primary definers such as politicians or the police identify a threat and cue the media (secondary definers) to a particular event. The media exaggerate and amplify the threat and the police and courts then act to eliminate the threat. Hall, in *Policing the crisis* (1978), saw the 'moral panic' over muggings in the early 1970s as a specific response to a more generalized crisis in society and a search for authoritarian solutions.

Negrine (1989) concludes his investigation of the issue by asking if the success of the media lies in the fact that, despite crude distortions, the media interpret and organize rather than create attitudes and myths:

> Studies which employ the concept of 'moral panic' leave one in no doubt that the media do reproduce the opinions of the powerful; but do the media also reflect public concerns? Is it possible to suggest, in other words, that whilst they unjustifiably exaggerate and accentuate news stories, the mass media at the same time are resonating unarticulated public concerns?

The debate on news and ideology ends, therefore, where the debate on media effects begins. The weight of evidence examined above suggests, nevertheless, that (as Fiske concludes) television news represents the '"unauthored" voice of the bourgeoisie' (1987).

NEWS NARRATIVE

In *Television culture* John Fiske explores the similarity between fictional and non-fictional (news) narratives. Taking Todorov's account of the basic narrative structure 'in which a state of equilibrium is disrupted, the forces of disruption are worked through until a resolution is reached, and another state of equilibrium is achieved'. Fiske notes that this constitutes the basic structure of a television news story, just as it does a sitcom or a cop show.

The similarity between fiction and news can also be seen in the news's treatment of character, adopting the conventions of classic realism. Central to the story are individual, goal-orientated characters, made recognizable through their social roles – the political leader, the unionist, the crime victim and so on. These social roles are then organized into narrative functions, for example: police officers ('heroes'), social workers ('helpers'), drug runners ('villains') and drug users ('victims'). Fiske quotes a study of drugs in the news in which the media

> posit heroes and helpers acting on behalf of the administrative arm of society in just the right proportion to allay any excessive threat that the villainy of racketeers and the weakness of victims might arouse (Bell, 1983).

Because news values the 'vox pop' so highly, despite various strategies used to contain 'oppositional, alternative or unruly elements', the narrative structure is not always powerful enough to dictate which of the voices we should pay most attention to. The montage of voices can, therefore, create a certain 'leakiness' in the presentation of any preferred ideological reading. Furthermore, the segmentation of the news undermines the structure given by its narrative and works to open up its meanings.

> The collisions, the lack of laws of cause and effect, and the surprising contradictions remain the manifest character of the news despite any latent ideological coherence. Grouping of stories into 'political', 'industrial', 'foreign', and so on is an attempt to minimise these collisions but is of limited strategic effect (Fiske, 1987).

The structuring of narratives around *binary opposites* such as

- unions–management
- Labour Party–Conservative Party
- euro-sceptics–euro-enthusiasts
- British government–European bureaucrats
- traditionalists–modernizers
- police–criminals
- Unionists–Republicans
- road protesters–road constructors

creates stories which can go on almost indefinitely. There is no suggestion that superficial narrative closure at the end of a story signals an end to the dispute. The conflict, in fact, lies *unresolved* and *ready to disrupt* the fragile equilibrium once again. Fiske compares news, in this way, to the series drama or sitcom, for in all three genres the basic situation is never finally resolved.

PRODUCTION PRACTICES – IN THE NEWSROOM

Preparation for news bulletins is an ongoing 24-hour-a-day process, with agency reports and other sources providing news directly to television stations. The BBC's first meeting of the day for the evening news bulletins is at 9 am. Around 20 people meet in the office of the managing editor, who talks through likely stories. An hour later the editor of the day will assign stories to around eight producers who will spend the next eight hours briefing reporters, deploying cameras, calling interviewees, and finally writing the item on their computers. The editor will join a phone conference at 10.30 am with the BBC's 13 regions. Each area summarizes what they are working on and the editor may take any stories which she or he feels is of national interest. There are 200 reporters, ten London-based camera crews, the foreign bureaux and a host of resources for the news-gathering operation to call on during the day.

News broadcasts have changed, over the years, to take on relatively standardized formats. They employ many of the same techniques as sports programmes in which a presenter introduces various clips, sometimes provides a commentary and is always prepared to improvize. The presenter speaks to camera from behind a newsdesk using an autocue (or teleprompter) which reflects the words over the lens of the camera so that it appears that she or he is looking at the viewer. The newsreader periodically looks down at typed notes, which act as a backup in case of autocue failure and therefore help to prevent the apparently direct eye contact of autocue reading from being too intense or threatening to the viewer. Messages, cuts and changes can be communicated to the newsreader from the control room via an earpiece.

Most newscasts involve the use of the presenter's voice over film, graphics, archive footage and photographic stills or drawings. The presenter may also interview guests in the studio (often pre-recorded) or via a link-up at another location – perhaps in another studio overseas. The presenter also introduces pieces by reporters who may be specialist correspondents, on location, at a 'live' link-up or reporting from abroad. These pieces may include interviews, live action, voiced-over sequences, reporter-to-camera speech or question-and-answer sessions with the news presenter.

The running order of news broadcasts may be changed up to the last minute, although, now, this usually only happens when a major story has broken. Each story is allocated an exact duration of time (for example 57 seconds) and it is the responsibility of the newsreader to ensure she or he reads her or his script at exactly the right pace so that stories do not overrun or underrun. Deviations from the script are not welcome as there is a need to achieve precise cueing-in of insert material which is taken from marked places in the script. In the event of the non-appearance of a film or videotape recorder item, a reserve story is held on a standby machine, the newsreader having a reserve script for these stories.

The presenters are frequently sitting alone in a studio space with only state-of-the-art robotic cameras to keep them company. The camera positions are static, and shots are modified by zooming. The director must ensure cueing of the right source, and coordinating contributors. Subtitles (identifying people, places or time) are added strategically when they will not detract from an important point in the story. The studio background may be real or partly computer-generated. Chroma key panels behind and to the side of newsreaders may display insert images or there may be a simple cut away to location footage.

The tone of the news broadcasts aimed for on British terrestrial channels is 'unremote' without being tabloid, although there is a tabloid-like interest in the Royal Family. The BBC's six o'clock news concentrates more on home news whereas 'the Nine' has a slightly more upmarket agenda and looks at world news and the activities of diplomats and leaders. Whereas the lunchtime news is still developing and things can be found out on the programme, for example, through interviews, by 9 pm the news is expected to be neatly packaged. There are usually around 15 items – far fewer than in the early days of television news – and some attempt to give background and context to the stories covered. ITN's Channel 4 news at 7 o'clock is, at an hour, by far the longest, most substantial and detailed and also the least downmarket of the news bulletins. There are currently strong commercial pressures to move ITN's 10 o'clock slot on ITV to a later time to prevent the interruption of films screened after the 9 o'clock watershed. Such a move could have profound implications for the future scheduling and resource priority given to news broadcasts on British television.

EXERCISES AND ESSAYS

Exercise: Bias Case Study

The ideological significance of news, particularly television news, is keenly appreciated by political groups. News output is closely monitored by party political interests of all shades who frequently bombard newsrooms with complaints when they feel they have been misrepresented or underrepresented. Prepare a letter of complaint to the ITC about a recent news item you have studied. You are advised to videotape one, or more, news broadcasts and look for examples of lack of balance or bias in the treatment of a story. You may wish to write the letter on behalf of a political party, pressure group, union or commercial company. You will need to produce evidence such as amount of time allocated to sides of an argument, bias in the use of language, images and so on. Note: such complaints are treated very seriously by television companies, particularly when directed via the ITC, and are usually passed on to the producers of the programme.

Essay

> News 'normalises' life, by reporting events from a position of assured normality in a way which may serve to reproduce the interests of those holding economic and political power (Corner, 1995).

How does news do this?

Essay

> TV exists in a defined period of time in a little square box. It is an emotionally loaded symbol. If you go to TV for your only news, then you're lazy. If you go to TV for the truth, then you're a looney (Richard Blystone, CNN's London correspondent).

Why should Richard Blystone say this?

Essay

Fiske (1987) writes of television news:

> The strategies of containment are many, subtle and tried and tested by time. They are essentially formal characteristics and thus bear the brunt of the

ideological work. But the intense need that the news has for such strategies should not be seen merely as evidence of the desire of the dominant ideology to impose and naturalise itself, but also as evidence of the strength of the forces of disruption. By the forces of disruption I mean those aspects of the text, of the real, and of the audience, which threaten the sense that it is used to contain oppositional, alternative or unruly elements.

Briefly outline some of the 'strategies of containment' that Fiske is referring to in the above quote, and/or take an example of a recent news report and show

- evidence of 'ideological work' or preferred readings;
- evidence of 'the strength of the forces of disruption'.

Practical Assignment

Produce a short (five-minute) local news bulletin for television. The story may, for instance, be based on developments in a local college or school (a problem such as break-ins; the success story of a department or group of students; a new building and so on). The following criteria must be adhered to:

- the bulletin must be no longer than five minutes;
- it must be clearly identifiable as a local news bulletin (i.e. it should use the conventions of television news and the story should be a local one);
- the bulletin must contain a minimum of three minutes' worth of investigative reports (including interviews);
- reports must be made entirely of news you have researched;
- groups of two and three people only should prepare the item.

Alternatively, produce a running script with links for a local story.

Sources

Allaun, F. (1988): *Spreading the news*. Spokesman.
Bell, P. (1983): Drugs as news: defining the social. *Australian Journal of Cultural Studies* **1**:2.
Branston, G. and Stafford, R. (1996): *The media student's book*. Routledge.
Bromley, M. (1994): *Journalism*. Hodder and Stoughton.
Burton, G. (1990): *More than meets the eye*. Arnold.
Corner, J. (1995): *Television form and public address*. Arnold.
Cumberbatch, G., McGregor, R., Brown, J. and Morrison, D. (1986): Broadcast Research Unit Report. Broadcast Research Unit.
Dutton, B. (1986): *The media*. Longman.
Eldridge, J. (ed.) (1993): *Getting the message*. Routledge.
Fiske, F. (1987): *Television culture*. Routledge.
Gill, D. and Adams, B. (1988): *ABC of communication studies*. Macmillan Education.
Goodwin, A. (1990): TV news: striking the right balance. In Goodwin, A. and Whannel, G. (eds), *Understanding television*. Routledge.
GUMG (1982): *Really bad news*. Glasgow University Media Group, Glasgow.

Hall, S. (1978): *Policing the crisis.* Macmillan.

Harrison, M. (1985): *Television news: whose bias?* Hermitage.

Hetherington, A. (1985): *News, newspapers and television.* Macmillan.

Hood, S. (ed.) (1994): *Behind the screens.* Lawrence and Wishart.

Lewis, M. (1993): Why is TV news so bad? *Daily Mail* 28 April.

Lewis, P. (1986): *Media and power: from Marconi to Murdoch.* Camden Press.

Millard, R. (1993): Back with a bong. *Guardian* n.d.

Momi (undated): *News and Newsreel.* Museum of the Moving Image information sheet. Momi
    Education.

Negrine, R. (1989): *Politics and the mass media in Britain.* Routledge.

Pilger, J. (1992): *Distant voices.* Vintage Books.

Said, E. (1993): *Culture and imperialism.* Chatto and Windus.

Schlesinger, P. (1987): *Putting reality together – BBC News.* Methuen.

Sherman, J. (1996): News at ten. *The Times* 23 August.

Stevenson, N. (1995): *Understanding media cultures.* Sage.

Wheen, F. (1985): *Television – a history.* Guild Publishing.

Woffinden, B. (1996): Fast and loose. *Guardian* 12 August.

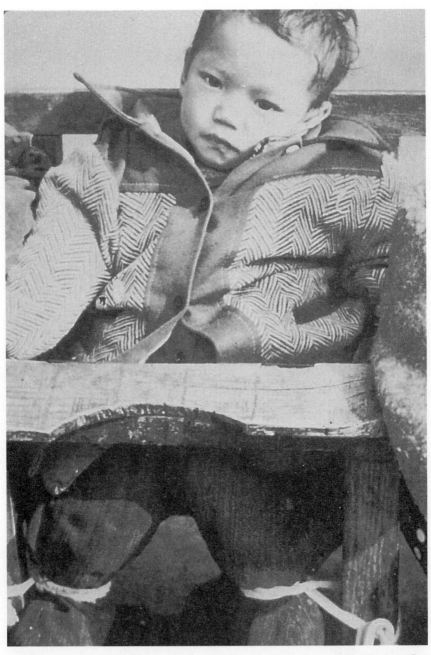

The Dying Rooms

10

Documentary

INTRODUCTION

Documentaries are so-called because they attempt to 'document' some feature of the 'real' world. They can be used to verify, or provide irrefutable 'proof', of an event or point of view – a function that may take precedence in the narrative organization of material. Like news programmes, documentaries deal with facts: real places, events and people rather than with fictional creations. The construction of a documentary is determined by assembled documentary evidence, such as written records, attributable sources and contemporary interviews. It is often suggested that the aim of the documentary should be to present an impartial narrative with no imaginary elements. The extent to which this aim can be achieved is, of course, questionable: 'factual' texts are as inevitably structured as their fictional counterparts through selection and omission and the need to present separate details and incidents as a coherent whole or documented argument.

Although it is sometimes claimed that 'the camera cannot lie', it is clear that the way a director decides to film any event – how it is filmed, what is recorded and what is ignored – can bias the presentation considerably. Kawin (1992) describes how in *Triumph of the Will* (1935) Leni Riefenstahl used many low-angle shots of Hitler, pointing her camera up at him to make him seem a powerful and imposing presence, and intercut close-ups of his face with long shots of excited crowds to suggest that Hitler was

> a galvanising speaker who could excite, control and lead his people. A British news company might have represented the same event (a Nazi Party convention) in a very different manner, giving the impression that Hitler was dangerous and erratic, a lunatic conqueror at the head of a pliable and frightening mob.

The documentary, in fact, is a far less objective genre than is commonly supposed. The author's views can either be heavily disguised or clearly fore-grounded depending on the style of presentation. Many documentarists deliberately keep the structure of their films simple and unobtrusive, or have little or no 'voice-over'. They want their version of the facts to suggest the same apparent randomness as life itself. Nevertheless, a totally 'impartial' narrative is *impossible* – the production of a documentary, as with any media form, necessitates the mediation of reality.

In fact, documentaries are frequently subject to controversy particularly where a single point of view is obviously signposted. These are sometimes described in the industry as *authored* documentaries. Michael Delahaye (1988) describes how such documentaries present problems for broadcasting organizations subject to statutory obligations to remain impartial, as with the BBC:

> An 'authored' anything in television is like a primed bomb, usually only defused by sticking 'A Personal View' belatedly across the titles. It's dangerous enough when the author – someone like James Cameron, say – is on screen and answerable to the extent that he is at least visible. But the director remains behind camera. Thus the idea of doing ... authored documentaries raises questions about objectivity, accountability, balance, and – not least – truth.

These questions rehearse many of the issues discussed in Chapter 9. They are also closely associated with the apparent *realism* of such programmes which, as Clarke (1987) remarks, like the realism of crime series or soap operas, has to be carefully contrived. An examination of the history and developing styles of documentary film-making from the earliest 'Actualities' which were filmed in a single continuous take through the Soviet experiments with montage, classic documentarists such as Flaherty and Grierson, Nazi propagandists, through to the 'candid' styles of the 1960s reveals how definitions of realism are historically and stylistically determined. As with fictional film, the codes and conventions of documentary have changed significantly throughout the twentieth century and, as Bill Nicholls remarks in his book *Representing reality* (1992), each change in style and format has produced claims of a closer contact with the 'truth'.

THE STATUS OF DOCUMENTARY

Documentaries have quite tiny viewing figures by comparison with other, cheaper genres, such as game shows. As many documentaries are comparatively expensive to make, it seems worth asking the question: 'why do television channels make them at all?' The answer lies partly in the public service broadcasting obligations that British television has towards its audience (Chapter 14). Film-maker Roger Graef (1993) informs us that, when it comes to documentary, 'British viewers may not appreciate that no other country in the world offers anything like such variety.' As the legislative responsibility for television 'to educate as well as entertain' dwindles, this position may change. Nevertheless, documentary remains a prestigious area of broadcasting, attracting critical attention in the press, and kudos for the film-makers and broadcasters. This may be a result, at least in part, of the type of audiences documentary regularly attracts: indicated by the 'upmarket' broadsheets and magazine supplements where such programming is most commonly reviewed.

That is not to say that only 'upmarket' audiences watch documentaries; far from it. The current-affairs documentary series *World in Action* in 1992 had average audiences of 7–8 million, and the composition of an audience for a one-off documentary or series of episodes is, arguably, more influenced by the scheduling and subject of the programme than anything else. *The Dying Rooms* and *Return to the Dying Rooms* (1996) produced by Brian Woods and Kate Blewett (probably Channel 4's single most successful documentary) has been seen by 100 million people in 37 countries. The documentaries were made in secret in Chinese orphanages where unwanted baby girls were found tied to their chairs, legs splayed over makeshift potties, or simply put aside in a separate room and left to die. The documentary caused such distress and uproar that a charity (The Dying Rooms Trust) was formed as a result and the Chinese government, under pressure from the United Nations, was forced to admit that it needed to raise 3.86 billion dollars to care for 100,000 orphans.

In many cases, however, documentaries continue to attract relatively small audiences. It has been suggested that the appeal of documentary to mass audiences may be influenced by the background of those normally associated with its production. Although there have been advances within documentary with regard to the representation of groups normally stereotyped in other genres, working-class voices are still regularly presented within a fairly superior, or mocking public-school and university-educated framework. As Clarke (1987) asks rhetorically:

> is the status of documentary something to do with a peculiarly British awe of experts, especially those of the right background? It is very noticeable that the vast majority of television experts distributed liberally throughout most documentaries are white, male, middle-class and middle-aged.

REALISM

> I use situations that are real. But the films are an imagined dream of what really happened (D.A. Pennebaker).

'Realism' has been defined in a variety of ways. For some critics, such as Raymond Williams, it is a *movement* with a clear historical development which can be traced back to the paintings, drama and novels of the nineteenth century. Williams suggests that this movement is characterized by a concern with everyday events, contemporary issues and ordinary people (i.e. middle-class and working-class people rather than nobility). For other critics, realism is a *style*, or set of techniques. Giannetti (1988), writing in relation to film, contrasts realist with formalist styles:

Generally speaking, realistic films attempt to reproduce the surface of reality with a minimum of distortion. In photographing objects and events, the filmmaker tries to suggest the copiousness of life itself. Both realist and formalist film directors must select (and hence, emphasize) certain details from the chaotic sprawl of reality. But the elements of selectivity in realistic films is less obvious. Realists, in short, try to preserve the illusion that their film world is unmanipulated, an objective mirror of the actual world. Formalists on the other hand, make no such pretense.

In film-making and television production this involves the use of particular *codes* and *conventions*, such as 'natural' lighting and sound, real locations, conversational dialogue, a simple, 'life-like' plot (that may include seemingly 'natural' digressions from the main storyline), the possible use of non-professional actors, and an unobtrusive camera and editing style. This mode of production, sometimes described as the *documentary look* is found in the work of the Italian neo-realists such as Roberto Rossellini and British social-realist film-makers typified by the work of directors such as Tony Richardson, Ken Loach and Mike Leigh.

This realist style is not to be confused with that of Hollywood, where films are made in a style described as *classic realism*, a style that has become pre-dominant, although not unchallenged, in international film-making. Here the effect of realism is achieved by attention to surface details such as period costume, or sets that look like real locations; characters that are consistent, if not predictable, in their behaviour; a tightly controlled narrative, a more or less plausible plot development (moving from equilibrium through disruption to a new equilibrium and closure), and the use of a series of techniques that help tell the story and allow the spectator to suspend disbelief. These techniques are also dominant in television. They include the use of continuity editing, granting the audience (who usually know more about the events unfolding than the characters involved) a privileged point of view in the narrative, hiding the means of production (cameras, mikes, crew) and keeping to an 'expected' or conventional pattern of shots, angles, lighting, set-ups and so on.

Broad definitions of term suggest that the 'effect of realism' is determined by the extent to which viewers can identify with, and accept, what is portrayed as being plausible and having some relation to the real world they know. In this sense realism is highly subjective and specific to cultures, historical moments and the media experience of the audience. Greta Garbo's acting, for instance, was regarded as realistic and powerful in the 1920s and 1930s, but is considered melodramatic by many modern audiences. What a Western audience considers realistic may appear totally puzzling and nonsensical to, for example, an Amazonian Indian not previously exposed to television. As Fiske and Hartley (1978) make clear:

Consider for a moment how easy it is for us, when watching the most realistic of programmes, to accept that at its beginning or end the oddest occurrences may take place. People's names appear in the sky, music emerges from nowhere, and suddenly the world we have been watching dissolves. We are unperturbed. It is easy enough to say that these manifestations are conventions to which we have become habituated, but the question remains: how is it that we accept these particular conventions so easily?

Furthermore, the codes and conventions that establish the realism of any text are genre specific. Graeme Burton (1990) illustrates the point with reference to what is 'acceptable' within a variety of media genres:

> For example, in situation comedy canned laughter is acceptable. In documentary, long shots of someone talking to camera are acceptable. In radio journalism recordings of someone talking through a poor telephone link are acceptable. In film fiction, sudden bursts of romantic music are acceptable – you can easily extend these examples. But generally we don't mix these sets of rules. So once we have locked into a particular set of rules for a particular kind of realism then we have set up particular standards for and expectations of the quality of realism in the product.

Hence, different genres operate according to different *modes* of realism. This wider view of realism, as a set of 'acceptable' or conventional media codes (what Brecht refers to, in relation to theatre, as self-effacing, seamless 'illusionism') leads some critics to describe realism as a 'bourgeois mode of representation'. For what is conventional, commonplace, self-disguising and taken-for-granted denies alternative ways of seeing or thinking. Realism, in this sense, conceals the fact that it is constructed, and prevents the audience from thinking critically about either the mode of representation or the actions represented. The role of the viewer of realist television is thereby confirmed as that of a non-critical consumer of escapist entertainment.

REALISM AND DOCUMENTARY

No matter how much we are drawn into the 'realisms' of genres such as soap opera or police series, we are ultimately aware that these are fictions – stories written, produced and broadcast for our entertainment with, at most, a limited relation to the world they mimic. This is not the case with documentary, which claims a direct relation to the real world. The evidence of documentary is certainly compelling. In *Hearts and Minds* (1975) directed by Peter Davis we see newsreel footage of Vietnamese children running from their village with their clothes literally burned off their bodies by napalm dropped by a US aircraft filmed moments before. Few would suggest that this event never occurred and only the most posturing academic could claim, as the French postmodernist Jean Baudrillard in fact does, that the subject of the documentary – the Vietnam War – 'didn't happen'.

However, this visual evidence can and has been interpreted in a number of ways. The commentary that accompanies this appalling event can suggest widely differing viewpoints of the specific atrocity, or the wider war, by anchoring the images to specific 'meanings'. In interpretation the bombing raid was described as 'accidental' – a justification used by US military sources following the outcry that followed the screening of the footage, despite the fact that villages were routinely bombed with napalm in this manner. The same commentary suggests that 'It was images such as these that eventually turned the majority of Americans against the war.' Hence, television 'images' of 'accidental' acts are held responsible for turning the tide of public opinion against involvement in Vietnam. Not, it is thereby implied, the 'fact' of thousands of young US men flown home in body bags, or with missing limbs, and not the possibility that Americans were revolted by the failed policy of bombing a faraway country 'into the Stone Age'. Finally, the same commentary concluded, in relation to the image of naked burnt children, that, 'in no other country except the United States would such self-damning footage be allowed on the public airwaves – which are controlled, or at least regulated by governments. No other country has a First Amendment.' In this way, the victims of a US napalm bombing become a celebration of US liberty.

REALISM AND TELEVISION 'RHETORIC'

So, although documentaries can provide evidence, such evidence can be faked, altered, or turned on its head by a commentary. The same film footage has often been used by enemy countries in a war as evidence of the other side's barbarity. Len Masterman (1985) argues that awareness of the following rhetorical techniques in the media can provide a method for interrogating any text and how its realism is constructed.

Selection

The first question to ask is: 'in the selection of a particular event as the subject of a documentary, whose interests are being served?' Selection is a central aspect of media production. This shot is chosen over that, that angle preferred to this, one interview recorded rather than another, this much of an interview used, this music chosen and a certain order adopted (as opposed to other possibilities). These are just a sample of the many choices made, both during filming and editing. As Masterman notes, the act of selection is, itself, evaluative:

> The media mark particular people and events as more significant than others simply by reporting them. For 'what is noted' to repeat an earlier observation of Barthes, 'is by definition notable'. The media, therefore, carry out what is perhaps their most important ideological role through a

process which is generally regarded as being ideologically innocent, the process of reporting 'the facts'.

Branston and Stafford (1996) make reference to the work of Frederick Wiseman who made documentaries about institutions such as a police force and a high school in the late 1960s. Wiseman spent a great deal of time in these institutions, filming enormous amounts of footage, and he found when it came to editing that he was forced to select, order and interpret his material for the audience. His mediating role became a crucial one in shaping the audience's understanding of the institutions represented. Wiseman's dilemma was, in fact, no different from any documentary film-maker's: most documentaries will shoot 20 or 30 hours for every hour screened. Recognition of the inevitably structured nature of documentary, like news or any media text, undermines any claim the genre makes to be an objective 'window on the world'.

The Rhetoric of the Image

Masterman argues that visual images are highly 'authentic' but at the same time 'ambiguous'. We can (almost) be sure that those events and people captured by the camera were there, although computer technology is making even this modest claim subject to doubt. For example, when Janet Jackson dives from the top of the Statue of Liberty in an MTV video, or when Forrest Gump shakes hand with President Kennedy in a feature film, we know that this is a special effect; but will we always know when events have been created in this way?

As previously discussed, the authenticity of images may be used to underscore a point of view which is highly subjective, or has no basis in fact. Anchorage may be provided by a commentary or visual text, but anchorage is also possible without either of these. British fly-on-the-wall director Paul Watson's film *The Fishing Party*, made in the late 1980s, made devastating use of juxtaposition and overlay (putting the protagonists' words over footage shot at another time and place) to point up the discrepancy between what the wealthy subjects were saying and what they were doing.

In fact, commentary is continuously supplied in documentary, and all television genres, without the use of spoken or written language at all. Images alone are quite enough to construct a point of view. The juxtaposition of images of, for instance, homeless beggars next to well-dressed passers-by, needs no voice-over to suggest a discrepancy in the distribution of wealth in a particular country.

Image and Text

The use of commentaries, or captions, in documentary has already been briefly illustrated. Masterman argues that sound is every bit as selective and open to manipulation as the image, and just, if not more, important to the construction of television's 'realism', or what he terms 'illusionism'. Sound, unlike images, provides continuity, and cues for how the images should be interpreted, the mood of a particular scene, and points of maximum interest. A daily example of this 'rhetorical technique' can be found as the camera zooms in for a close-up 'reaction shot' at the end of a scene in a soap opera. Dramatic music invariably accompanies the moment so that there can be no mistaking the scene's significance.

Masterman (1985) gives several examples of how sound can be used to construct a point of view. In the coverage of the 1984–85 coal dispute, for example, wildtrack 'riot' sounds were used to cover images shot at different times and places, and news commentators described those who remained loyal to their union as 'militants', and those who disregarded union policy as 'moderates'. In relation to documentary, a simple choice such as the placing of microphones in a school classroom may illustrate the intentions of the film-maker:

Give dominance to the teacher's mike (as in the BBC's series on the public school Radley) and you get a very different impression from the chaos of sounds which results from the dominance of a mike in the middle of a classroom.

The Effect of Camera and Crew

The well-known book on photojournalist technique, *Pictures on a Page*, by the former *Times* editor Harold Evans, shows a photograph of a young woman next to an unconscious figure, surrounded by a crowd of spectators and a doctor, or nurse. The picture is bizarre because although the woman is clearly associated with the unconscious person, she is smiling at the camera. Similarly, a dull party, or dreadful holiday will be transformed for a moment by the appearance of a camera as everyone dutifully smiles. The arrival of a television camera and crew at virtually any location or institution will create a far greater stir than a lone photographer. Behaviour, dress, speech, even the location itself, are likely to be altered for the benefit of the camera. Bob Woffinden (1988), writing in *The Listener*, contends that what appears on the screen in a documentary can sometimes amount to little more than a sanitized public-relations job:

A government agency might spend thousands of pounds on image-building with a promotional film in the middle of *News at Ten*. On that scale, an access documentary could represent millions of pounds-worth of free publicity. How many recruiting ads was John Purdie's *Sailor* (1976) worth? After that series – shot aboard the Royal Navy's Ark Royal aircraft carrier – all branches of the armed forces started putting out the welcome mat for the BBC. The less edifying aspects of service life –

bullying in the army, perhaps – could always be resumed once the cameras had left.

Set-ups

It is not at all unusual for television film-makers working outside a studio to set up a situation that will be more photogenic than the everyday reality they initially encounter. Flaherty's training of the Aran islanders to hunt basking sharks with harpoons (a tradition which had died out decades before) for a spectacular sequence in his famous documentary *Man of Aran* (1934) is an extreme example of standard media practice in this respect. Sometimes, such set-ups will be for speed and convenience. A radio journalist was invited into a classroom in which I was working to record a burst of sound for a piece on local education. Without a moment's hesitation she asked if I could chalk some words on the board and say these words to the class. The sound was duly recorded and she left satisfied. The students were disappointed that they would not hear their own voices on the radio, and I felt that the set-up had been a 'cheat' as I never used the blackboard, and the sound reinforced the notion of teaching as 'chalk and talk'.

What is expected of a particular institution or event may be just as influential in the outcome of a documentary as what actually occurs during film-making. A director entering a comprehensive school will be heavily influenced in what they record, or 'ask to see', by their private views of state education. A hostile director will concentrate on any evidence of graffiti, broken equipment, noise, violence, disillusioned or lazy teachers and signs of poor educational standards generally. These elements can easily be amplified and subtly encouraged in the film-making process. A director who (privately) supports comprehensive education will of course look for and find evidence of a positive, clean, friendly, hard-working, progressive, well-run institution with high educational standards and ideals. Not all set-ups are necessarily dishonest if they help recreate a typical situation, although giving stones to children in Northern Ireland to throw at soldiers, as a French film crew were once alleged to have done, would be an example of a wholly unwarranted 're-creation'.

Film and Sound Editing

In editing, the film-maker creates new meanings from fragmented and often unrelated occurrences. Masterman argues that the meanings of a piece of film are not implicit within the original events which they represent but are the product of the film itself. This is related to the other effects of editing which are: to select, compress and omit a range of material; to falsify the dimension of time; and to organize the text 'according to a narrative, thematic or aesthetic logic which, again, is the creation of the filmmaker rather than an inherent quality of the original events'.

Fiske (1987) argues that another effect of *motivated* (continuity) editing is what is called *suture*. This literally means 'stitching', and works by rendering the construction of the film invisible so that our experience of it is one of 'seamlessness', thereby 'stitching' the viewer into the narrative. Although this theory is usually applied to examples of classic realism such as Hollywood films,

> This attempt at seamlessness is not confined to fictional realism. In news or current affairs programmes location interviews are normally shot with a single camera trained on the interviewee. After the interview is finished, the camera is then turned onto the interviewer who asks some of the questions again and gives a series of 'noddies', that is, reaction shots, nods, smiles, or expressions of sympathetic listening. These are used to disguise later edits in the interviewee's speech. When a section of this speech is edited out, the cut is disguised by inserting a 'noddy', thus hiding the fact that any editing of the speaker's words has occurred. Without the 'noddy', the visuals would show an obvious 'jump' that would reveal the edit.

Interpretative Frameworks

Anchor persons, interviewing strategies and pre-broadcast reviews are some of the means that may be employed by television makers to 'nudge' audiences towards a particular interpretation of what they watch. We are sometimes warned that a documentary may contain graphic language or disturbing scenes. The words an anchor uses to introduce a documentary-drama film such as *Threads* or *War Games*, about the effects of nuclear war, will have a strong influence on the way people view those films and may even have many people reaching for the off button on their televisions before they view a single minute of the programme.

Visual Codings

Television employs specific visual codes, such as the use of direct address (the speaker making 'eye contact' with the viewer), appearance (such as shaven or unshaven), dress (compare the 'meanings' of suit and tie against jeans and T-shirt), and framing (tight, claustrophobic close-ups, more 'comfortable' medium shots, or more 'objective' and distanced long-shots). Masterman quotes Hood (1981):

> The convention is that in 'factual' programmes they (subjects) should be shot from eye-level and not from above or below, since shots from either of these angles would represent an image slanted in more senses than one. The other convention deals with the question of how 'tight' a shot may be. Generally, important figures will be shown in medium close-up which shows them from the waist up. This may be replaced by a close-up which shows only the subject's head and shoulders. It would be very rare for a big

close-up – a shot showing only the head – to be used of an important person. Just as in our normal social intercourse we observe certain conventions about how close we come to other people and how close we allow them to come to us, so when choosing their images, television cameras keep a certain distance from their subjects. ... It is almost inconceivable that one should see on the television screen a big close-up of a figure of authority – of a prime minister or international statesman. The camera stands back from them. But in the case of ordinary people it is not unknown for the camera to come close in, particularly if the subject is in a state of emotional excitement, grief or joy.

Masterman also draws attention to the role of location. Following Margaret Thatcher's studio grilling by an ordinary viewer, Mrs Diana Gould, over the sinking of the Argentinian ship *General Belgrano* in the Falklands War, both Margaret Thatcher and her successor John Major were shy of studio confrontations. The Prime Minister is now more commonly interviewed only on special occasions and under carefully controlled conditions. Ideally, this will occur at 10 Downing Street where the interviewer is generally more reverential.

Finally, Fiske (1987) describes a particularly powerful aspect of the visual coding of documentary which helps construct the specific 'realism' of the genre: what he calls the 'visibility of form' – a technique he contrasts with the invisibility of 'dramatic' (classic) realist modes:

the documentary appears to use an objective, but recognized camera, and thus uses conventions like the hand-held camera, the cramped shot, and 'natural' lighting, often supported by unclear or inaudible (and therefore 'natural') sound. The documentary conventions are designed to give the impression that the camera has happened upon a piece of unpremeditated reality which it shows to us objectively and truthfully: the dramatic conventions, on the other hand, are designed to give the impression that we are watching a piece of unmediated reality directly, that the camera does not exist.

Narrative

Documentary, like any other genre, tends to package its content as stories. Directors are usually careful to find the narrative structure: in basic terms – the beginning, middle and end of their proposed programme – before they begin filming. In the absence of a clear narrative pattern, a structure may be imposed or borrowed, as is suggested by some of the titles adopted by documentarists: *Sunday Times – A Life in the Day*, *Ten Days in Holloway*, *Fourteen Days in May*, or *Culloden: A Year in the Life of a Primary School*.

Where no clearly defined closure can be imposed for the narrative of events, the documentary may, instead, rely on the narrative of drama to be found in relationships and between characters, which are most interesting when in a state of tension or crisis. Hence the popularity of institutions as the subjects of documentaries such as *The Family*, *The Duty Men* (customs and excise officers), *The Chosen Few* (the civil service), *Dolebusters* (Department of Employment), *Police*, *The Ark* (London Zoo) and *Turning the Screws* (prison). The most memorable moments of these documentaries tend to be where tensions and crises are emphasized, as in Roger Graef's celebrated *Police* series (1982) which became infamous for a scene in which a rape victim was interviewed in an apparently hostile manner. The controversy which the programme caused resulted in changes to interview procedures in suspected rape cases and also in the temporary loss of access to several institutions for many documentary film-makers.

CASE STUDY: INDEPENDENT PRODUCTION

The following is an insider's view of independent television. Andrew Devonshire currently (1997) works for Anglia Television as an Associate Producer but has also made a number of independent productions on a 'freelance' basis for Channel 5, amongst other companies. The following account is his summary of the institutional and financial background to contemporary documentary production. It also includes a concise description of the physical process of making an independent documentary film for a regional ITV network.

Financial and Institutional Context: The Threat to Television Documentary in the 1990s

The present state of documentary is indicative of the television industry as a whole. As each channel is pushed towards the attainment of 'targets' (i.e. viewing figures), the scrutiny over the content and audience 'accessibility' of a documentary adds to the growing pressure on the film-maker. This pressure constantly to increase, or at least maintain, viewing figures against an ever-growing industry (and therefore shrinking share of the available audience) cannot fail to influence the judgement of the programme editors.

The series *Cutting Edge* (Channel 4) and *Modern Times* (BBC2) both explore the quirks of modern life. Both compete against each other for the space to portray British life at the turn of the millennium. In the face of rapidly fragmenting audiences the documentary 'ticket' for the minority channels is rapidly becoming a luxury that is difficult to afford.

The arrival of a fifth terrestrial channel, Channel 5, on Easter Sunday 1997 may yet herald a new era of broadcasting. When Channel 4 was launched it met with harsh criticism and scorn. Its role as a minority channel was questioned, and its 'survivability' thrown into doubt. Yet this was a channel launched with what was essentially a public service remit into a market yet to face the true onslaught of satellite and cable broadcasting. Channel 5, as a commercial channel, has to compete in a fiercely competitive 'open' market against the background of the growing popularity of non-terrestrial channels, as well as the looming threat of digital television. It will be interesting to see how the channels cope with this threat. No matter what the quality of Channel 5, the result will inevitably be the reduction in audience size. The further the market is split, the more strain will be placed on the companies to perform. Its budgeting of network programming, on what are modest regional programme budgets, remains to be proven as a viable strategy.

Since the franchising of the late 1980s, and the growth of satellite television, ITV, Britain's most popular channel, has seen its dominance diminished. Channel 5's target of being the 'younger ITV' may further isolate ITV's audience as an ageing one less attractive to advertisers. The greatest threat to all the terrestrial channels, however, lies elsewhere. As research has shown, the male in the household is most likely to control the television. With this in mind, BSkyB aggressively stamped their mark on the traditional televisual entertainment of the British male by buying up television rights for a whole range of major sporting events. Once sport is exclusively on satellite television, the pressure is on the average household to buy or rent satellite equipment. The BBC were heavily criticized when they entered into a joint deal with BSkyB over coverage of Premiership football. Sky had exclusive rights to the top football league, whereas the BBC had rights only to the highlights. The truth seems to be that this was Hobson's choice for the company. As sport will be restricted to a subscription-only channel, the future of British television can only follow the US model of pay-per-view.

Channel 4's market share has grown healthily in recent years. Its marketing strategy – a mixture between the seemingly esoteric minority programming and highly popular 'cult' ventures – combined with a highly successful investment in feature film making (*Four Weddings and a Funeral*, *Trainspotting*, *Shallow Grave* and so on) has given Channel 4 credibility and emergent market share.

The Production Process

Every regional ITV company has to bid for a franchise to have its broadcasting licence. The franchise agreement pitched (along with a levy in a blind auction) contains an overview of programming commitments. These are broken down into programme types and an allocation of hours per year that these programmes will occupy. The regional slate of programmes is broken into segments: current affairs, religious and arts programming, and so on. Its yearly target must be met or exceeded to comply with the ITC agreement.

Anglia's '*marquee*' strand is part of the allocation of independent commissions (approximately 25 per cent of the output must be made by independent programme makers). As part of the regional 'arts' strand, it must include films based and made in the region, mainly by regional filmmakers.

My film, *Mad Dogs and Englishmen*, was an affectionate look at the British obsession with dog ownership. The proposal for the film was submitted (as part of a regional arts documentary series). A two-page treatment was submitted and the film shortlisted. Following an interview, the film was commissioned and the production schedule started.

A budget had to be agreed with the company (Anglia TV). A budget – and detailed breakdown – was submitted and then approved. In agreeing the budget, certain decisions had to be justified. In taking the decision to shoot the programme on film, for example, the accounts department had to be persuaded that the extra cost was reasonable.

On a modest budget, the staffing of the shoot had to be kept to a minimum. On a seven-week turnaround the process was broken down into six days' filming, two weeks' editing, and three-and-a-half weeks' research. Although some general research had been done to submit the original proposal, the components of the show and its participants had to be found and coordinated. Making the decision to research, produce and direct myself meant that I saved the money of employing other staff, and could put the saved money into the film – to shoot on film cost basically around 7.5 per cent of the budget. The crew consisted of a camera operator, camera assistant, sound recordist, sound assistant and a production runner. I hired a 'dolly' (a wheeled camera truck, to let the camera move, operated by a grip) for a day, and had a 'suitcase dolly' (a very basic dolly, which opens out to be a flat, four-wheeled platform running on a plastic or metal track to carry the camera on its tripod). These are generally regarded as luxuries on a regional programme, but I felt the costs were justified within the programme budget.

Making a film is an exercise in logic. The week's schedule was based around a coordinated journey around the Anglia region, via the most sensible route, to include each of the participants. The suitability of a character for a film is obviously the most crucial – but there are a host of other considerations: availability, location and temperament being the principal precursors. Practicality is a frequently forgotten part of film-making. . . . In the middle of the shoot, a character – and her twelve prize-winning dogs that she had washed and groomed for the arrival of the crew – was dropped, simply owing to pressures of time. The morning's work had brought us into half of cliché number 1 of film-making – never work with animals – and so we had to displease a very disappointed dog breeder.

The single most expensive part of the process is the editing. This made up around 30 per cent of the budget. The editor brings a fresh pair of eyes to the film – working so closely to the material clouds the objective eye, and it is in the edit that the film is made. The role of the editor is, therefore, crucial to the success of the film. With film the raw footage is first printed on to a 'rush' print. This is then cut to be compiled, scene by scene, to make its programme. The disadvantages of using film are the time needed and awkwardness of the format. A 25-minute film is approximately 1000 feet of celluloid. At a ratio of

8:1, 8000 feet of stock have to be cut down to make the eventual programme. This process is carried out on a Steenbeck® in an edit suite on what is essentially very primitive equipment, which makes it cheap but time-consuming. To edit on video carries the disadvantage of having to edit in a linear way, having to re-record each version as changes are made.

The new methods are computer-based, non-linear edit systems: Light-works® or Avid® are two such systems. The rushes are stored as digital information that can be 'cut and pasted' and assembled like a document on a word processor. This system has all the advantages of editing on film, as well as the picture reproduction and user friendliness of working on video. The principle disadvantage is, however, expense. The cost of the equipment means that one hour's use of Lightworks costs around the same as a week's hire of a Steenbeck. The addition of music and the layering of a soundtrack make the final texture of the film.

The edit process culminates in a viewing by the executive producer. A few minor alterations are suggested and discussed, debated and then made. The decision as to whether a programme is rejected or accepted lies with the executive producer, which makes him or her a very powerful presence in an edit suite and any viewing an uncomfortable time for the programme maker. Once approved, the sound dub – a day's work – makes the piece complete.

£27,500, seven weeks' work – all this for two showings on a regional network.

EXERCISES AND ESSAYS

Exercise

Watch a documentary. Make notes on the following elements in the programme:

- subject
- 'story'
- 'argument' (there may be more than one)
- conclusion (if there is any)
- number of interviews and interviewees
- locations used
- use of voice-over, talking heads, montage editing, continuous shots, sound (including music) and, taking all these elements into consideration, the 'style', or mix of styles used (i.e. 'classic', 'direct', 'vérité', etc.)

How successful do you think the documentary was in marshalling all these elements? Was the film a coherent piece of work?

Practical Assignment

Script and/or produce a short (five-minute) investigative documentary on a topic of public interest to your local community. The programme must be clearly identifiable as an investigative documentary programme and should include interviews and/or vox pop.

Alternatively, script and/or produce a short (five-minute) documentary on the problems of homelessness and unemployment among young people in your town or city.

Sources

Branston, G. and Stafford, R. (1996): *The media student's book*. Routledge.
Burton, G. (1990): *More than meets the eye*. Arnold.
Clarke, M. (1987): *Teaching popular television*. Heinemann Educational in Association with the British Film Institute.
Cook, D. (1981): *A History of narrative film*. W.W. Norton.
Cooke, T. (1993): Documentary student pack. Oldham Sixth Form College (unpublished).
Crisell, A. (1994): *Understanding radio*. Routledge.
Delahaye, M. (1988): Camera! Life! Action! *The Listener* 1 December.
Evans, H. (1978): *Pictures on a page*. Heinemann.
Fiske, J. (1987): *Television culture*. Routledge.
Fiske, J. and Hartley, J. (1978): *Reading television*. Methuen.
Francke, L. (1994): Nothing but the truth. *The Guardian* 13 March.
Giannetti, L. (1988): *Understanding movies*. Prentice-Hall.
Graef, R. (1993): Inside story of a fight for survival. *The Times* 17 February.
Hood, S. (1981): *On television*. Pluto Press.
Kawin, B. (1992): *How movies work*. University of California Press.
Kaye, M. and Popperwell, A. (1992): *Making radio*. Broadside Books.
Kenvyn, M. (1992): *Documentary realism*. Haywards Heath College. Unpublished.
Masterman, L. (1985): *Teaching the media*. Routledge.
Momi (undated): *News and newsreel*. Museum of the Moving Image information sheet. Momi Education.
Nicholls, B. (1992): *Representing reality*. Indiana University Press.
Rentschler, E. (1996): Germany: Nazism and after. In Nowell-Smith, G. (ed.), *The Oxford history of world cinema*. Oxford University Press.
Rotha, P. (1952): *Documentary film*. Faber and Faber.
Sklar, R. (1993): *Film: an international history of the medium*. Thames and Hudson.
The Dying Rooms Trust (1996): *Newsletter* no. 1 (June), no. 2 (December).
Woffinden, B. (1988): Inside out. *The Listener* 20 October.

Part III

Related Concepts and Debates

Harry Enfield's 'Old Gits'

11

Representation and Stereotyping

The media have

> the power to represent the world in certain ways. And because there are so many different and conflicting ways in which meaning about the world can be constructed, it matters profoundly what and who gets left out, and how things, people, events, relationships are represented (Stuart Hall, 1986).

INTRODUCTION TO REPRESENTATION

A representation is an image, likeness or reproduction of something in the 'real' world. It may be an object, person, group or event that has been *re-presented*, or *mediated* in some way. With a written text this mediation is clear to see. The thing has been re-presented as marks on a page, or 'words', which are not easily confused with the thing itself. With media such as tapes, compact discs, film and television, however, the re-presentation appears to resemble far more closely our own experience of reality. A video recording of a wedding, for instance, *looks* in many ways like the thing itself, certainly far more than a written diary entry describing the event (although the diary may later seem to be a more 'honest' recording of the occasion).

In this way, television re-presents the real world, at a superficial level, in ways that are analogous to how we 'interpret' experience through our senses of seeing and listening. We, rightly, assume that a television picture of Tony Blair approximates to a real-life impression of the living politician. We might never have met the man yet we are very likely to recognize him in the street because of exposure of his image on television. Similarly, Tony Blair's voice will be 'known' to us from what we have heard in news reports and interviews with the man.

Nevertheless, our television experience of him will be based not on Tony Blair 'the man' but on information stored and transmitted as electrical pulses and fired at a phosphorescent screen in our living room as a series of coloured, or black-and-white, dots. These images will have been selected from hours of footage and reduced to a few minutes (at most) of meticulously edited sound and visual 'bites'. Images of the politician at a conference, for example, will have been carefully framed, lit, juxtaposed with other material and placed within the frame of a report, with comment and analysis to guide the viewer. Just as with our sensual experience of any event or person, a massive amount of information will be excluded from this representation. What has happened just outside the literal screen frame? Perhaps there is a glass autocue from which he is reading. There may be someone wandering about aimlessly just out of shot, or yawning, or clapping wildly. At a political meeting there is often a large crowd of hecklers, but the audience at home will not hear a single murmur from them as the unidirectional microphones 'hear' only what the Prime Minister is saying.

We can go beyond this to consider how all representations, even those of our own senses, can never contain or exhaust the whole of the represented scene. Hence we rarely stop to consider what the newsreader looks like from above, or behind, or at a microscopic level. All representations contain only a fraction of what could have been presented, thus all are *selective abstractions*. Equally, all representations must, at any one time, have a single point of view (one camera in one position, one writer, one or more microphones giving a single 'perspective').

This is all so obvious that it is easy to miss the implications of the fact that all representations are (a) selective, (b) limited or framed, (c) univocal (i.e. from only one position), and (d) the result of mechanical processing or mediation. Far from representing the whole scene or context, representations 'contain' an almost infinitely small percentage of the totality. Nevertheless, because this is true of the way in which we represent the world to ourselves (television and other mass media mimic our own perception processes) we tend to accept it without question and are quite capable of entirely forgetting that such representations have been mediated, or processed, by anyone but ourselves.

Richard Dyer (1985) identifies four different connotations of the term *representation* in relation to television. The first use of the word is, in the sense outlined above, as a *re-presentation* of the world, subject to television's selection, emphasis and technical and aesthetic codes. The second sense is as being *representative of*, or *typical of*, the real world. Are television representations of women, children, ethnic groups, different classes and so on typical of how those groups are in society? The third meaning of representation implies a democratic notion of *being spoken for*, or fairly represented. The question arises here of who is speaking on our behalf. Dyer illustrates this point with reference to representations of women in a male-dominated media:

> For every image of a woman, it is important to ask who is speaking for women at that point. In the vast majority of cases, the answer would be a

man. The same is true of other groups excluded from the mainstream of speech in our society. Television so often speaks on our behalf without letting us speak for ourselves.

Finally, when considering representation, questions of *audience* are important because what the programme represents to them is, arguably, the crucial meaning of the text (Chapter 12). The questions Dyer suggests we ask of any television programme are therefore:

> What sense of the world is this programme making? What does it claim is typical of the world and what deviant? Who is really speaking? For whom? What is represented to us, and why?

REPRESENTATION BY TYPE

The media construct representations by the use of a kind of shorthand which involves various easily recognizable types and conventions. It is, after all, fundamental to all media processes that representations are limited, simplified and made sense of through recognizable codes. Without these codes or conventions the representations would be 'unreadable' because they would each be idiomatic (i.e. unique). Imagine, for instance, a news report shot from every possible camera angle, or a soap opera with characters utterly unlike anyone ever encountered on the screen before.

According to Burton (1990) the media are responsible for the representation of social groups by building certain types of people, made up of *repeated elements* such as appearance and behaviour. These elements carry meanings about character, relationships and about how we are meant to view and value the types. Burton distinguishes three levels at which this process occurs:

Types found on television such as the shopkeeper, or the eccentric old lady who solves crimes, are frequently recognizable without necessarily being stereotypes. This may be, as Burton suggests, because they are not drawn 'strongly' enough – they may lack a clear set of characteristics reinforced by years of repetition (such as the beret-wearing Frenchman riding a bicycle with a string of onions around his neck) – or because (as in the case of the elderly female detective) they are so particular, and drawn in such detail, that they cannot be easily applied to any real group in society.

Stereotypes are always closely bound up with issues of representation. A stereotype was originally a piece of metal plate that was used to make sure that all subsequent pieces of metal were cut to exactly the same size. The term 'stereotyping' today has come to mean the continuous repetition of ideas about groups of people in the media. It involves taking an easily grasped feature or characteristic assumed to belong to a group and making it representative of the whole group. These simplified representations of human appearance, character and beliefs become established through years of repetition in the media, as well as through assumptions in everyday conversation. Stereotypes have qualities of being instantly recognizable, usually through key details of appearance. They have attached to them implicit judgements about a group (covert value messages). As Burton notes:

> Stereotypes are not necessarily bad in themselves – it depends on how they are used and what value judgements they unlock. For example, a 'safety in the home' advertisement including a comfortable Granny in a rocking chair, which is used to make children aware of the dangers from electric sockets in the home, could be said to be OK. It represents Granny as kind and careful. It is being used for a socially approvable purpose. Whether older females wish to be seen in this way is another matter, of course.

Where the image of a group of individuals is distorted to the point that it appears ridiculous, grotesque or evil such stereotypes may also be described as *caricatures* (a term usually reserved for exaggerated or deliberately humorous images of individuals). Nazi images of Jews, for example, or *Spitting Image* puppets of tabloid journalists (shown as pigs) are clear examples of caricatures.

Archetypes, Burton suggests, are the most intense example of types and are also very deeply embedded in culture. They are the arch heroes, heroines and villains who epitomize the deepest beliefs, values and perhaps prejudices of a society. Superman is an archetype, just as all the heroes from mythology are archetypes. Archetypal characters are not limited to a particular genre:

> For instance the power-hungry villain who wants to destroy the world might turn up in spy thrillers, science fiction or horror stories. Qualities of courage or beauty, goodness or evil, are drawn most firmly and sharply in these archetypes. They are the stuff of comic strips (Jane), of cheap television (Buck Rogers), of low budget film (the Mad Max series). They may be enjoyable in the story, whatever the medium, but they also take us into the realms of fantasy (Burton, 1990).

STEREOTYPES

For media and cultural studies, as well as social psychology, the most important of the three common types of representation described by Burton is the stereotype because stereotypes illustrate crucial power relations and attitudes towards categories of people in a particular society at a given time. These categories include nationality (e.g. the Scots), 'race' (e.g. Latin), gender (male or female), class (e.g. middle-class), age (e.g. teenage), sexuality (e.g. bisexual), occupations (e.g. social workers) and deviant groups (e.g. illegal drug users). For more detailed examples of stereotyping, refer to Chapter 5, pp. 42–3; Chapter 6, pp. 58–60; Chapter 8, pp. 84–6.

Tessa Perkins (1979) defines stereotypes as group concepts (held by a social group, about a social group) which give rise to simple structures that often hide complexity, based on an 'inferior judgemental process' (i.e. one which is in some sense less than fully rational). She argues that, against commonsense notions of stereotypes:

- Stereotypes are not always 'false': cowboys do wear hats, some gay men do grow moustaches, many businessmen do smoke cigars and so on. The interesting question is to what extent social groups consciously adopt stereotypical signs in order to identify themselves, and to what extent the mass media orchestrate or amplify these deliberate social acts of communication.
- Stereotypes can, at least in part, be positive: Germans are stereotypically efficient, the French great lovers, black people good at sport and so on. However, these are nearly always backhanded compliments – the Germans may be seen as ruthlessly efficient, the French obsessed with sex, and blacks good at sport because it is a physical rather than an intellectual quality.
- They can be held about one's own social group: the English have several stereotypical images of themselves (from lovable Cockney rogue to upper-class twit). By the same token women can hold stereotypical images of women, blacks can hold racist views, and so on.
- They are not always concerned with oppressed groups: there are stereotypes of aristocrats as arrogant and stuck up, Americans as loud, brash and vulgar, males as chauvinist pigs and numerous others that are in various ways socially dominant.
- They are not always about minority groups of which we have little direct experience: stereotypes of women and men, with whom we all have experience, are widespread. To see stereotypes as applying only to distant and alien minorities obscures the ways in which stereotypes affect our everyday dealings with people.
- They can be simple and complex at the same time: the 'dumb blonde' stereotype, of which Marilyn Monroe was the most famous representative, paradoxically combines lack of intelligence and wit; child-like innocence and sexuality; naivety with the power to manipulate; an exploited, subordinate position and cult status.
- They are not rigid or unchanging: the cloth-capped, Labour-voting, constantly-striking British worker stereotype of the 1960s became the affluent, consumerist, Conservative-voting, self-serving 'Loadsamoney' stereotype of the working class in the 1980s. Stereotypes evolve and adapt since they relate to struggles around power which may differ in scale and change over time. A general stereotype (the Latin man) took on a specific and negative focus during the British and Argentine war of 1982. This negative stereotype was quickly forgotten by the media that fostered it (such as the dropping of the *Sun*'s 'Argie-Bargie' cartoon strip) as memories of the war faded.

- We do not simply 'believe' or 'disbelieve' in stereotypes: they can 'work' for us or communicate to us without our necessarily 'agreeing' with them. An Irish person can 'get' an 'Irish joke', or even laugh at it, without liking it or agreeing with what it says about the Irish.
- They do not necessarily influence our behaviour and attitudes: it is possible to 'hold' a stereotype without believing it to be true. The reaction of a viewer to a stereotype will depend on a complex set of social, historical and individual experiences. Watching Harry Enfield's 'Old Gits' may produce revulsion at such a crude stereotype, or hilarity at the comic excess of their portrayal, or a combination of the two. It may reinforce a notion of old people as miserable, bad-tempered and socially useless, or it may challenge the commonly employed comic stereotype through crude caricature.

Perkins insists that her rethinking of stereotypes is not a denial of the significance of stereotypes amongst the various mechanisms of ideological control. Stereotyping, as has been shown, works in relation to groups, usually to the advantage of the dominant groups. Furthermore, stereotyping often makes such dominant views seem 'natural' or 'normal' and not the result of a systematic process of construction. Despite her qualifications to common-sense assumption, stereotypes, for Perkins, remain both inaccurate (because they are selective in important ways) and a source of social oppression (because they conceal the true causes of social domination). [For the above summary of Tessa Perkins's essay I am indebted to Andrew Goodwin's chapter 'Understanding stereotypes' which appears in *Media studies for adults* (1988).]

CONTENT ANALYSIS

Much of the research conducted into stereotypes in the media has used *content analysis*. Content analysis is a statistical method for gathering data about a number of texts. This might be as simple as counting the number of times a woman or man appears in a kitchen in a given number of television adverts. The figures are usually expressed as percentages. Hence a study by Dominick and Rauch (1972, quoted in Fiske, 1994), for instance, found that 3 per cent of men compared with 14 per cent of women appeared in kitchens in television advertisements. Those using content analysis have sometimes claimed that is an *objective* and *empirical* research technique. Critics point to the problems of agreeing on the categories to be used. How can anybody make a scientific claim to have counted the number of married, single, attractive or unattractive, middle-class or working-class characters in a number of programmes? How are these terms agreed upon or applied to texts where the information is not available (where the marital status of the person is not made explicit, for example)?

Furthermore, there are sometimes problems with using raw statistics to draw conclusions. If Jerry hits Tom 18 times over the head with a frying pan, does that mean 18 'violent acts' must be added to the day's tally of on-screen violence? If one politician is found to use the word *peace* more often than another (an exercise performed during a Nixon–Kennedy televised debate) does that suggest their policies are more likely to promote peace? Some of these problems will be seen in relation to the various studies that have been conducted into stereotyping in the media.

GENDER STEREOTYPES

The earliest content analysis research on the representation of women simply counted the appearance or mention of women on television, radio or in newspapers and magazines. In a famous article in 1978 Gaye Tuchman summarized this research over a 25-year period, arguing that women are 'symbolically annihilated by the media through absence, condemnation or trivialisation'. On prime-time television it was found men outnumbered women by 3 to 1. Women counted for only 26 per cent of characters in all soaps, serials and dramas. Game shows and quizzes were, almost without exception, presented by men and where there were panels they were invariably made up of three men and one woman (Gill, 1988).

Other researchers have arrived at similar conclusions. The sociologists Sternglanz and Serbin conducted an analysis of popular children's television in 1974 and found that males outnumbered females 2 to 1. Males were typically aggressive, constructive and rewarded for action, whereas females were passive, deferential and rewarded for reaction. In research for a BBC *Heart of the Matter* in 1987 it was shown that in news only 1 per cent of the news items were regarded as 'women's issues' (the difficulty of categories is apparent here), and only 9 per cent of experts interviewed were women, and that of those interviewed because of their occupation, such as pensioners, students, managers, trade unionists and nurses, only 1.2 per cent were women.

In 1990 Guy Cumberbatch carried out an extensive research project for the Broadcasting Standards Council and found that men outnumbered women by 2 to 1 in advertisements and that the vast majority of adverts – 89 per cent – used a male voice. Youth and beauty were found to be distinctive features of women in the adverts: only a quarter of women shown were judged to be over 30 years old, compared with three-quarters of men, whereas the slim, model or 'ideal' category applied to more than 1 in 3 women, compared with 1 in 10 men. Furthermore, men were more than twice as likely to be shown in paid employment, and when men were shown in work settings, how they performed in those jobs was an integral part of the advertiser's message. By contrast, when women appeared in work settings their relationships were emphasized.

What all this content analysis research has in common is a concern that women are not being portrayed accurately, that representations of women in the media do not reflect real women and their roles in contemporary society. Researchers have asked why, for example, advertisers continue to use a representation of 'the family' (working husband, 'housewife' and two children) when only 5 per cent of British people live in such a home?

As Barratt notes, the findings of such content analyses are rather crude measures of sex stereotyping. They do not account for the wide range of stereotypes of gender such as the 'mother-in-law', the 'secretary', the 'call-girl' and so on. Nor do they capture the subtleties of stereotyping. Some of the *limitations* of content analysis have been recognized by the researchers themselves, and in some cases properly addressed. Guy Cumberbatch's study of advertising surprisingly found men more likely to be cooking than women – 32 per cent against 24 per cent. However, when men cooked it was shown as a special and skilled activity, as in an Oxo advertisement, where candles on the table signalled it was a special occasion.

Despite this kind of recognition that is emerging in content analysis, quantitative research will always miss the subtleties drawn out by qualitative research. More women may have been shown in boardroom settings in recent years, for example, but *how* have they been shown? The journalist Judith Williamson, writing in the women's magazine *Cosmopolitan* in 1990, takes up the issue:

> Feminists have long campaigned against images of women as wives, mothers, cooks, providers: we know we're capable of more than dishing up fish fingers and baked beans. But the women of today's ads are like the Seventies' dream turned into a nightmare. Where once we longed for the image of a woman with a briefcase, chairing a meeting or answering two phones, advertising now seems to be packed with glamorously dynamic, crushing women who can invariably beat men at their own game.
>
> But there is something disturbingly brittle about this creature of the late Eighties: she is portrayed simultaneously as cutting, yet always on the brink of snapping herself. One of the most telling ads was the K Shoes commercial ('for the well heeled'), where a woman marches through an office to staple a 'private and confidential' goodbye note on to the boss's tie, snips two balls off his executive toy and then almost spoils her exit by catching her heel on a grid at the door. The man is shown starting to smirk – but she pulls up the piece of metal, detaches it from her shoe and hands it to his secretary, regaining her cool. The slogan: 'Whatever you break off, it won't be one of our heels'.
>
> Ms Tough-as-Nails triumphs in this particular scenario. But what the ad really plays on is the fear of tripping up. Only K heel saves her from humiliation; no other ending is allowed. We are meant to get a kick from the fact that she wins. But no one asks, who wants to play Being Spiteful anyway?

What this article points up is how 'objective' content analysis (that might show an increase in the number of women in positions of power) can only ever give a part of the picture. Research at the Centre for Contemporary Cultural Studies, with its theoretical roots in semiotics and structuralism, has used *qualitative* methods to investigate representations of women in the media and found them to contain the kind of contradictions described (in a different 'style') by the *Cosmopolitan* article. Feminist language and aspirations were found to be co-opted or incorporated into a masculine world. Advertisers used the vocabulary of women's rights – words such as *rights, choice* and *freedom* – in such a way as to empty them of their progressive meaning, in order to sell a product. Gill (1988) suggests that advertisers use traditional feminist language, as in 'the right to choose' (for abortion) so that:

> what was essentially a collective political demand is reduced to an individual personal one . . . . This transformation of meaning has turned the feminist idea that 'the personal is political' on its head – by reducing the political to personal choices.

The various fantasy roles played by many women in advertising, including that of 'the boardroom director' who outsmarts her male colleagues, have been criticized as bearing no relation to the real world. Few women are top executives and the impossibly slim and attractive business women may say more about male desires than female ones. These criticisms have been made against 'liberal' feminists, some of whom have argued that by changing the representations of women in the media, society can, in time, learn to change traditional sex roles. According to its critics, what liberal feminism, like the content analysis with which it is often associated, fails to recognize is that in many cases apparently negative stereotypes may express at a simplified and symbolic level real social relations. Hence the dumb blonde stereotype, according to Tessa Perkins, refers to the subordinate status of women in Western societies and in that sense is quite accurate. Barratt (1986) summarizes this position:

> Women typically *do* find themselves in roles that are seen as less intellec-tually demanding. Women *are* often defined in terms of their physical attractiveness to men. But, as Richard Dyer argues, the stereotype goes further to suggest that such differences are inborn – they imply 'natural' differences between the sexes. It suggests, or reinforces, the view that women's social position is *caused by* differences in their aptitude and ability. In doing so it conceals the possibility that such differences may be the *effect* of their inferior position in a male dominated society. Thus it confuses cause and effect, and in doing so, serves the ideological function of making female disadvantage seem just, acceptable, and legitimate. The 'dumb blonde' stereotype is not, therefore, necessarily inaccurate, it reflects back the reality of women's exploited experience, but in doing so makes it seem inevitable and natural (emphasis in original).

Clearly, this is a controversial area and one where it is easy to argue a chicken and egg case without any clear resolution. The position of liberal feminists can, at any rate, be contrasted to that of 'radical' feminists, for whom gender inequalities are systematic and rooted in patriarchal relations. These fundamentally sexist relations, radical feminists argue, are the key defining characteristic of society and cannot be changed merely by improving equality-of-opportunity legislation or putting more women into more visible or senior roles in the media. The media, it is suggested, are owned and controlled by men and are used to reflect the images of women which they desire. The issues which affect women, including discrimination at work and in education, sexual harrassment, the problems of baby care, social isolation and the attitudes of police towards rape cases are marginalized or trivialized.

'Socialist' feminists, on the other hand, blame capitalism (rather than simply men) as an economic structure responsible for the exploited and disadvantaged position of women in society. Trowler (1989) summarizes the perspective of socialist feminism:

> Women give their labour cheaply. They serve as a reserve army of workers who can be called on when the need arises and then sent back into the home. They are also useful to the capitalist class for breeding purposes; they bring the next generation of workers into the world. In addition they help to sustain and pacify the male workers by providing a comfortable home, meals and sexual services for them. Finally, they are super-exploited by capitalism as consumers and as sex objects.

PORNOGRAPHY

Pornography, many women argue, is the clearest expression of patriarchal–capitalist exploitation and degradation of women. The richest man in Britain in the mid-1990s was Paul Raymond, who controlled 50 per cent of the pornography market and had accumulated a fortune of £1,700 million (Davies, 1994). The industry today is worth over £52 million a year, and video sales are one of the fastest growing areas of the 'entertainment' industry. A major concern is that as pornography becomes more 'acceptable' a climate in which the abuse of women and children is commonplace becomes created. According to Nick Davies, who investigated the issue for *The Guardian* in 1994:

> The pornography industry in Britain has been riding on an escalator and as Soho and the illegal dealers have moved towards more bizarre and violent material, so the legal 'top shelf' dealers have moved up behind to take their place. They now sell, through newsagents, material that would once have been hard to handle under the counters of Soho. So far from being different and distinct, the two markets – the respectable and the hard core – have

been intimately connected. And, as time goes by, the distinction is increasingly hard to spot.

Scotland Yard noticed this escalation at work last year when the then head of the Obscene Publications Squad, Michael Hames, analysed a small stack of paperwork which he had seized from hard-core mail order firms. 'We looked at the material which was being ordered and found that about 70 per cent of the requests were for material at the extreme end – rape, torture, eating of excrement, urination. This was not about consensual sex, heterosexual or homosexual. This was much more bizarre than it had been.'

Davies continues that 'top-shelf', 'respectable' magazines such as *Penthouse* carry advertising for hard-core pornographic videos, 'For example, SFP Trading from Brighton are using their columns to distribute 65 videos of women being beaten up.' From legal pornography it is a short and easily negotiated path to the illegal, sometimes imported material, of violent rape, child and animal sex and 'snuff movies' where the victims are killed on camera. Pornography, many women's and victim support groups argue, acts like advertising implying that these women and the things they are doing or having done to them are the desirable norm. A further implication is that women enjoy these acts, no matter how bizarre or violent.

Liberal, radical and socialist feminists all agree that pornography *degrades women*. The cause of such a phenomenon may be debated, but feminists of all persuasions agree that they are symptomatic of *much wider* degrading and biased representations of women in the media and that such portrayals have a negative effect.

PLURALISM

Pluralists, and those who support an unrestricted media market, argue that if women's bodies have been objectified, so have men's, and that, as far as pornography is concerned, the industry only meets a demand that already exists in society. Furthermore, they contend, the media cannot be held responsible for all the ills of society. The media does not create or perpetuate inequality but merely *reflects* it back to us. Hence, if images of women in a domestic setting occur more often than images of men, for example, then this is because it is women who buy these products, and advertisers should not be blamed for attempting to reach their 'target audience'.

Pluralists believe that although the media used to be sexist, they no longer are. Quite the opposite; the media, in a desire to be 'politically correct', actually overcompensate for women and frequently allot them roles in the media which do not reflect the reality of male–female relations outside television studios. Many of these arguments are found in conservative-leaning newspapers and magazines. 'Television adverts declare war on men' is the headline of one such article that begins:

> Advertisers have declared war on men. A new wave of television com-
> mercials is wooing female consumers by portraying the male as oafish,
> insensitive and incompetent. In the latest, for Prudential pensions, millions
> of viewers see a young couple sitting on a sofa. He is insipid, she is bouncy.
> He has greasy hair, she is fresh-faced.
>
> 'We want to be able to live a little', he says in a thick Birmingham accent.
> 'I want to be able to live a lot,' she replies. 'We want to be able to enjoy the
> garden,' he says. 'I want to be able to stuff the garden, buy a big yacht and
> disappear around the world,' she replies. 'We want to be together,' he says.
> Contemptuously, she is silent.
>
> The commercial has achieved the rare distinction of attracting a com-
> plaint to the Independent Television Commission, the industry watchdog,
> on the grounds of discrimination against men. The ITC expects more to
> follow as television advertisers continue the image war against men.

Pluralists also counter feminist objections to the use of women's bodies in advertising by pointing out that since Nick Kamen stripped to his boxer shorts to wash his jeans in a Levis advertisement in the mid-1980s the uncovered male body has become a central feature of modern advertising, aimed both at men and at women. As with the image of slim, young women found in advertising, these are not representations of ordinary men, but tall, handsome and muscular models.

In *Washes Whiter*, a television retrospective on advertising up to the early 1990s, the programme makers make clear how representations of women and men have changed dramatically since the early 1950s. Amongst a welter of types and bizarrely contradictory representations of men, for example, certain broad trends were shown to have emerged. The sober 'family man' gave way to a rugged (James-Bond-inspired) 'independent' image in the 1960s and a more blatantly 'macho' image in the 1970s. The 'yuppie' or business executive mode was popular in the 1980s and a more sensitive 'new man' is shown emerging in the 1990s (characterized by the Audi driver who dashes to the hospital with his son to witness the birth of a second baby).

Feminists and pluralists alike would agree that these changing represen-
tations of men and women signal changes in the society that produced them. Pluralists would argue they show how sexism is a thing of the past and that men and women now enjoy broadly equal status in the media. Feminists, by contrast, would argue that although some gains have been made the outward appearance of equality that manifests itself in television is a smokescreen, which disguises enduring inequalities, exploitation and violence towards women.

REPRESENTATION OF AGE

The term 'ageism' does not carry nearly the same value, or weight, as the equivalent terms 'sexism' and 'racism'. There is, as yet, no Age Relations Act, or Commission for Age Equality, and few industrial tribunals bother to deal with biased selection procedures or unfair dismissal on the grounds of age. Perhaps this is because we are all 'of an age', and will all (it is hoped) grow old. Nevertheless, ageist assumptions, not only affect old people, they affect everybody.

Age in Western industrialized societies is very closely associated with economic activity. The young and the old, it is assumed, do not work, and their status reflects this basic economic fact. In reality, millions of children have part-time work, and retired persons are economically active in a number of ways, increasingly because they have no choice. In developing countries children and old people contribute significantly to the welfare of the community. Children may carry water, serve food, work in the fields, produce handicrafts or sell things on behalf of their family. Old people may do any of the above and also advise and teach younger generations. The status conferred by age is a reflection of the respect for experience given to older members of closely knit communities. Only in developed countries, where factories have long replaced the family as the main site of production, is it considered normal for the generations to be cut off from each other quite so dramatically. Isolation and institutionalization – the young in schools, and the old in 'homes' – widens the generation gap further every year.

This particular set of economic circumstances, as Alvarado *et al.* (1987) argue, has produced an ideology and a characteristic set of representations for different age-groups. These, broadly, are that: children are helpless and innocent; teenagers irresponsible and rebellious; middle-aged people responsible and conformist; and old people vulnerable and a 'burden' on society. Of course these representations vary across and between the age-groups. Therefore television aimed at a 'young' audience, for instance, such as *DEF2*, *The Word*, *The Passenger* or *Rough Guide* will project 'youth' in a different way from the less frequent mainstream representations of youth, which tend to concentrate on acts of deviancy such as drug taking.

Children

Children's television, and the changes in its content and presentation over the years, is an interesting measure of how society regards children. Three main strands of children's television can be detected. First, there is a *commercial* strand, which targets children as consumers of action and formula cartoons, humour, quizzes and games. This is the dominant mode of address and in the USA (where much of the material originates) was for many years the only type of programming available. Wheen (1985) quotes Peggy Charen who founded the US pressure group Action for Children's Television (ACT):

> when ACT began there were about sixteen minutes of commercials per hour for children . . . . Saturday mornings were wall-to-wall monster cartoons filled with a lot of messages to eat sugary food and buy expensive toys.

These genres and messages still form the backbone of children's programming which regularly exploits children's identification with action and cartoon heroes to sell 'spin-off' toys. Commercial programming is usually highly stereotypical with an enduring emphasis on aggressive or dominant male characterization, passive, sentimental female representations, 'brainy' characters who wear glasses, working-class villains and so on.

The second strand in children's television is an *educational, public service* element which is now somewhat in decline. At one time children's television in Britain was insistently 'educational', with the schedules full of somewhat patronizing and 'worthy' programmes such as *Blue Peter, Magpie, How* and *Why Don't You?* (which had the apt subtitle *Just Switch off Your Television and Do Something Less Boring Instead*). These often assumed that children had the inclination and resources to engage in endless pseudo-craftwork sessions. The highly successful *Sesame Street*, a programme initially rejected by the three commercial networks, was exported to 50 countries and was typical of the move to integrate commercial elements (cartoons, puppets and various advertising techniques) into attempts to teach basic literacy.

The third, and most recent strand, came from the long-delayed recognition that many 'children' enjoy, or even prefer, *'adult'* programmes. The scheduling of US situation comedies aimed at young audiences and the similar re-orientation of cheap daytime soaps (often from Australia) at times previously regarded as the domain of children is evidence of this shift in attitudes. The phenomenon is also, at least in part, a reflection of budgetary constraints (these imports are very cheap), but it does signal an acceptance that children can deal with complex and sometimes controversial issues. Phil Redmond's *Grange Hill* was one of the earliest signs that television companies could make representations of, and to, children that were honest about their lives, their problems and their pleasures. It is this last strand which has only begun to challenge the traditional representations of children as 'inactive, apolitical, asexual, classless, raceless, and, above all, totally dependent' (Alvarado *et al.*, 1987).

Youth

The break from these traditional definitions of childhood marks out much of the representational territory of 'youth': class, race, sexuality, politics, action and independence have long been hallmarks of media images of youth. However, what *is* 'youth'? In certain respects the term is a concept exclusive to industrial consumer cultures, an extension of the teenage phenomenon – that

came into being, or was created (depending on your point of view) in the 1950s
– as a market for mass media products such as rock and roll music and
'teenage' movies. Before this time, and in most countries around the world
today, adulthood was, and is, the state directly after childhood. Children
become 'young' men and women. Only in the West do they become 'teenagers',
a kind of limbo state between childhood and adulthood, frequently and
sneeringly described as 'having all the freedoms of adults and none of the
responsibilities'.

In this sense, 'youth' represents the *boundary* between child and adult.
Children, it is assumed, belong to their family of origin, do not work, are
single, asexual and not responsible for their actions. The assumptions
regarding adults, on the other hand, are that they are sexual, married, in work
and are responsible for their actions. Youth transgresses all of these 'binary
oppositions'. Young people often neither live with their families of origin, nor
their families of destination, but are found in bedsits, halls of residence and
shared houses. They frequently socialize in anonymous spaces such as night
clubs, are working sporadically, or not at all, and are in relationships that
mean they are neither married nor single. In many cases this limbo extends to
sexual identity as this is a time when cross-dressing and sexual experimentation can occur. They are always being told to act responsibly, but are not
seriously expected to do so. This, it should be stressed, is the 'assumption' or
stereotype of youth.

Some observers have suggested that a characteristic of modern industrial
society is that this space, or boundary, between child and adult (which we call
'youth') has widened considerably and now extends well beyond the teenage
years. As Edmund Leach has remarked, it is the ambiguous boundaries
between two 'unified fields', in this case 'child' and 'adult', that are most often
hedged about with ritual and *taboo*, and are subject to society's closest
inspection. Hence the fascination with 'youth', and youth's transgressions.
This goes some of the way towards explaining sensationalist representations of
young people in the media. As Hebdige (1979) points out, for example, the
most common depiction of young people in news and documentary is with the
image of 'youth-as-trouble'.

> in our society, youth is present only when its presence is a problem, or is
> regarded as a problem. More precisely, the category 'youth' gets mobilised
> in official documentary discourse, in concerned or outraged editorials and
> features, or in the supposedly disinterested tracts emanating from the social
> sciences at those times when young people make their presence felt by going
> 'out of bounds'. Resisting through rituals, dressing strangely, striking
> bizarre attitudes, breaking rules, breaking bottles, windows, heads, issuing
> rhetorical challenges to the law, all these constitute 'going out of bounds'.

A glance at other television and film representations of young people would
seem to bear this observation out. Films such as *Rebel Without a Cause, East*

of Eden, The Wild One, The Blackboard Jungle, West Side Story, Christiana F, Quadrophenia, Scum, Trainspotting, Kids and many others are regarded as definitive and highly influential, precisely because they deal with issues of sex, violence, criminality, dissidence, rebellion, drug taking and deviancy. These powerful, if stereotypical, representations of youth are often considered to be more challenging than equivalent representations on television. For instance, the film *Scum*, about life in Borstal, started life as a television drama but was not screened as it was regarded as too controversial. Nevertheless, these films construct the essence of the stereotypical 'youth' which are finally reinvented for the small screen in a more containable form, as the countless misfits, hooligans, drug addicts, loners, gangs, rebels and young lovers that populate various fictional and non-fictional television genres.

Old People

Representations of old age, in many cases, constitute a return to the stereotypical characteristics of childhood listed previously. Growing old is no longer (if it ever were) a state where an individual can enjoy the respect of their community and the material rewards and comforts of a lifetime's labour. It is, instead, a condition to be delayed and avoided, through plastic surgery and hormone treatment if necessary. The media is full of images of youthful faces which are used to sell virtually everything down to the pleasure of living itself. As with women, there is evidence of a 'symbolic annihilation', or 'structuring absence', of older people, with 11 per cent of the population who are aged over 65 years, reduced to only 2.3 per cent of the television population. These remaining images are dominated by those older white men who are still in positions of power. Women and black men past retirement age, in particular, if shown at all, are usually seen as needy, vulnerable, unhealthy or mentally regressive. Alvarado *et al.* (1987) continue this point:

> Beyond the likes of 'youthful' Joan Collins, images of women over 40 are almost non-existent, unless you count mother-in-law jokes. Older women indeed constitute almost a sub-class within older people, as they often lack the occupational pensions of men and also live considerably longer. Women who have raised families find it almost impossible to rejoin the labour market except in low-paid jobs. Patriarchal sexual relations mean that youth is an intrinsic component to women's sexual value (whereas the older, experienced and middle-class male is considered sexually attractive) so that the older woman is deemed to be, paradoxically, either asexual or rampantly frustrated. Not surprisingly, a significant proportion of the cosmetic industry's profits are made by encouraging women to keep young and beautiful.

Only in soap operas are older women regularly found as permanent characters, and even here they are often portrayed as vaguely 'comic', bad-tempered, forgetful, nosy and interfering. When older men appear they are almost invariably irascible (Percy Sugden, Victor Meldrew, 'The Old Gits' of Harry Enfield fame and Old Steptoe). The sexuality of these older people, where it occurs at all, is always used for humorous purposes – as in *Last of the Summer Wine*. As the population at or beyond retirement age continues to grow it will be interesting to see if these overwhelmingly negative, comic or grotesque images continue to dominate television representations of old people.

REPRESENTATION OF RACE

The term 'race' is a problematic one because there is little or no biological evidence to support the use of the term at all. The British 'race', for example, is made up of generations of invaders and migrants: Britons, Celts, Romans, Angles, Saxons, Vikings, Normans, Slavs, Jews, Italians, Afro-Caribbeans and Asians being amongst the most numerous. Almost every nation is made up of a similar 'mix' of races who intermarry and share elements of their culture and language. Only in the remotest parts of the world such as the Kalahari desert or Amazon jungle is it possible to find relatively 'pure' races. Nevertheless, Nazi 'theories' of eugenics – based on racial 'superiority and purity' – still hold considerable sway over far-right parties such as the British and French 'National Front'.

There is a long and shameful history of representations of 'race' in 'Western' nations, stretching back through the Third Reich to the days of British and US slavery and beyond. These representations have been closely identified with efforts to dehumanize, ridicule, exploit, and, in the case of European Jews, 'exterminate' a group, for no other reason than their racial origin. In Britain and the USA images of black people have remained an area of ongoing controversy. Hollywood movies and cartoons, many still shown on television today, are full of black people portrayed as cheerful, rolling-eyed simpletons. In *The Black and White Minstrel Show* white performers 'blacked-up' to sing and dance, perpetuating degrading Hollywood stereotypes of black people. The show, which ran until 1976, was until that time, according to Milner (1983) 'the single most regular exposure of "black" people on the television screen'.

Racial stereotypes have also been frequently found in situation comedy, a form which abounds in stereotypes of many groups, arguably because the half-hour format demands easily recognizable characters and situations. O'Sullivan *et al.* (1994) observe that

the 'simple' and 'quaint' delivery of English by ethnic minorities has been a constant source of ridicule, as in *It Ain't Half Hot Mum* (Indians living under colonial control), *Fawlty Towers* (Manuel, the half-witted Spanish waiter) and *Mind Your Language* (a foreign student class containing several crude stereotypes). All of these are 1970s British television sitcoms, frequently repeated since.

Other racial representations within situation comedy, as O'Sullivan *et al.* note, include the black characters of *Rising Damp* and *In Sickness and In Health* who are the focus of racial bigotry by the lead characters. Although the audience is supposed to laugh at these bigots for their foolishness, some audiences, it is suggested, will enjoy the racial insults, producing an 'oppositional', racially prejudiced reading. Instead of becoming the focus of racial conflict, some commentators argue, black characters should appear in 'normal' situations where the colour of their skin is not an issue.

The other concern about representation of ethnic minorities is that black people are seen too often as a 'social problem'. Images of black criminals, drug takers, rioters, gangs, dysfunctional families and troublemakers have been far more common than any positive or neutral representations. Despite journalistic codes which advise that the colour of a person's skin need only be mentioned if it is relevant, negatively defined news values which play on popular fears often result in a stress on skin colour in stories. Furthermore, black pressure groups have accused the media of underplaying racially motivated attacks and overplaying 'muggings' perpetrated by black people (see the work of Stuart Hall outlined in Chapter 16).

Research by Hartmann and Husband (1974) supports this view and has shown that white children in areas with few blacks see race more in terms of conflict than those in areas of high black residency. The researchers explained this partly in terms of news values, in particular the preference for presenting the news in terms of 'drama', problems and conflict. In the case of race, such values can lead, as has been said, to a strong emphasis on events such as 'muggings', 'riots' and 'illegal immigration'. As a result, children whose ideas of black people come mainly from the media tend to build up a negative stereotype of black people.

However, the media also stand accused of being unrealistically overpositive as well as negative. It has been argued that many programmes, especially on television in the USA, which frequently present black people and women as having successful, independent careers do not reflect the real composition of high-earning professions, which are still dominated by white, male, middle-class Americans. *The Cosby Show* and *The Fresh Prince of Bel Air*, about wealthy black families, have been criticized in these terms. Criticism has also been made that racial issues such as discrimination and abuse are ignored or underplayed in these series. The representation of the Huxtable family in *The Cosby Show*, for example, is unrealistic, according to some, as racial issues would certainly arise at some point with a 'regular' black family. Virginia Mathews points out this dilemma of the 'burden' of representation in an article in *The Listener*:

> When we reflect society as it is – with all its prevailing class, sex and racial bigotry – we are accused of pandering to ignorance. But when we attempt to challenge stereotypes, we are accused of peddling fantasy, not reality.

John Tulloch (1990) argues in his essay 'Television and black Britons' that only when black people are more fairly 'represented' in terms of numbers of actors, journalists, directors and producers will the issue of screen representation be resolved:

> The objective of proponents of 'integrated casting' is for greater black representations in broadcast fiction and news programmes, with a range, not of black characters, but characters who happen to be black.

He nevertheless concedes that the situation has improved, with programmes such as Channel 4's multicultural situation comedy *The Desmonds*, BBC2's drama *Shalom Salaam* and *Eastenders* in which a number of black characters play a more balanced range of roles, from petty criminals to parents and couples in love. Nevertheless, Tulloch points to the continuing lack of black faces, in television advertising in particular, and the underrepresentation of black people in television production generally, to make the controversial case that 'blacks have little to lose and much to gain' from the loss of the old 'corporate' public service model of television that has, in his view, been responsible for this situation (Chapter 6).

OTHER STEREOTYPES

In many ways television can be said to stereotype *all* groups in society. *Yes Minister* and *The New Statesman* offer examples of the comic representations and stereotypes of dominant elites. Nevertheless, some marginal groups are either absent entirely from television (handicapped characters, for instance), or are reduced to crude caricatures. There are a series of stereotypes of sexuality – homosexual men are quickly identified by a mincing walk and camp voices, for instance, and a common stereotype of lesbians (where they appear at all) is as butch, dungaree-wearing feminists. Regional characteristics are routinely boiled down to a few tired clichés – straw-sucking West Country yokels, bitter-supping northerners and toffee-nosed southerners. The cast of *Eastenders* and *Coronation Street*, for example, is largely composed of middle-class actors imitating what they imagine to be authentic accents and characters. For the most part they are a collection of stock representations, so it is refreshing to see sympathetic local actors breathing life into their characters when they are given roles in these soaps.

The rare images of dissent by unionists, feminists, poll-tax demonstrators, road protesters, environmental activists, anti-racist marchers, students and so on (where they occur at all) are generally brief, negative and dismissive. The camera often picks out the images that are easiest and most recognizable: placard-waving workers, protesters being pulled from trees, braided hair and nose rings, violent clashes with police – there are the 'image bites' that sum up, in a single minute of news reporting, complex and critical issues. It represents what Fiske (1987) has described as 'inoculation' – the process whereby mass audiences are 'exposed' to a tiny dose of the 'threatening agent', to strengthen society against its effect. In this way, grass-roots activity, away from the stage-managed political theatre of Westminster, can be ridiculed and rejected.

Stereotyping, therefore, is an ideological process which obscures fundamental arrangements in society made in the interests of the more powerful (Chapter 16). Stereotyping makes these 'arrangements' (such as sexual, racial, regional and class discrimination) appear natural rather than cultural. Stereotyping has been described as one strategy amongst many used to secure the power and influence of the dominant groups in society. As such it is vital, according to this reading, that the means of representation (the mass media and television) which are so essential to the democratic health of a country ultimately lie in the hands of the public and not a wealthy and unelected elite.

EXERCISES AND ESSAYS

Exercise

Conduct an investigation into the representation of men. Consider how far you think these binary opposites, adapted from Nelson (1985) are useful as a means of explaining the construction of gender difference on television:

masculine–feminine
active–passive
presence–absence
primary–secondary
independent–dependent
intellect–imagination
logical–illogical
head–heart
mind–body
culture–nature

Exercise

RESIDENT: What are you rebelling against, Johnny?
JOHNNY: Whaddya got?

(Marlon Brando in *The Wild One*, 1954)

Try to find examples of 'youth rebellion' on contemporary television. Does it exist any more? If not, how is 'youth' represented?

Exercise and Essay

The cartoon *Beavis and Butthead* plays with and reworks contemporary stereotypes of young males. What are these stereotypes?

Exercise and Essay

'Women are enslaved to the beauty industry' (Naomi Wolf).

What evidence is there for this view in the media's representations of women?

Exercise and Essay

Examine the representation of any group in a recent television programme or news report.

Sources

Alvarado, M., Gutch, R. and Wollen, T. (1987): *Learning the media: an introduction to media teaching*. Macmillan.

Barratt, D. (1986): *Media sociology*. Routledge.

Burton, G. (1990): *More than meets the eye*. Arnold.

Cole, T. (1989): Researching race and racism. *Social Studies Review*. November.

Cooke, T. (1990): Mediation, representation, stereotyping. Pendleton Sixth Form College (unpublished).

Cumberbatch, G. (1990): *The portrayal of violence in BBC television*. BBC Publications.

Davies, N. (1994): Under cover kings. *Guardian* 28 November.

Dyer, R. (1985): Taking popular television seriously. In Drummond, P. and Lusted, D. (eds), *Popular TV and schooling*. British Film Institute.

Fiske, J. (1987): *Television culture*. Routledge.

Fiske, J. (1994): entry on 'content analysis'. In Hartley, J. *et al.* (eds), *Key concepts in communication and cultural studies*. Routledge.

Gill, R. (1988): Altered images?: women in the media. *Social Studies Review* September.

Goodwin, A. (1988): *Media studies for adults*. British Film Institute.

Hall, S. (1986): *Bending the reality: the state of the media*, quoted in Nicholas, J., Price, J. and Moore, B. (eds) (1996): *Media communication and production*. Nelson.

Hartmann, P. and Husband, C. (1974): The mass media and racial conflict. In Cohen, S. and Young, J. (eds), *The manufacture of news*. Constable.

Hebdige, D. (1979): *Subculture: the meaning of style*. Methuen.

Kennedy, H. (1988): Women on show. *New Society* 25 March.

Leach, E. (1976): *Culture and communication*. Cambridge University Press.

Leach, E. (1982): *Social anthropology*. Fontana.

Milner, D. (1983): *Children and race ten years on*. Ward Lock; quoted by Tulloch, J. (1990) in *Understanding television*. Routledge.

Nelson, C. (1985). *Envoys of otherness: Difference and Continuity in Feminist Criticism.* In Treicher, P., Krameral, C. and Stafford, B. (eds), *For alma mater: theory and practice in feminist scholarship.* University of Illinois Press.

O'Sullivan, T., Dutton, B. and Rayner, P. (1994): *Studying the media – an introduction.* Arnold.

Perkins, T. (1979): *Rethinking stereotypes.* In Barrett, M., Corrigan, P., Kuhn, A. and Wolff, V. (eds), *Ideology and cultural production.* Croom Helm.

Trowler, P. (1989): *Investigating the media.* Tavistock Publications.

Tuchman, G. (1978): *Hearth and home: images of women and the media.* Oxford University Press.

Tulloch, J. (1990): Television and black Britons. In Goodwin, A. and Whannel, G. (eds), *Understanding television.* Routledge.

Wheen, F. (1985): *Television – a history.* Guild Publishing.

Williamson, J. (1990): Ads nauseam. *Cosmopolitan* January.

Audience – the great unknown

12

Audience

INTRODUCTION

Art that cannot rely on the joyous, heartfelt assent of the broad and healthy mass of people is intolerable (Adolf Hitler).

The audience for television is enormous and, to a large extent, unknown. To be a member of this audience is to consume, interact with and, in a sense, be 'constructed by' television programming. McQuail (1969) suggests that this engagement with television and other mass media constitutes 'at least a mark, and possibly even a requirement of membership of modern society' (quoted in Hartley *et al.*, 1994).

Audiences – the individuals and groups watching television – may be defined by the particular programme they watch, such as the audience for *Dr Who* or *Star Trek*. They may also be defined according to the genre, or type of product, they consume – such as the audience for sports programmes or soap operas. Finally, audiences may be identified according to their 'social profile' – their age, gender, class, racial group, sexual orientation, lifestyle and so on.

Research into audiences has, until quite recently, been largely confined to determining the *effects* of exposure to the mass media (Chapter 13). Social scientists, often funded by governments, have been more interested in what television does to people than what people do with television. As Masterman (1985) suggests, this is because so much study of the media, like literary criticism, has traditionally been based on the belief that textual meanings are produced by authors (writers, directors, producers) and are inherent within the 'texts', rather than actively produced by 'the reader' or member of the audience.

'Uses-and-gratifications' research (Chapter 13) was an early advance on the idea of audiences as merely the receivers of messages. This research was a move towards the idea of an 'active reader' because it claimed that audiences used television, and other mass media, to meet individual needs. These needs include the need for escape from routine or worry, the need for information about the immediate and more distant world, the need for 'company', the need for 'advice' about how to deal with personal problems or relationships, and the need of individuals to measure their sense of identity against the values and lifestyles of others. Uses-and-gratifications research, much of which came from psychological studies in the USA, suggested that individuals used the media in unique ways – by selecting a particular range of material, to satisfy particular needs. This brought to the fore the idea that the meanings and pleasures audiences obtained from television could be quite different from those intended by the makers of the programmes.

Following upon uses-and-gratifications research there have been a range of approaches to the study of audiences. These have attempted to redescribe the viewing behaviour of audiences to show how television viewing is a process of negotiation between the text and reader. These studies have shown how the response of any given viewer to television messages is determined by a large number of factors. These factors might include apparently trivial issues such as the viewer's mood or degree of attention at a particular time. Studies of viewing behaviour, which have included installing video cameras in the television set, have revealed that people engage in a remarkable variety of activities in front of the television set, including eating, talking, working, reading, playing, fighting and making love. According to one study by Peter Collett people have their eyes on the screen for only about 65 per cent of the time they are in the room (O'Sullivan *et al.*, 1994) and for much of the time that viewing is taking place there is talk, which may or may not relate to the programme being watched. Such talk may be about some obscure part of the programme such as the newsreader's tie, the similarity of a character to a friend or acquaintance or an unusual name in the credits.

FEMALE AUDIENCES

Studies of audience behaviour also noted gender-specific viewing patterns. Many men, it was found, preferred to watch television in silence whereas women were often engaged in more than one activity, such as ironing, and were quite happy to talk during a programme. It was also found that men frequently determined, or controlled, what was being watched when in the room, preferring particular types of programming – such as news, sport, documentaries and action films – over romantic stories or films, soap operas and other 'women's fiction'. Men often exercised this power through possession of the remote control.

Research has demonstrated that use of other television-related technology is equally gender related. An investigation by Ann Gray (1992) into the use of video recorders in the home showed that women were less confident in using the apparatus, particularly the timer function, to record programmes and films. Whereas women were found to be quite able to deal with equally 'difficult' technology in the kitchen (such as microwave ovens) that men struggled with, the video recording of programmes was often regarded as a 'male activity', along with the use of computers and computer games. Women were also found to use the video cassette recorder in a different way, usually 'time-shifting' favourite programmes which were watched once only, whereas men frequently kept a 'library' of favourite films and programmes which they watched several times over.

A study by Ien Ang (1985) of attitudes of Dutch women to the soap *Dallas* highlights some of the differences in viewing between the sexes. Ang found that whereas *Dallas* was widely criticized in Dutch society as an example of US cultural imperialism (Chapter 16, pp. 239–41), and that Dutch men generally ridiculed the programme as an 'unrealistic' melodrama, many women enjoyed it and found it to be 'emotionally realistic'. By this term Ang suggested that female audiences identified with experiences in the serial such as rows, family problems, extramarital affairs, emotional abuse, and characters' occasional happiness set against their more sustained misery. Family life in *Dallas* was shown to be less of an ideal state than a condition continuously 'shattered' by events within the drama. Stevenson (1995) writes of Ang's study:

> The world of *Dallas* was felt to be realistic by certain sections of the audience because it took for granted the workings of patriarchal society. The tragic structure of feeling not only symbolically opened up a world where the celebration of happiness is always short lived, but represented those with power as most often being men.

Women were found to adopt an ironic or humorous disposition towards the programme as a means of defending their enjoyment of the programme. The 'language of the personal' – emotional honesty and exploration of relationships, including the possibility of a more equal, caring relationship (Bobby and Pamela Ewing) set against the recognition of male dominance (J.R. and Sue Ellen) – gave the soap its popular appeal to many women. Ang linked the popularity of *Dallas* amongst women to the empowering right of setting aside time for a programme which offered pleasures not always identified, or even shared, by males in the domestic setting.

Ang's conclusions echo those of earlier research by Dorothy Hobson (1981) into the audiences of the soap opera *Crossroads*. *Crossroads* was scorned by critics and people working in the television industry for its low-budget production values, 'wooden acting' and 'creaking scripts'. The show was notorious for its tiny budget which frequently did not even stretch to editing out fluffed lines. Despite huge ratings the soap was reduced from five to three episodes a week and was finally pulled altogether from the schedules. It has been widely acknowledged that although *Crossroads* attracted one of the largest audiences of any television programme after *Coronation Street* this audience – principally middle-aged and elderly women – was not attractive to advertisers or television executives.

Hobson's study looked at the reaction to a decision by a single (male) television executive, Charles Denton, to write the central character Meg Mortimer out of *Crossroads* in 1981. People wrote and telephoned the television company ATV in their thousands to defend Meg Mortimer who had been played by Noele Gordon ever since the first episode. Unmoved by the 'Save Meg' campaign which dominated several tabloid newspapers for days, scriptwriters arranged for her to sail to a new life in Australia aboard the *QE2*. Hobson read all the letters ATV received which were written mainly by female pensioners and contacted several to watch the programme with them in their home. Her work revealed how many women saw *Crossroads* as 'their' programme – not something selected by their husbands or other men – and they articulated, usually with great clarity, how important the programme was to them. Hobson concludes that a programme that draw an audience of 15 million was equally valuable as single plays or documentaries, which traditionally gained critical attention and respect but might attract an audience of only four million. As Hobson noted, 'Neither is better nor worse than the other. They are simply different programmes and each is dependent on the understanding which the audience brings to it for its ultimate worth.' For Hobson, television provided a vital service in providing entertainment and a sense of contact for a large group of people virtually ignored by the rest of society, a responsibility television executives could not shrug off (Chapter 5, pp. 42–3).

ETHNOGRAPHIC RESEARCH

Dorothy Hobson's study of *Crossroads* is an example of ethnographic field-work research because she attempted to enter the culture of the women who enjoyed *Crossroads* and provide an account 'from the inside'. Other ethnographic studies have investigated audience response to programmes in a variety of cultures and countries. A study by Katz and Liebes (1985) found that various ethnic groups viewed *Dallas* differently from US audiences. Many Arabs, for example, viewed the soap as evidence of US immorality and the corrupting effect of wealth. Many thought that Sue Ellen had returned to her father and not her former lover when she left J.R. with her child, because such a scenario was unthinkable in Arabic culture. Similarly, a Moroccan Jew says:

> I learned from this series to say 'Happy is our lot, goodly is our fate' that we're Jewish. Everything about J.R. and his baby, who has maybe four or five fathers, who knows? The mother is Sue Ellen, of course, and the brother of Pam left, maybe he's the father . . . . I see they're almost all bastards (Katz and Liebes, 1984).

Significantly, in light of concerns about media imperialism, Katz's and Liebes's study, like Ang's, argued that it was the melodramatic nature of the narrative and the importance of everyday experiences in the soap, rather than the glitter of consumerism, that captured the attention of the audience.

Shohat and Stam (1996) sum up the conclusions of many ethnographic studies, that different reactions to television material are symptomatic of different historical and social experiences:

Perception itself is embedded in history. The same filmic images or sounds provoke distinct reverberations for different communities. For the Euro-American, shots of Mount Rushmore might evoke fond memories of patriotic father figures; for the native American they might evoke feelings of dispossession and injustice.

Gender, race, religion, class, sexuality and age are all major determinants in the way a given audience is likely to view a programme. *Dynasty* and *The Professionals* are just two programmes that have gained a cult following amongst specific gay communities for reasons that could not have occurred to the programme makers. In *Dynasty* Alexis, played by Joan Collins, has been seen as 'a destroyer of sexual difference', and the high-style, high-fashion 'bitchiness' of the serial is regarded as a source of camp humour, with video loops of cat fights between Alexis and Krystal being played in gay bars in Los Angeles (Fiske, 1987). *The Professionals*, by contrast, has gained cult status in the USA amongst gay audiences, at least partly because of the extreme macho characterization of Bodie and Doyle.

By contrast, in Australia, market research found that schoolchildren enjoyed *Prisoner Cell Block H* because they identified the series with life at school, which they saw as resembling the institution of a prison in many important respects:

Schoolchildren and the prisoners live under a single authority, are treated alike in a tightly scheduled order imposed from above, and have their activities co-ordinated by the rational planning of the institution. The schoolchildren also articulated a number of points of similarity, between the school and the prison, in terms of the way they are often shut in, separated from friends, have no rights, wouldn't be there unless they had to be, and are made to suffer rules they see little point in keeping. The pupils' own self-perceptions resembled those represented by the prisoners, who were reduced to 'childlike' roles within the programmes. Similarly, the teachers and the prison warders were often positioned together (Stevenson, 1995).

Prisoner Cell Block H has also been acknowledged as having a strong cult status amongst many lesbian women, although this appeal is likely to be significantly different from that of Australian schoolchildren. That is not to say, however, that the reading of any programme is determined only by the 'reader's' social profile. Gramsci (1971) has argued that human personalities are not the 'unified boxes' we often imagine them to be, but are full of very contradictory elements – 'progressive' elements and 'Stone Age' elements. Fiske quotes Morley (1986) who illustrates the possibility of contradictory subject positions within a single personality:

the same man may be simultaneously a productive worker, a trade union member, a supporter of the social Democratic Party, a consumer, a racist, a homeowner, a wife beater and a Christian.

Hence each individual is capable of contradictory or even multiple readings of media texts.

ENCODING AND DECODING

In 1973, in a famous essay entitled 'Encoding and decoding in the TV discourse' Stuart Hall developed 'meaning systems', outlined initially by Parkin (1972), to show how television messages are 'encoded' (produced) and 'decoded' (understood by audiences) according to three main categories. This coding: 'dominant', 'negotiated' and 'oppositional' corresponds, in Hall's model, to the class backgrounds and social experience of the producers or audience members concerned. Hence most television programmes are encoded in a dominant meaning system because the people who make such messages are privileged, middle-class professionals with a stake in the dominant ideology (Chapter 16).

It follows that although most television programmes or 'texts' may be open, to a greater or lesser extent, to a number of different readings by the audience, the 'preferred reading' (i.e. that preferred by the text) will generally be a dominant or dominant-hegemonic one. If a member of an audience agrees with the preferred reading – in other words, if they agree with the assumptions of the encoder – then such a reading is dominant-hegemonic; for example, if a person watching a documentary celebrating the royal family were a royalist, their reading would most likely be dominant-hegemonic.

In a negotiated text or reading, elements of the dominant ideology may be challenged. 'Official' or 'establishment' positions may be questioned, for instance, in relation to the need for privatization of major utilities, currently agreed by the major political parties. Corruption may be shown to exist within the police, unions shown to have a positive role to play in defending workers' rights, or homelessness and unemployment explained against a backdrop of social inequality. In an example of a negotiated reading of the documentary celebrating the royals a viewer might, along with the programme (and its makers), wish to see a continuation of royalty in Britain but oppose the amount of money spent on them by the taxpayer, or, for instance, find their love of hunting objectionable.

An example of an oppositional text would be Newman's *Law and Order* series (Chapter 8) which represented the police and judiciary as rotten institutions. The director Ken Loach is known to have made a series on the history of the trade union movement in the 1980s – as being a betrayal of the working class by union leaders. To this day, the film has neither been broadcast nor allowed to be taken away for private screening performances by the director. Ken Loach claims that the message – that powerful union leaders colluded in the destruction of the union movement – was too radical, or 'oppositional', to be allowed. Similarly, in an oppositional reading, a person watching the same celebration of the royal family may hold fast to their republican views and find even more to dislike about the royals as a result of it.

Hall's thesis was important because it suggested that the variety of readings different audiences brought to a text protected them from the direct influence of television. In 1978 David Morley's study of audience responses to the daily news and current affairs programme *Nationwide* challenged some of the assumptions implicit in Hall's 'encoding–decoding' model. Morley, in his study of occupational and social group responses, found, for instance, that some of the audience's readings did not accord with their objective class position. For example, apprentice engineers who were at the bottom of the wages ladder and had the least material 'stake' in society were surprisingly giving dominant readings that allied them with management positions. Morley found that print management trainees were capable of 'rightist oppositional' readings. Other, previously overlooked, factors such as gender and ethnicity were sometimes found to be the major determinant of a given reading and in some cases the message of *Nationwide* was completely ignored or misunderstood, particularly if it failed to engage with the experiences of the viewers.

Morley therefore adapted Hall's dominant, negotiated and oppositional terms to mean that such readings were aligned with, or set against – to a greater or lesser extent – the interpretative framework of the programme itself. This allowed for the fact that the audience were sometimes more conservative than the programme makers and could oppose a more 'progressive' preferred reading. Hence an oppositional reading, in Morley's terms, was not necessarily the same as an 'anti-establishment' reading. Another conclusion was that different audiences brought different 'cultural competencies' to their readings. Morley hoped to show how that not just class but other economic, social and cultural factors within an audience could 'determine' the decoding of the message for different sections of the audience. However, Morley concluded as a result of his research that textual decoding could not simply be 'read off' class, ethnic, gender or subcultural positions, suggesting 'that social position in no way directly, or unproblematically, correlates with decoding' (Morley 1983; see also Chapter 16, pp. 236–7, 241–4; Chapter 17, pp. 263–4).

FISKE AND 'SUBVERSIVE' READINGS

John Fiske ascribes huge power to audiences, arguing that popular culture is, in fact, produced by audiences, not by media industries. He places great emphasis on the subversive and oppositional readings of people, who, in his view, transform the uniform products of the 'dominant power blocs' into 'resistant practices'. The explosion of communications and media messages has, according to Fiske, paradoxically weakened the grip of the 'power bloc' over audiences and the range of interpretations available to them.

Fiske points out the importance of talk or 'gossip' in audience research. Oral culture has an important role to play in promoting diversity, equality, tolerance and understanding. It creates 'audience-driven meanings' and nurtures the communities in which these popular meanings can circulate. Critics of Fiske's position accuse him of mistaking consumerist 'choices' and 'pleasures' with access to the information necessary to make informed democratic choices, and confusing his own sophisticated oppositional readings with the decoding strategies of wider audiences. Shohat and Stam (1996) take up this point:

> Resistant readings, for their part, depend on a certain cultural or political preparation that 'primes' the spectator to read critically. In this sense we would question the more euphoric claims of theorists, such as John Fiske, who see TV viewers as mischievously working out 'subversive' readings based on their own popular memory. Fiske rightly rejects the 'hypodermic needle' view that sees TV viewers as passive drugged patients getting their nightly fix, reduced to 'couch potatoes' and 'cultural dupes'. He suggests that minorities, for example, 'see through' the racism of the dominant media. But if it is true that disempowered communities can decode dominant programming through a resistant perspective, they can do so only to the extent that their collective life and historical memory have provided an alternative framework of understanding.

AUDIENCE POSITIONING AND SCREEN THEORY

Fiske's notions of resistant audiences and subversive readings lies in opposition to theories of textual determination and 'audience positioning'. According to these theories, which emerged in the 1970s, particularly in the film journal *Screen*, audiences are metaphorically 'stitched' or 'sewn' into the narrative of film and television by a variety of conventional production techniques. These techniques, derived from the classic realist style of Hollywood (the dominant stylistic influence on television, worldwide), include the use of shot and reverse shot, the 180 degree rule, reaction shots, inserts, motivated cutting and a host of other conventions designed to 'suspend disbelief' and involve the audience. These techniques, it was claimed, effectively allowed only one reading of events, the reading 'preferred' by the film or television makers.

The stitching or 'suture' (a French term used in screen theory) of the audience into the narrative can be seen at a shot-by-shot level. A reaction shot, for example, will give the viewer an intimate insight into the emotional response of a character to developments in the narrative by showing that person's face in extreme close-up. Shot-reverse-shot allows us to observe two or more characters in conversation from nearly the same point as the other character (it is often filmed over the shoulder). This allows us to see the full range of expressions, to observe in detail the changing mood of the speaker, to judge their every action and word, without ourselves being the object of their gaze (as occurs with the direct address of the newsreader, for example). An insert will show us exactly what a character is looking at, which could be, for instance, the time on their watch, a dog barking at them, a beautiful landscape or an exploding car. All these techniques are designed to grant the audience a privileged point of view and make them forget they are watching a production filmed and edited painstakingly over weeks or months. We are, in this sense, 'positioned' to look at certain things, in a certain way, whether we like it or not. The 'privileged point of view' might also be the legs of the heroine as she walks through the door, or a violent attack where we see the pain of the victim from the point of view of the person attacking. In this way members of the audience are often positioned as masculine spectators of women, or as voyeurs of violence.

Screen theory has been challenged by Fiske and others as too text-centred and dismissive of audiences. The theory fails to take account of the reality of differing viewers' reactions to a single text, and is closely associated with the monolithic view of audiences proposed by hypodermic effects (Chapter 13). Nevertheless, audience positioning does occur and it is important to be aware of the *preferred meanings* (how we are expected to view a series of events or characters) presented in television programmes.

MODE OF ADDRESS

Audiences are 'addressed' in different ways by television programmes. The *mode of address* is the way a text is constructed that establishes a relationship between addresser and addressee. Dramas, usually produced in the classic realist style described above, normally use an impersonal or unseen mode of address. There may be first-person narration in, for example, historical dramas or literary adaptations where we are guided through the events by a single character within the story. News, game shows, magazine programmes or any television form using presenters adopt the 'direct address' (direct eye contact with 'the viewer', who is openly acknowledged) for much of the programme. The audience may also be addressed as concerned consumers, sophisticated connoisseurs, highly literate readers, young, cynical music fans, potential financial investors, families, children, devout Christians, film buffs, 'ordinary members of the public' and so on. Each will use a different *discourse*, or language, just as people adopt different discourses, or ways of talking and writing, for different events and people. The mode of address, therefore, may be formal, informal, serious, humorous, sincere, ironic, personal, impersonal, just as with any other communication. The presenters or mediators of MTV, for instance, are usually in their 20s, are slim, attractive, vaguely 'transatlantic' rather than belonging to any region, casually dressed, direct, informal, irreverent or even conspiratorial in their manner, often ironic or detached from their scripts, 'cool', musically aware – everything, in fact, that is designed to include, rather than exclude, MTV's target audience.

AUDIENCE POWER

Mode of address is one technique whereby television producers 'construct' their audiences. The popular music industry is interested in young, relatively affluent, audiences with spending power that they are prepared to direct towards their products. They are less interested in older audiences, who only occasionally buy music, or very young audiences with limited spending power. According to some media theorists, therefore, the major product of a music channel such as MTV or Channel V is the audience power they attract. Undoubtedly, commercial television makes its money by selling audiences to advertisers. According to Dallas Smyth (1981), the Canadian Marxist economist, the mass media were 'beckoned into existence' by their ability to create audiences that advertisers wanted to buy. These audiences are constructed in order to 'consume' and to market themselves more effectively to advertisers. Masterman quotes Smyth on the working of 'consciousness industries' which produce audiences who are ready to buy consumer goods, pay their taxes and continue working in their alienating jobs in order to continue buying tomorrow:

> The full grocery store of 1900 is long gone with its telephone order-filling, charge accounts, sales persons showing customers the merchandise, and delivery service. In its stead we have customers waiting on themselves with a paucity of relevant information provided by the supermarket, then waiting in line at the cash register to pay cash and transport the groceries home by their own means.

Advertisers today are often more interested in who the audience is rather than how large it is, as the example of *Crossroads*' 15 million strong audience has already illustrated. Media marketing is about identifying audiences according to income, social class, sex, age, 'lifestyle' and a whole range of classifications so that advertisers can more easily reach their 'target audience'. Programmes on commercial television, then, are regularly devised with advertisers' needs in mind. A programme such as *Wish You Were Here* will obviously appeal to holiday firms whereas *Home and Away*, *The Chart Show* or *The Word* will attract advertisers trying to reach a younger audience.

SCHEDULING

Scheduling is the placing of programmes in such an order that will gain the largest audience. An example of this is the policy of putting popular soap operas at the beginning of an evening's schedule. It is hoped they will keep an audience watching that channel through new or less popular material. The so-called 'inheritance factor' of such programmes has been used to maintain audiences through low-ratings items such as documentaries. 'Hammocking' a weaker programme between two more popular ones is also common. 'Cross-trailing' refers to the use of common junction points in the schedules to advertise programmes on another channel not regarded as a rival (BBC1 promoting a programme on BBC2, for example). Another feature of traditional scheduling techniques has been to account for the different age profiles of a television audience at any given time. Between 4 o'clock and 5.30, for instance, most programmes on British terrestrial channels are aimed at children. Between 5.30 and 9 o'clock programming is supposed to be suitable for a family audience. After the 9 o'clock 'watershed' material may be of a violent or sexual nature and contain explicit language and is usually made for an older audience.

Scheduling is designed to create viewing 'routines' – fixed points in the ordering of programmes with which the viewer can become familiar. If the same audience can be guaranteed at the same time very week, programme production can be more easily planned and budgeted and audiences sold to advertisers on a more reliable and regular basis. Television companies, there-fore, hope to offer, wherever possible, 'guaranteed audiences' to their advertisers, which explains the popularity of serials and series. For this reason, in the USA, where commercial pressures on the television industry are that much sharper, the networks are interested only in long programme runs of at least 52 episodes – one for every week of the year. A series such as *Fawlty Towers*, of which only 12 episodes were ever recorded, creates problems for US broadcasters because a large, regular weekly audience cannot be guaranteed to draw revenue from sponsors and advertisers.

Nevertheless, whereas early television broadcasting was aimed principally at mass audiences (particularly in the USA) the situation has slowly changed since the 1970s. Television executives and advertisers have become increas-ingly interested in audiences with high spending power – the middle and upper classes and young 'upwardly mobile' viewers in particular. For this reason it is possible to run a channel such as Channel 4 as a commercial concern, with only 10 per cent of the total viewing figures, or an entire 24-hour satellite station such as Asia Business News with high production values, on a tiny fraction of the Asian television market. Maltby (1989) notes this development in relation to the type of programming developed on the US networks:

In the developed world further expansion of the media involved the exploitation of increasingly specialised markets for higher-priced media commodities such as financial information or 'quality' television. These appealed to the more privileged social groups. A 1979 survey identified 14 separate audience groupings among the consumers of American television. MTM sustained the most impressive record among American producers of 'quality' television, aiming series such as *Lou Grant* and *Hill Street Blues* at a liberal professional audience, who preferred programmes that they felt were more sophisticated, stylistically complex and psychologically 'deep' than ordinary television fare. 'Quality' programmes such as *M*∗*A*∗*S*∗*H* could reach 'quality' social groups (the metropolitan, the upwardly mobile, the wealthy), and this offered advertisers an alternative strategy to the constant quest for a larger share of the ratings.

What such systems of scheduling demonstrated is that in an increasingly diverse media economy there can only be profit in supplying products aimed specifically at the upper end of the market. As the hardware costs of broadcasting continue to increase, however, many analysts argue that only the pursuit of international mass audiences can sustain the investment in both equipment and programming. This leads to the prospect of a diet of least objectionable programming, sport, music, videos, news and reruns (Maltby, 1989).

Increasing market pressures, the fragmentation of the family audience (many households have more than one television), the arrival of remote-control devices, video recording and the proliferation of channels resulting from satellite, cable and digital television have each put their strains on scheduling policies. As audiences 'surf' the various channels available to avoid adverts, television makers have moved towards incorporating the advertising message into the programming. This has occurred in the form of sponsorship (the use of explicit messages within the programme), 'product placement' (displaying or incorporating branded products within a programme) or, more insidiously, in the *type* of programme made. CNN's *Future Watch* reports, sponsored by IBM, are typical of the merging of advertising and programming, with promotional features on the latest computer programmes and hardware available on the market a major feature. This incorporation of advertising material into programming is a key aspect of the experience of contemporary television as being a continuous 'flow':

> The greater the competition for viewers in order to increase revenue directly the more marked the flow character of television becomes. This is because the flow helps to disguise the breaks in programmes and mask potential channel-switching moments (Paterson, 1990).

Moreover, the commercial broadcasting environment described above is not confined to commercial broadcasting. A glance at the schedules of the BBC reveals a range of programming that is explicitly promotional, particularly 'magazine' programmes such as *The Clothes Show*, *Top Gear*, *Holiday* and *Food and Drink*, but also in other popular programmes such as *The National Lottery Live*, or *Top of the Pops*.

With the dramatic increase in the number of television channels, and no corresponding increase in advertising revenue available, it has been suggested that advertisers and sponsors will put more financial pressure on programme makers to incorporate their messages into the programme content. The result of these pressures can already be seen in the blurring of programming with advertising. When CNN runs a three-minute report on Depeche Mode's latest album release, for instance, the question arises: is this news? In the commercially determined world of contemporary television the answer is, apparently, yes. In this sense, the lack of clear programme and advertising boundaries will become more marked, with important implications for scheduling policy. Programmes which are too distinct from, or challenge, the advertising that surrounds them, or that are markedly different from the programmes that follow and precede it in the schedules, will be dropped. Television output, according to this model, will become a seamless, 'commercially friendly' whole; and the fragmentation of audiences with their 'distinct' needs, programmes and channels little more than an effective marketing strategy.

EXERCISES AND ESSAYS

Task

Research the use of television by the people in your home. Look at:

- who is watching
- when they are watching
- how they are watching

Who in your opinion 'controls' what is being watched at any one time?

Task

Conduct a survey of at least 10 male and 10 female viewers on their favourite programmes and viewing habits. Does any 'gender-determined' pattern emerge from the survey? Does it support, or refute the findings of other academic surveys?

Exercise

Look at how any television programme attempts to 'position' its audience. What techniques are employed? Are they successful?

Exercise

Interview people of a particular age or background about a specific programme that they have recently watched. Did they like or 'agree with' all of it, or were there parts they disliked? Did they think the programme had any 'message' (either explicit or implicit)? Did the viewer accept, partly accept or reject this message? What type of reading have they, in your opinion, given of the programme – dominant, negotiated or oppositional?

Essay

How and in what ways can audiences 'resist' the preferred meaning of a text?

Exercise

Make or photocopy a list of programmes from a day's schedule. Summarize in a single sentence the 'mode of address' for each.

Essay

Audiences, whether they are 'mass' or 'niche', are targeted carefully. With reference to specific examples, show how this is achieved.

Essay

> Any media text that may be termed 'popular culture' is bound to be of low worth.

Discuss this view, basing your answer on at least one example of a programme you have studied.

Exercise

Michael Grade made his fortune by his skill at manipulating the schedules and drawing bigger audiences back to the BBC in the 1980s.

Cut up an existing schedule from any television listings and remove the times given. Rearrange the programmes in a different order and justify your decision in terms of some of the scheduling strategies outlined above. How is the schedule different now? What kind of audiences will now be drawn at peak hours? How could you defend your changes in terms of advertising revenue and/or public service commitments?

Essay

Write an essay on one of the following:

- What recent technological and organizational changes have affected ideas about broadcast scheduling and flow?

- New technologies, such as video recorders, satellite, cable and digital television, have made possible the disruption of 'broadcast flow'. How has this affected the use of traditional scheduling methods by the BBC and ITV companies?

Essay

In America, unbridled competition between the major networks has produced so called 'jugular' scheduling in which each network seeks to win as large an audience as possible (Paterson, 1990).

In what ways is British scheduling distinct from the US tradition? Are there any other models for television scheduling?

Sources

Ang, I. (1985): *Watching 'Dallas': soap opera and the melodramatic imagination.* Methuen; quoted in Stevenson, N. (1995): *Understanding media cultures.* Sage.

Branston, G. and Stafford, R. (1996): *The media student's book.* Routledge.

Fiske, J. (1987): *Television culture.* Routledge.

Gramsci, A. (1971): *Selections from the Prison Notebooks.* Lawrence and Wishart.

Gray, A. (1992): *Video playtime: the gendering of a leisure technology.* Routledge.

Hall, S. (1973): Encoding and decoding in the TV discourse. Occasional paper 7 of the Centre for Contemporary Cultural Studies, University of Birmingham.

Hartley, J. *et al.* (eds) (1994): *Key concepts in communication and cultural studies.* Routledge.

Hobson, D. (1981): *Crossroads: the drama of a soap opera.* Methuen, quoted in Masterman, L. (1985): *Teaching the media.* Routledge.

Katz, E. and Liebes, T. (1984): *Once upon a time in Dallas.* Intermedia.

Katz, E. and Liebes, T. (1985): *Mutual aid in the decoding of Dallas.* In Drummond, P. and Paterson, R. (eds), *Television in transition.* British Film Institute.

Maltby, R. (ed.) (1989): *Dreams for sale – popular culture in the 20th century.* Equinox.

Masterman, L. (1985): *Teaching the media.* Routledge.

McQuail, D. (1969): *Towards a Sociology of Mass Communications.* Macmillan.

Morley, D. (1983): *Cultural transformations: the politics of resistance.* In Davis, H. and Walton, P. (eds.), *Language, image, media.* Blackwell.

Morley, D. (1986): *Family television.* Comedia.

O'Sullivan, T., Dutton, B. and Rayner, P. (1994): *Studying the media – an introduction.* Arnold.

Parkin, F. (1972): *Class inequality and political order.* Paladin.

Paterson, R. (1990): *A suitable schedule for the family.* In Goodwin, A. and Whannel, G. (eds), *Understanding television.* Routledge.

Shohat, E. and Stam, R. (1996): Media spectatorship in the age of globalisation. In Wilson, R. and Dissanayake, W. (eds), *Global/local – cultural production and the transnational imaginary.* Duke University Press.

Smyth, D. (1981): *Dependency road.* Ablex.

Stevenson, N. (1995): *Understanding media cultures.* Sage.

Kowabunga!

13

Media Effects

The media, indisputably, have 'effects' on audiences. Bob Geldof's *Live Aid* (1985) raised millions of pounds for starving people in Ethiopia in a single day. The BBC's *Crime Watch* series has been responsible for the capture of criminals as witnesses have come forward to provide evidence as a result of its crime reconstructions and appeals. Television advertising has boosted the sales of thousands of brands including some, such as the margarine Krona, from their launch to market leader in a matter of weeks. That television has 'effects' on audiences cannot, logically, be denied. Nevertheless, media analysts are far from sure as to the extent and kinds of effects the media have, or as to how these effects occur.

The control of television stations, in addition to other organs of the media such as radio stations or printing presses, has always been a priority for those seeking power, as can be seen most clearly at times of civil wars or military coups. The power of television for social control has been clearly grasped, in this sense, by those who exercise such control directly. Many of the complex issues which relate to the ideological power of television are covered in more detail in Chapter 16. The popular debate on the effects of television, however, from which it is often difficult to escape, are more commonly concerned with the far narrower issues of violent or sexual content and the effect of exposure to such material upon audiences, particularly younger audiences.

HISTORICAL BACKGROUND TO THE EFFECTS DEBATE

Concern about the 'harmful' influence of the media can be traced back as far as the days of Shakespeare when the content of plays, and even the location of theatres, was very strictly controlled. In the nineteenth century cheap, sensationalistic fiction, referred to as 'penny dreadfuls' in Britain and 'dime novels' in the USA, were held responsible for a variety of social ills. Similarly, street theatres and music hall of the turn of the century were blamed for street crime and 'loose morals', and cinema was being subject to censure and censorship from the earliest screenings (which were frequently pornographic, even by today's standards). Crime and horror comics were the object of outrage and legislation in the 1950s as Communist, Labour and Conservative

MPs in Britain united to curtail severely the 'depraved' content of such comics. The same fears have been repeated in relation to paperback novels, jazz, rock and roll, rap music, video nasties, video games and, most recently, the Internet.

Television has taken centre stage in this debate because of its place in the home, widespread (and frequently heavy) usage and easy access by all age-groups. The title of Marie Winn's book *The Plug-in drug* (1977) sums up many of the fears expressed about the medium, particularly in relation to children: namely, that television can be 'addictive' and 'harmful' to those who watch it. The specific negative claims most commonly made against television are that by seeking mass audiences it has caused a decline in aesthetic tastes and standards of popular culture; that it promotes escapism, passivity and dependency; and that it encourages habits of violence and delinquency. Research goes on continuously into the last of these accusations, and it is the area most commonly debated in the mass media, including, ironically, television itself. There are, however, other issues such as the role of television in stereotyping groups, or setting the agenda for debate, that are less commonly debated, at least in the popular, public realm but which can equally be regarded as an aspect of the 'effects' controversy.

THE 'HYPODERMIC EFFECT' MODEL

The perceived effectiveness of the mass media in the propaganda campaigns in Europe and the Soviet Union from the First World War to the end of the Second World War led to a widespread belief in the power of the mass media to control men and women against their will. The relative novelty of cinema, radio and early television combined with rapid urbanization and the weakening of traditional social relationships may, at least in part, have given substance to the common assumption that audiences were relatively passive, naive and easily manipulated in the face of such media. The Frankfurt School (see Chapter 16, pp. 232–3) share some of these assumptions about the power of the media and the compliant nature of audiences.

This view of the audience as broadly undifferentiated in their response to a media stimulus or message, a response which was assumed to be immediate, has been described as the 'hypodermic effect', or simply, 'effects model'. Although this behaviourist 'myth' of media omnipotence has since been rejected by most researchers, there remains some evidence for a fairly straight-forward stimulus–response model for particular audience effects that cannot be lightly dismissed. The often quoted example for this is *The Martians Have Landed* (1938), Orson Welles's radio adaptation of *The War of the Worlds*, a science fiction novel by the nineteenth-century writer H.G. Wells. What was unusual about the drama was the documentary style, which simulated news bulletins and interviews with 'real' experts such as government officials and army doctors. Because many people missed the announcement at the beginning of the programme, telling listeners that what they were about to hear was a fictional reconstruction, there was, according to several testimonies, widespread panic, 'sightings' and even reported rapes by the alien invaders:

> Long before the broadcast had ended, people all over the United States were praying, crying, fleeing frantically to escape death from Martians. Some ran to rescue loved ones. Others telephoned farewells or warnings, hurried to inform neighbours, sought information from newspapers or radio stations, summoned ambulances or police cars. At least six million people heard the broadcast. At least a million of them were frightened or disturbed (Cantril, 1971, quoted in Braham, 1987).

Other critics claim the extent of the panic had been exaggerated by the media and Orson Welles himself who, it is suggested, revelled in the publicity. Furthermore, as Burton (1990) notes, there were other crucial factors contributing to the night of panic, such as people's knowledge of the imminence of real war, which had them in a state of high anxiety anyway.

Further evidence of the 'hypodermic effect' was provided in a famous experiment by Bandura *et al.* (1961) when children were allowed to observe an 'adult model' under several conditions, one of which involved the adult attacking a Bobo doll (an inflatable clown) with a hammer. Children were then taken to a room that contained toys such as a tea set, crayons, a hammer and a Bobo doll, and given the opportunity to play for a while. The results showed that children who had watched an aggressive model were more aggressive than children who had watched a non-aggressive model or those who had watched no model at all, and then been given the same play materials. Critics of these experiments have pointed out that the situation is an unrealistic and artificial one, and has no relevance in explaining real-life aggression (Davies and Houghton, 1991).

Media power has also been held responsible for several dramatic political developments such as the civil rights campaign in the USA in the 1960s, anti-Vietnam demonstrations in the USA and Europe; the spread of 'terrorist' activity (given the 'oxygen' of publicity for a range of activities, notably in a series of hijackings in the 1970s); the fall of communist regimes in the former Eastern Bloc; and street riots in Britain in the early 1980s and in Los Angeles in 1992. Clearly, the screening of a group of police viciously beating Rodney King was instrumental in provoking civil unrest in the last case. In many of these examples it is arguable whether television acted as a catalyst for the violent expression of deep-rooted public resentment rather than as a cause of the violent unrest in itself.

Such claims should be balanced by an alternative view of the media as an 'undeclared arm of the establishment', particularly at times of social and political crisis. To take only one example, some critics, such as John Pilger, have demonstrated how television helped to sustain the war in Vietnam for many years, until the weight of public opinion, and a series of humiliating US military defeats, forced television stations to give expression to alternative viewpoints of the conflict.

Finally, it is worth considering briefly the 'hypodermic effect' at a personal level in terms of the effectiveness of advertising and other messages. Most people have experienced, at some time, the effect of watching a product such as coffee, chocolate, cigarettes or a cold drink being consumed on television (whether it be a film, television programme or advertising break) and wanting that product immediately. In some ways, the less conscious we are of being 'manipulated' in these circumstances the more effective the message becomes. It is for this reason that particular 'subliminal' advertising techniques remain outlawed, such as inserting images of a product that are only a few frames, or less than an eighth of a second, in duration. Such limitations are evidence of a general acceptance of the potential of television to elicit a desired response with, or without, the conscious knowledge of the audience.

CHALLENGES TO THE 'HYPODERMIC EFFECT' MODEL

US media analysis of the 1940s and 1950s attempted to establish the measurable impact of the media of mass communication on human behaviour through laboratory experiments and social surveys. Its conclusion – that the media was, on the whole, harmless, or merely reinforced the norms and values of a pluralist society – was an almost complete reversal of previous opinion. A variety of reasons were given for this conclusion, including the preconceptions of the audience which, it was argued, acted as a powerful filter of media messages. For example, those with strong political convictions, or a religious upbringing, might react against a given media message as completely as audiences were previously assumed to have accepted them. The prevailing image in this model is of an audience composed of sociological and psychological groups who 'expose themselves to, understand and remember communications selectively, according to prior dispositions' (Curran et al., 1977; quoted in Braham, 1987). In this sense, the media, including television, were seen to be acting far more as an agent of reinforcement than as an agent of change.

Two-step Flow Theory

Katz and Lazarfield (1960) argued that people lived in groups, and that groups, and opinion leaders within groups, were the 'determinant' of, or a crucial factor in, the formation of social attitudes. They stressed that audiences respond directly to information given through the media, even in news and current-affairs material which presented relevant social and political information. It was argued that respected members of our peer group were more influential than the media themselves, even though the media may have influenced them in the first place. This approach was influential in much of the research of the 1960s and 1970s, particularly into the influence of television and election campaigns on political opinions.

Uses-and-gratifications Model

According to this theory, which first found expression in the USA in the 1940s, audiences use the media to gratify certain needs, such as a need for entertainment, information, personal identity and social interaction. As Fiske (1987) remarks, 'Television and its programmes do not have an "effect" on people. Viewers and television interact.'

This functional approach to audience behaviour tends to reduce the manipulative, 'ideological' role of the media and to some extent denies or underplays the long-term effect of the selective presentation of 'facts' and approved actions – or 'normative consensus' predominantly expressed in mass media texts. The 'uses-and-gratifications' model does, however, accord mass audiences with far greater 'reading' powers than did previous models. These readings are seen to resist the power of the dominant ideology – as in feminine readings of soap operas set within, yet against, patriarchy. Fiske (1987) is a keen proponent of this view:

> There is a power in resisting power, there is a power in maintaining one's social identity in opposition to that proposed by the dominant ideology, there is a power in asserting one's own subcultural values against the dominant ones. There is, in short, a power in being different.

CURRENT EFFECTS RESEARCH

Media effects are researched in different ways. Advertising agencies and advertisers closely monitor the results of their television campaigns, through extensive market research. 'Independent' researchers rarely make use of this information, mainly because they do not wish to be associated with studies paid for and conducted in the interests of commercial concerns. In any case, much of the evidence of the multimillion pound advertising industry remains confidential. Areas of 'effects' which do not benefit from expensive market research surveys include advertisers' generally accepted role in reinforcing a broad range of stereotypes and the extent to which advertising creates 'false needs', encouraging an anxiety-driven consumer culture which is detrimental to society and, particularly, those on low incomes.

Media 'effects' are also researched by a number of media institutions. The BBC and ITV jointly control The Broadcasters' Audience Research Board (BARB) which provides viewing figures and more detailed audience responses to terrestrial, satellite and video recorded programming through electronic monitoring, interviews and questionnaires. Automatic meters are connected to

4500 homes which continuously record which sets are on and which channels are being watched. Other research is commissioned by television stations through, for example, the BBC-run Television Opinion Panel which ask 3000 people a week to complete a booklet rating on all the programmes they watch. Questions relating to the audience's response to, for example, violent or sexual matter may be (and often is) included in any of this research.

The government, in addition to requiring terrestrial broadcasters to keep themselves informed on the state of public opinion about the programming and advertising they broadcast, have set up other bodies to monitor television output and register public concerns. The Independent Television Commission (ITC), which takes advice from 10 regional viewer consultative councils, enforces licence conditions, including rules on taste and decency. However, unlike the body which it replaced – the IBA – they do not pre-vet programmes. The Broadcasting Complaints Commission (BCC), set up in 1981, deals with complaints of unfair treatment or alleged infringement of privacy both by television and by radio programme makers. The Broadcasting Standards Council (BSC) was established in 1988 'to act as a focus for public concern about the portrayal of violence and sex, and about standards of taste and decency' (Central Office of Information, 1993). The BSC monitors programmes, examines complaints from the public and undertakes research.

In addition to media and government-sponsored surveys there is a large body of research conducted by 'independent' bodies such as sociology, psychology, media and communication, or cultural studies departments of universities. The type of research conducted includes content analysis of the media products, experimental studies in the laboratory, correlation studies and field studies of attitude and behavioural changes amongst diverse television audiences.

In an experimental study there is an organized attempt to measure the effect of a stimulus on an experimental group, which is then compared with a set of results taken from a control group – where all aspects of the experiment are replicated (with the exception of the stimulus). An example of this type of research is the 'Bobo doll' study of Bandura *et al.* (1961). The problems that are commonly recognized with this kind of study are that only immediate, short-term effects can be measured, and that experimental situations are, in fact, wholly artificial and different in a number of respects from real-life situations. A field study is conducted away from the 'laboratory' in an attempt to record audience behaviour as it occurs in more domestic environments or to obtain reactions and opinions soon after the media experience. This may involve observing audiences as they view programmes or simply recording viewers' responses in a questionnaire. Correlation studies attempt to show a link between two factors such as watching violence on television and behaving violently. Examples of this type of research include Belson's survey of adolescent boys in London, and Milavsky's survey of US teenagers which came to diametrically opposed conclusions about the effects of exposure to television violence (Braham, 1987). Even in those studies where there appears to be a link between watching violent material and violent behaviour it is difficult to establish if violent people choose to watch more violence on television than others or whether they are made more violent by their viewing habits.

TELEVISION AND VIOLENCE

More than 1000 pieces of research, covering psychology, psychiatry and sociology, have been commissioned in the area of media effects, making it one of the most studied questions in mass communication, but there appears to be no firm conclusion about whether violence on screen breeds real-life violence or crime.

Measured on the basis of violent acts per hour, and contrary to popular belief, Britain has less than half as much violence on television today as it did in the 1940s or 1960s. In fact, there has been a steady decline in the 'amount of violence', as measured in this way, since the Second World War. The country with the highest number of violent acts in prime-time dramatic fiction is Germany (8.6 per hour) with more than three times as much violence as the United Kingdom (2.5). Curiously, Japan, with 7 violent acts per hour compared with 5.5 for the USA, is regarded as one of the safest countries in the world (Cumberbatch, 1989).

In fact, research indicates that there is far less violence on British screens than elsewhere in the West. Guy Cumberbatch, of Aston University, who has undertaken one of the most detailed reviews of research available, has found that British viewers are subjected to about half the volume of violence shown in the USA, Canada, Australia and much of Europe. 'In that context, the concerns about on-screen violence here seem a bit misplaced', he claims.

Nevertheless, such attempts to measure levels of 'sex' and 'violence' on television are virtually meaningless without some knowledge of the type of act recorded, or the context in which it takes place. In this sense these figures, and any correlation studies that might relate to them, suffer from the shortcoming of all content analysis. A simple 'body count', or 'violent act' tally, for instance, would make *Dr Strangelove* (in which the world is destroyed) or *Independence Day* (in which whole cities are wiped out) amongst the most 'violent' films of all time, despite their innocuous reputation. In a film, video or television programme, a rape or torture scene may either be presented, for example, as an appalling act, or as glamorized fun. In Britain, but not in all countries, the latter presentation is subject to censorship by the guidelines of broadcasters or the British Board of Film Classification (BBFC) because of the fear that sexual violence or sadism presented as entertainment influences a significant minority of men. These examples usefully illustrate the proposition that there is no such thing as 'sex and violence' on the screen, but that there are only 'ways of showing sexual or violent encounters'.

Context, again, is a crucial determinant of the reaction to violent material. As the television journalist and arts presenter Melvyn Bragg (1993) makes clear:

> There are certain areas – for instance, documentaries and arts programmes – where violence of action and language has been admitted for some time, on the understanding that these are specialised areas which have earned special treatment. So the *Arena* on Edward Said recently showed the most contemptuous cold-blooded killing of Algerians by French soldiers; the *South Bank* showed what Berlioz, as a young medical student, experienced so traumatically gazing at the abattoirs in Paris. The c-word was used on arts programmes more than 12 years ago with no fuss. In that sense, distinctions between programmes are well made.
>
> News also receives, and deserves, special treatment. Care is taken with early bulletins, and warnings are given in late bulletins, but it is a matter that merits constant debate. Given the horrors in the former Yugoslavia, ought we to be protected from the worst that is happening to the distraught Muslims? The violent effect on our consciences of the starving in Africa testifies to television's duty and power to portray unwelcome and all but unacceptable 'truths'. These lead to a serious and continuing discourse about the portrayal of the world through film reports on the news. And we are right to have those debates.

One theory that is frequently referred to in public debates about screen violence is the 'desensitizing effect' of such material. This relates even to images of wars or disasters in the news, as mentioned above. News organizations talk about 'war weariness' or 'compassion overload' in relation to charity appeals. It is also suggested that exposure to fictional violence hardens us to the image of real violence. A special-effects-aided close-up of a violent death may well have greater emotional impact than a shaky, grainy image of someone falling in battle, who has been actually killed in front of the cameras. However, the desensitization of 'inoculation' theory remains largely an anecdotal or commonsense assumption and Burton (1990) reminds us that research has found no evidence to support this theory.

In fact, studies conducted into the effects of watching violence in fictional material have, on the whole, come up with contradictory, and incomplete evidence. There seems to be an acknowledgement that particular disturbed individuals, some one or two per 1000, clearly imitate violence on television. There is also some evidence that a much larger number of people become more fearful, developing a heightened and perhaps unjustified sense of danger in the outside world. However, even this tentative suggestion has been countered by the possibility that heavy viewers may bring with them a more simplistic or a more alarmist view of the world in which they live rather than adopting such perspectives from watching television. The problems with so many correlation studies, as Braham (1987) points out, is that 'they produce correlations, the development, connections and direction of which are insufficiently elaborated'.

CHILDREN AND TELEVISION VIOLENCE

The young have always been felt to be particularly vulnerable to the effects of 'harmful' material, and the history of concern in this area stretches back to the ancient Greeks who debated whether particular stories or dramas corrupted youth or provided purgation and 'catharsis'. Early studies of media effects concentrated on young people and the cinema in the USA in the late 1920s. The most famous, established by the Payne Fund in 1928, examined the relationship between film watching and juvenile crime. Although no causal links were established, such studies did little to dispel popular fears that the media could, and did, deprave young audiences. Therefore, when teenagers appeared to ape the surly, rebellious manner of Marlon Brando in *The Wild One* (1954) or 'rioted' in the cinemas when Bill Haley's 'Rock Around the Clock' was played over the opening titles of *The Blackboard Jungle* (1955) these were thought to provide clear proof of how mass media content might make audiences more delinquent or violent.

This charge has been supported by a number of social scientists. According to a study by Wilson the media can act as a destabilizing influence on those with an 'antisocial disposition'. The mass media, he claims, provide these audiences with vivid fantasies, stimulate criminal, violent, sensational and salacious appetites and, in so doing, present a set of values which 'stand in stark contrast to the values entrenched in our existing social institutions – the family, the work place, the school, the law courts, the church – and in our social relationships' (Wilson, quoted in Braham, 1987).

Some studies have indicated that the level of aggressive behaviour could be predicted in young adults by using a knowledge of the kinds of television programmes they viewed as children (Eron *et al.*, 1972). Belson's (1978) survey of teenage boys in London found that participation in acts of serious violence had been, apparently, increased by heavy exposure to violence on television. However, this survey was subsequently criticized for methodological flaws. Boasting plays a part in many of the responses of young people to research questions, and in several studies where made-up titles for films had been given the participants claimed they had seen them.

It is also difficult to separate the effects of other variables such as a child's disposition and the environment in which they were raised. Not only can it be shown that children who watch more violence on television are more aggressive, but it is also the case that children with aggressive dispositions are more likely to watch violent television programmes (Eron, 1987), and, furthermore, that 'aggression-prone' children are likely to become even more aggressive when watching programmes with a violent content (Stein and Friedrich, 1975, quoted in Davies and Houghton, 1991).

The possible link between violent video films and the horrific killing of James Bulger by two 10-year-old boys brought a fierce debate over these issues into the public domain. Passing sentence on the two children, Mr Justice Morland drew attention to a possible connection between the crime and films in the family house. It was, by this time, common knowledge that *Child's Play 3*, an 18 certificate film, was hired by Jon Venables's father less than a month before James's abduction and murder. The film features a doll called 'Chucky' which is possessed by an evil killer and dressed in toddler's clothing. The judge said that although it was not for him to pass judgement on their upbringing he suspected 'exposure to violent video films may, in part, be an explanation'.

However, according to newspaper reports of the time, detectives involved in the case rejected suggestions that the two boys transferred the role of Chucky to their victim. There is no proof that either Venables or his codefendant, Robert Thompson, saw the film. Mr Venables said the film was hired for himself and that his son only watched cartoons. Detective Superintendent Albert Kirby, who led the inquiry, said that he had seen no evidence to suggest the boys had access to videos any worse than might be found in many households. Asked whether violent films may have influenced the boys' actions, he said, 'The area of videos was one we looked at and we cannot find any specific thing which highlights that.'

Following the Bulger case, Professor Elizabeth Newson, head of the child development unit of Nottingham University, produced a report called 'Video Violence' suggesting that researchers had 'underestimated' the harmful effects of violent videos. The report, which received wide publicity, particularly as it had been endorsed by 25 psychologists, paediatricians, educationalists and other academics, turned out to be only nine pages in length, contained no original research and concluded, as most surveys do, that more research was needed. In much the same way, Guy Cumberbatch reviewed the existing literature on media effects and concluded that there was nothing that had been proved empirically. Although 77 per cent of the research seemed to support a causal link between media violence and crime, in most respects the research, in his view, had been quite inadequate and did not concur as some reviewers suggested. Cumberbatch cited one study of 1500 boys aged 13–16 years which concluded that boys with high levels of exposure to television violence commit 49 per cent more acts of serious violence. In fact, on closer inspection, the study showed that those with the highest exposure to violent television were found to be the least violent of all the children.

There appears, therefore, to be highly debatable evidence for the potentially harmful effects of programmes on children. Some representations of violence, Branston and Stafford (1996) suggest, may even have a positive effect in creating revulsion at certain kinds of assault, or military power or bullying.

Meanwhile, other studies have been conducted into the wider positive effects of television. Some researchers have suggested that prosocial behaviour, such as helping and sharing, can be learnt from various sources, including television. Stein and Friedrich (1975), for example, observed increases in prosocial types of play in young children who watched programmes in which behaviour such as sharing was emphasized (Davies and Houghton, 1991). Presumably, these studies would be open to the same kinds of questions and complications as research into negative effects.

It may seem reasonable to conclude, then, as Braham (1987) does, that there has been little advance beyond the findings of studies as far back as 1948, that 'some kinds of communication, on some kinds of issues, brought to the attention of some kinds of people, under some kinds of conditions, have some kinds of effects'. This may be a result, however, as Lewis (1990) remarks, of the limits of the investigative methods of effects researchers than with television's lack of power and influence.

CULTURAL EFFECTS THEORIES

Cultural effects describe the ways that collective audiences, rather than individual members of an audience, are influenced by the media. In this respect researchers are interested in the defining role of the media on society and culture. Such effects may include stereotyping, moral panics, agenda setting, socialization and, encompassing all of these, the endorsement and reproduction of ideology. There is a fundamental disagreement amongst theorists and researchers as to whether the media, in this respect, act as agencies of social control, imposing dominant class values on subordinate groups (a Marxist perspective), or whether they merely act to reinforce consensual norms and values (a liberal 'pluralist' perspective).

Stereotyping

Although there is much discussion about the possible effects of the media, and even of the very existence of 'effects', at the very least it is generally agreed amongst researchers that the media tend to present a stereotyped view of people and society. This artificial way of presenting types of people whether in, for example, soap operas or in comedy, can affect the way people view different social groups, or themselves (Chapter 11). Evidence of effects might include the massive growth of Ku Klux Klan membership following D.W. Griffiths's *The Birth of a Nation* (1915), which celebrated the Klan's activities against crudely stereotyped black people (usually played by white actors in black face paint) who were shown to be corrupt, ignorant and evil.

Although racist activity in the USA increased dramatically following release of *The Birth of a Nation*, in most cases the effects of stereotyping are regarded as gradual and long-term rather than immediate. Gillian Dyer (1982) writes of advertising in the following terms:

> It is more likely that an advertisement's effects are diffuse and long term, and there is some evidence that advertising plays a part in defining 'reality' in a general or anthropological sense ... for instance, the sex-role stereo-typing common to many advertisements – the 'little woman' as household functionary thrilling to her new polished table or whiter-than-white sheets, or the masterful, adventurous male – acts, many social scientists argue, as an agent of socialisation and leads many people, young and old, to believe in traditional and discriminatory sex roles.

Moral Panics

Jazz, rock and roll, punk rock, feminism, black muggers in the 1970s, welfare scroungers, video nasties, drugs, joyriders, single-parent mothers, falling educational standards and new age travellers are all examples of issues which have been the focus of 'moral panics' in the media. It is the *disproportion* between what takes place and the reaction to it that endows the response with the character of a panic. Hence, although much research shows that general educational standards have risen substantially since the Second World War, the media have been instrumental in perpetuating the myth of falling standards – a useful device for attacking the principle of free, universally available and well-funded comprehensive education. Similarly, the financial cost of welfare fraud is completely dwarfed by the scale of insurance and investment fraud that characterized so much of the 1990s, the cost of which is rarely debated in the media.

Moral panics have tended to occur at times when society has not been able to adapt to dramatic changes, such as during the upheavals of the Industrial Revolution or the modernizing trends of the 1960s. When the old system of values has difficulty explaining new developments, society and individuals within it can experience a sense of loss of control, and in these circumstances single issues can quickly become the focus of fear and 'panic'. Moral panics are usually led by the popular press but are then picked up by the broadcast media as an 'issue of public concern'.

Political Influence of Television

> No Prime Minister can afford to quarrel with the Media because it is difficult to win (Margaret Thatcher).

The fact that, for 20 years, the BBC banned *The War Game*, a dramatization of the effects of a nuclear attack on Britain, and during the same period banned, delayed or doctored more than 50 programmes critical of government policy in Ireland is testimony to a belief in the potential of television for changing people's political opinions.

Politicians are clearly concerned about the political effect of media coverage of their activities. Advertising takes up more than 80 per cent of the campaign expenditure of the major political parties, compared with less than 3 per cent for public meetings. Harold Wilson, a Labour Prime Minister in the 1960s and 1970s, threatened unspecified action against the BBC for alleged anti-Labour bias. Before the 1987 election Norman Tebbit, then the Conservative Party chairman, prepared a dossier seeking to prove anti-government and anti-US bias in the BBC's coverage of the US bombing of Libya the previous year. Alasdair Milne, the BBC's director general, issued a vigorous rebuttal – but a few weeks later he was fired.

Research into the political effects of television has reflected general trends in effects research. Early research conceived of the political influence of television in dramatic terms: capable of 'brainwashing' people to conform to any given message without much questioning about why they do so. George Orwell's novel *1984* reflects some of these assumptions of how television could be used for 'thought control' and was based on Orwell's views of actual totalitarian regimes such as the Soviet Union under Stalin's leadership.

A reaction to this monolithic view of the media and audience reaction, particularly in the area of political influence – such as voting in general elections – took place in the 1950s. Trenaman and McQuail's survey of the 1959 General Election seemed to show that the media affected neither the floating voter nor more stable electors. Floating voters were found to be shielded by their own indifference to, and avoidance of, politics from any media message, whereas loyal voters tended to reinforce their prejudices through what was called 'selective exposure' to political messages.

The 1980s and 1990s have seen the erosion of traditional voting patterns, with working-class loyalty to the Labour Party a major casualty and a new breed of floating voter emerging, less indifferent to parliamentary politics than simply volatile, or unpredictable, in voting behaviour. Under these circumstances the media have been seen by several observers to have a far more crucial role to play in successive election campaigns. Television's 'impartial' role in this process has come into question by a number of critics. In the run up to the 1992 election and with a new director general, John Birt, making changes to news and current-affairs coverage, the BBC was warned by Kenneth Baker, the Home Secretary, in an interview with the *Observer* that they had 'to be very careful over the next eight to ten weeks ... The country expects the BBC to be absolutely impartial as it is a state-funded body' (quoted in Williams, 1994). They had to be careful, as Granville Williams (1994) suggests, not to upset the Conservative Party because the organization was facing an uncertain outcome over negotiations regarding its new charter. ITN was also facing a difficult period as the ITV networks as a whole were facing the rundown of the old ITV franchise system.

Against this background, Williams argues, in 1992 as in 1987, broadcasters appeared to have their agenda set for them by the predominantly Conservative supporting press. He also examines coverage of the economy and the way in which the reporting of financial and city news worked to the disadvantage of Labour in those elections:

> By the end of the 1980s financial and city news had become central areas of media reporting, especially on television. This was one consequence of Conservative promotion of the merits of share ownership, entrepreneurs and business dealing in general. Consequently movements in the City were routinely reported and 'experts' from merchant banks and finance houses were consulted for their apparently neutral opinions on the latest trade or financial news. This gave them an important status as 'impartial commentators'. 'Good news' for them, which they projected through the TV medium, was a healthy stock market and rising shares.

Of course as Labour policies have moved closer to the interests of 'the City', this apparent party bias in television news coverage has disappeared.

Some 20 million people watch the news on television every day. For the whole population, news and current affairs are increasingly responsible for providing our picture of social reality, and it is a picture which many accept as impartial and authoritative. The importance of broadcast media in providing checks and balances against excesses of the state and other powerful interest groups, or of simply providing reliable information for the citizens of a country, is widely recognized. It is television, and not the press, which is relied upon by the majority of people for an 'impartial' perspective. In 1992 an opinion poll commissioned by *The Independent* showed that two-thirds trusted both BBC and ITN to tell the truth, compared with only 29 per cent who believed the newspapers. Williams (1994) quotes from a MORI poll to illustrate this point:

> In *We British: Britain Under the MORIscope*, Bob Worcester and Eric Jacobs asked people what influenced their thinking on a range of key issues and concluded: 'On the vast majority of twenty-four issues, television was chosen by the greatest number of people as having the greatest influence.'

Set against this view is the fact that in 1987 Labour was supposed to have had a great television campaign coordinated by Peter Mandelson who was the Labour Party director of communications, and Labour was widely believed to have won the campaign as a result of the coverage. The Conservative Party thought they had performed so badly on television that the central office held an inquiry into the television campaign, resulting in a highly critical report. However, despite that, the result of the election was that Labour was heavily defeated.

'CULTURAL NORMS'

> The eddies and currents of dissent in popular consciousness find virtually no representation in media interpretations of the world (Westergaard, 1977).

From the 1960s onwards there was a return to the concept of a powerful and influential media and a shift in focus away from short-term influences towards the longer-term effects of the media in consensus, proscribing limits and setting the agenda for political debate. The idea that the media influence our views of social reality by selective presentation and emphasis of information is referred to as the 'cultural norms theory'.

Closely associated with the cultural norms theory, is the process of 'agenda setting' whereby the boundaries, or terms of reference, of a debate are fixed to suit the interests of the dominant power groups in society. Other perspectives may be briefly voiced, but they are usually presented as peripheral, or marginal, to an assumed 'consensus', and are frequently reported negatively. This type of reporting is referred to as 'inoculation' by Barthes, as it allows a small dose of a 'disease' that threatens the existing order to be 'inserted in such a way as to ensure that the social body is strengthened and not threatened by the contrast between it and the radical' (Fiske, 1987).

Hence, road protesters, for example, are rarely given the chance to articulate their point of view fully against the policies of the government. Instead their cause is usually only given television coverage when they are in direct conflict with the police, bailiffs or road constructors. Similarly, the subject of 'animal rights' is only briefly discussed when activists commit a crime or 'outrage' public opinion by threatening animal researchers directly. Although road building and animal experimentation (like nuclear power and other 'environmental concerns') face considerable public opposition, discussion of such topics between activists and senior politicians in the 'respectable' space of a television studio hardly ever takes place. Some critics suggest this type of non-coverage by the media causes these groups to resort to more direct types of conflict to draw any kind of recognition for their cause. In this sense, the media can, ultimately, be seen as providing the 'oxygen of publicity' for terrorism.

The critical approach to media effects suggested by cultural norms and agenda setting regards television as providing an illusory or at least highly compromised platform for genuine democratic debate. The 'dominant discourses' (Chapter 16), in fact, carefully limit and qualify what can and what can *not* be discussed in the public forum of television and the mass media in general. Thus, as Fiske concludes:

> Television does not 'cause' identifiable effects in individuals; it does, however, work ideologically to promote and prefer certain meanings of the world, to circulate some meanings rather than others, and to serve some social interests better than others. This ideological work may be more or less

effective, according to many social factors, but it is always there, and we need to think of it in terms of its effectivity in society at large, not its effects upon specific individuals or groups. 'Effectivity' is a socio-ideological term, 'effect' an individual-behaviourist one.

EXERCISES AND ESSAYS

Exercise

Societies appear to be subject, every now and then, to periods of moral panic. A condition, episode or group of persons emerges to become defined as a threat to society. The moral barricades are manned by editors, bishops, politicians and other right-thinking people.

List as many moral panics as you are aware of. Can they be put under any headings or grouped together in any way? Who exactly 'manned the barricades'? Was television coverage critical or supportive of such 'right-thinking people'?

Essay

This is the age of the moral panic.

Consider in detail a recent moral panic.

Exercise

Every year more research appears on the subject of media effects. Look through newspapers and/or databases of the past 12 months to find summaries of any such research. What, if anything, does such research add to the evidence given in this chapter?

Essay

Answer one of the following three questions:

- David Alton and 100 MPs signed a motion condemning the granting of a certificate for the video release of Oliver Stone's *Natural Born Killers* in the United Kingdom. Alton suggested the film was an advertisement for shooting, burning and killing. What evidence could be produced to support or reject this motion?
- According to the television arts presenter Melvyn Bragg:

  Through self-censorship and well-established practices (Britain's terrestrial channels) are in fact the most regulated television networks in the free world. Coincidentally, they are also the most popular. In ITV, for instance, besides the laws of the land, we have the Independent Television Commission patrolling sex, violence, 'language' and impartiality; the Broadcasting Standards Council as a public appeal court; the Broadcasting Complaints Commission; lawyers inside each of the 15 companies bound to detailed guidelines on the taste and decency of every single programme; and widely observed rules such as the 9pm watershed, which is seen by many parents as a sacred trust.

Is there any justification for such strict controls of television output?

- The technology exists to fit a V-chip – or violence chip – into new television sets to censor brutality, bad language and sex scenes. The chip is operated by remote control whereby parents can set the permissible levels of language, sex and violence on a scale of one to five. Introduction of the technology has been opposed by various groups, including the traditionally conservative National Viewers' and Listeners' Association. What reasons might the NVLA have for opposing the censorship device? What justifications could manufacturers or legislators present for the introduction of this technology?

Sources

Bandura, A., Ross, D. and Ross, S. (1961): Transmission of aggression through imitative learning. *Journal of Abnormal and Social Psychology.*

Barker, M. (1992): Sex, violence and videotape. *Sight and Sound.*

Belson, W. (1978): Television violence and the adolescent boy. Saxon House.

Blumer, J. (1970): The political effects of television. In Halloran, J. (ed.), *The effects of television.* Panther Books.

Bragg, M. (1993): *The Sunday Times Culture Supplement.* 14 March.

Braham, P. (1987): *Media effects.* Open University Press.

Branston, G. and Stafford, R. (1996): *The media student's book.* Routledge.

Burton, G. (1990): *More than meets the eye.* Arnold.

Cantril, H. (1971): The invasion from Mars. In Schramm, W. and Roberts, D. (eds), *The process and effects of mass communication.* University of Illinois Press.

Central Office of Information (1993): *Broadcasting.* HMSO.

Cumberbatch, G. (1989): *The portrayal of violence in BBC television.* BBC Publications.

Curran, J., Gurevitch, M. and Woolacott, J. (eds) (1977): *Mass communication and society.* Arnold.

Davies, R. and Houghton, P. (1991): *Mastering psychology.* Macmillan.

Dyer, G. (1982): *Advertising as communication.* Methuen.

Eron, L. D., Huesmann, L. R., Lefhovitz, M. M. and Walder, L. O. (1972): Does television violence cause aggression? *American Psychologist* **27**.

Eron, L. D. (1987): The development of aggressive behaviour from the perspective of a developing behaviourism. *American Psychologist* **42**.

Fiske, J. (1987): *Television culture.* Routledge.

Furedi, F. (1995): A plague of moral panics. *Living Marxism* November.

Katz, E. and Lazarfield, P. F. (1960): *Personal influence*. The Free Press.

Leapman, M. (1992): The heavy breathers. *The Independent on Sunday*. 1 March.

Lewis, J. (1990): In Goodwin, A. and Whannel, G. (eds), *Understanding television*. Routledge.

Stein, A. and Friedrich, L. (1975): Impact of Television on Children and Youth. In Hetherington, E., Hagen, J., Kron, R. and Stein, A. (eds), *Review of Child Development Research* **5**. University of Chicago Press.

Westergaard, J. (1977): Power, class and the media. In Curran, J. *et al.* (eds), *Mass communication and society*. Arnold.

Williams, G. (1994): *Britain's media – how they are related*. Campaign for Press and Broadcasting Freedom (CPBF).

Winn, M. (1977): *The Plug-in drug*. Penguin Books.

Rupert Murdoch at the launch of Sky's new services. Where now for Public Broadcasting?

14

Public Service Broadcasting and the Future of the BBC

INTRODUCTION

The history of broadcasting in the USA and Britain has, until recent years, been shaped by quite different forces. Commercial imperatives have been virtually the only determinant of US television. British television, by contrast, has operated under relatively strict public service requirements since the 1925 Crawford Committee made its long-term recommendations about the scope and conduct of British broadcasting.

John Reith, the first director general of the BBC, in his presentation to the Crawford Committee, made a vigorous defence of the public service ethos in broadcasting, a defence made in direct contrast to US market-driven philosophy. Scannell (1990) summarizes the main points of Reith's 1925 manifesto for public service broadcasting:

> The service must not be used for entertainment purposes alone. Broadcasting had a responsibility to bring into the greatest possible number of homes in the fullest degree all that was best in every department of human knowledge, endeavour and achievement. The preservation of a high moral tone – the avoidance of the vulgar and the hurtful – was of paramount importance. Broadcasting should give a lead to public taste rather than pander to it: 'He who prides himself on giving what he thinks the public wants is often creating a fictitious demand for lower standards which he himself will then satisfy.'

Reith's view of the general public has been widely criticized as paternalistic. Reith sought to 'educate' and elevate his audience's tastes away from the 'popular' and 'vulgar', particularly imported US material which he regarded as a corrosive influence. Under Reith the gulf between 'high' and 'low' culture remained unbridgeably wide with 'low' (popular) culture effectively denied recognition in the public realm of broadcasting.

The creation of ITV in 1955, a commercial channel funded by advertising, forced the BBC to respond to its collapsing ratings with a more populist content and open style of presentation. The changes at the BBC, generally agreed to be improvements in quality, sprung from the sudden realization that its audience would not tolerate being force fed the kind of 'improving' programming they had endured for years if there was an alternative. Nevertheless, Scannell suggests that ITV, created with significant public interest responsibilities and 'subject to state regulation and control by an authority charged with maintaining high standards of programme quality ... was an extension of public service broadcasting, not an alternative' (Scannell, 1990).

The 1960 Pilkington Committee report, and both the government's and the broadcasters' response to its conclusions, provides solid evidence that ITV was subject to stringent public service requirements. The Committee concluded that ITV and the regulatory body ITA had confused 'quality with box office success' and had 'failed to live up to (their) responsibilities as a public service' in their programming (O'Sullivan et al., 1994). As a result the eagerly awaited third channel was awarded to the BBC, which launched BBC2 in 1964.

Commercial television had to wait a further 18 years before it was awarded the fourth terrestrial channel. The Annan Report, published in 1977, had found BBC and ITV broadcasting to be a cosy 'duopoly' that no longer reflected the diversity of tastes, interests and needs of an increasingly diverse society (Scannell, 1990). The imaginative conclusion was to create a fourth channel that would provide programmes with a distinctive character appealing to tastes and interests not generally catered for by the other channels. Once again, public service ideals seemed to underpin broadcasting legislation with Channel 4's remit to 'present a suitable proportion of educational programmes and encourage innovation and experiment' (Central Office of Information, 1993).

However, as Stevenson (1995) notes, since the end of the 1970s notions of public service broadcasting have been showing signs of crisis. World economic recession, the rise of the New Right and attendant public spending cuts, combined with the arrival of new technologies capable of global penetration have opened new cultural markets for private investors and weakened government commitments to public service ideals.

Of course, changes to the existing broadcasting system could not be carried out overnight, even under the free market zeal of Mrs Thatcher's Conservative administration. British television was widely admired around the world and the disastrous experience of deregulating Italian television, with its degrading strip quiz shows often quoted as typical of what to expect in a broadcasting free-for-all, served as brake to the kind of developments advocated by ultra-Conservative 'think tanks' such as the Adam Smith Institute and the Institute of Economic Affairs.

The Peacock Committee (1986) served to test the water of public opinion by advocating the eventual destruction of public service television. The Peacock report's suggestions for a three-stage transition towards a free market in broadcasting, including the introduction of advertising and a 40 per cent 'independently' (i.e. commercially) produced programming target for the BBC predictably caused uproar. Nevertheless, the report, in a sense, served its political purpose by softening the general public and Parliament to the more limited, but nevertheless revolutionary, changes contained in the 1990 Broadcasting Act and its subsequent amendments.

PUBLIC SERVICE V. COMMERCIAL BROADCASTING

Subscription systems make access to cultural and information resources conditional on ability to pay, creating a substantial strata of people who are locked out of the new cultural and information marketplaces – an exclusion that represents a reduction in their rights as citizens. Because a television set is the one major consumer durable that almost every household has, public broadcasting is central to the safeguarding of these rights (Murdock, 1991).

Public service broadcasting has been viewed throughout its history in two lights. Those who defend the principle claim that broadcasting has a crucial role in the development of an informed and educated public who can make a mature and reasoned contribution to a democratic society. This is a view of the media as 'a liberating force for human enlightenment and progress, informing, entertaining, nurturing creative talent and being financially and editorially independent from powerful vested commercial or political interests' (Williams, 1994).

The second view of public service broadcasting comes from those who argue that commercial forces will ultimately provide the best broadcasting service. Public service broadcasting, according to this view, is a restriction of the freedom of the market. The tight regulations under which the BBC and ITV operated until 1990 – with responsibilities to 'inform, educate and entertain' the public – were condemned as restrictive and monopolistic. Public service principles in broadcasting, according to its critics, created an elitist system, closed to new voices and deaf to the wishes of viewers. This, to some extent, was the view of the Conservative government and the Peacock Committee in the run up to the 1990 Broadcasting Act.

THE BRITISH BROADCASTING SYSTEM

Broadcasting in Britain comes from two sources: the public sector British Broadcasting Corporation (BBC) and the commercial 'independent' industry.

The BBC is the largest UK-owned media organization. Its television interests include two national channels (BBC1 and BBC2) attracting 44 per cent of average viewing figures (Peake, 1992) the international World Service and the teletext channel Ceefax.

In the United Kingdom there is tight state regulation of public and private sector television (as there is of all broadcasting). Commercially financed television, satellite and cable services operating within Britain are regulated under the National Heritage Department by the Independent Television Commission (ITC). The BBC is authorized to regulate its own programming, although indirect and direct political pressure is exerted by the governing party, which ultimately controls the BBC's finances by setting the level of licence fee. Such pressure is frequently seen, especially in relation to coverage of 'controversial issues' such as Northern Ireland, labour relations and the dominant political parties.

THE 1990 BROADCASTING ACT

The BBC chairman Marmaduke Hussey has described the post-1990 period as 'the third era of broadcasting' (BBC, 1992) – the first being from the BBC's origins in the 1920s until the start of ITV in 1955 and the second from then until the 1990 Broadcasting Act. Many within the industry have described the new era as one of 'deregulation', 'casualization' and 'commercialization'.

The origins of this new era can be traced to the launch of Channel 4 in 1984. Channel 4 was radical in that it created a new industrial model in British broadcasting: the publishing house. This change from 'integrated-factory pro-duction to the publisher model' (Tunstall, 1993) allowed the rapid growth of an initially tiny independent production sector. By the late 1980s this sector was strong enough for the government to set a 25 per cent independent production target for ITV, which became a legal obligation (for the BBC as well) in the 1990 Act.

The Act was based on findings of the 1986 Peacock Report. The free market economist Alan Peacock made two key recommendations that were taken up by the Act:

- the sealed bid auctioning of the ITV licences and the opening of the holders to the takeover market;
- an independent production target for the BBC and ITV.

Peacock's 40 per cent production target, one apparently 'plucked from the air' by the Committee, was reduced to 25 per cent following intense lobbying and the 1988 House of Commons Home Affairs Committee inquiry into broad-casting. Other proposals made by the Peacock Report were also watered down, but the Act still transformed British broadcasting.

The principal aims of the Act – to encourage the private sector and break up the 'comfortable duopoly' of ITV and BBC – can be seen in the changes made by the legislation.

Changes introduced by the Act:
- Both the BBC and commercial licensees were required to commission at least 25 per cent of their original television programmes (except news-related output) from independent companies by 1993–94.
- ITV franchises were to be decided by auction – the bids presented by the competing companies in sealed envelopes to the ITC, subject to certain quality thresholds.
- Some of the ITV's public service obligations were lifted. The new ITV licences no longer required the ITV network to show current-affairs programmes or documentaries at peak time, or *News at Ten* at 10 pm. Obligations to transmit religious programming on Sundays were relaxed.
- Channel 4 became a public corporation selling its own advertising time. This put it in direct competition with ITV and subjected it to direct commercial pressure by ending its guaranteed income from the network.
- The Independent Broadcasting Authority (IBA), with its direct involvement in scheduling, was replaced by the 'lighter regulatory touch' of the Independent Television Commission (ITC). The major change was from a system which included pre-vetting of programmes and schedules to one of monitoring services regulated in the first instance by the licensees themselves.
- Opportunities were provided for a new national independent television station (Channel 5). The new channel would have similar, though less stringent, programming requirements to 'Channel 3', although it would not be required to show either regional or local programmes.
- Provisions for, potentially, hundreds of local television stations. Licences to be awarded by competitive tender without quality thresholds. 'Proper persons' eligible to hold licences were to include religious groups.
- The IBA's television transmission networks were privatized and transferred to a new company, National Transcommunications Limited (NTL).

Nevertheless, even a government ideologically committed to the free market recognized the dangers of a wholly deregulated system. The value of public service broadcasting, particularly that of the highly respected BBC, was admitted. It was further recognized that advertising would not provide sufficient funding for the BBC and would jeopardize the financial stability of the ITV companies. Hence:

- Despite radical changes to the organizations themselves, the essential programming remits and public service responsibilities of the BBC and Channel 4 remained *unchanged*.
- Safeguards to prevent 'undue concentration of ownership' were extended. Non-European-Community organizations were prevented from gaining a

controlling interest in domestic television licences (not including local licences or, vitally, satellite services not using British broadcasting frequencies). A 20 per cent maximum stake in DBS channels by national newspapers was fixed.

- Welsh and Gaelic language and culture were to continue to be promoted in the form of direct government assistance to S4C (Wales) and a small Gaelic Television Fund.
- A Broadcasting Standards Council (BSC) was established in 1988 to 'act as a focus for public concern about the portrayal of violence and sex, and about standards of taste and decency'. The BSC monitors programmes, examines complaints from the public and undertakes research. The BSC has drawn up a code of practice which the BBC and other broadcast bodies are legally obliged to reflect in their own codes of conduct. The BSC works alongside the Broadcasting Complaints Commission (BCC) which was established in 1981 to deal with complaints of unfair treatment in broadcast programmes and of unwarranted infringement of privacy in programmes or in their making.

INITIAL CONSEQUENCES OF THE ACT

Auctions for the ITV licences in 1991 witnessed successful bids by existing companies for as little as £1000 (Channel Television). This was not an isolated case – Scottish Television and Central TV both made successful offers of £2000 knowing there would be no rival bids.

Some 3 of the 15 regional companies, however, were successfully outbid and lost their licences. Carlton Television's huge £43,000,000 bid for the London weekday franchise previously held by Thames effectively saw the destruction of the company that had enraged Mrs Thatcher by producing *Death on the Rock*, an investigative documentary about the shooting of Irish Republican Army (IRA) suspects in Gibraltar. Concerns that the size of Carlton's bid would mean a reduction in the quality of programming have, according to most critics, been borne out by Carlton's downmarket schedules. A major criticism of the Act has been that it creates instability and unnecessary commercial pressure in the market by forcing the companies to generate massive cash sums for the franchise bids. This shifts the focus of attention away from the needs of the viewers to the needs of the advertisers – the source of the independent broadcasters' finance.

The other two companies to lose their regional franchises were TVS Television and TSW broadcasting who were outbid by Meridian and Westcountry Television, respectively. Perhaps the biggest surprise of the ITC awards, though, was when TVam lost the franchise for national breakfast television to GMTV with its £35,000,000 bid. TVam, which had led the field in deunionizing television broadcasting, was sacrificed in the auctioning process – drawing, for the first time ever, a written apology from Mrs Thatcher to TVam's director Bruce Gyngell.

The Act *failed to prevent* an almost immediate increased concentration of ownership. A series of mergers followed the passing of the legislation:

- Carlton took over Central TV (and its 20 per cent stake in Meridian);
- Yorkshire and Tyne Tees merged;
- Meridian and Anglia merged;
- Granada made a 'hostile bid' for LWT.

For many observers the takeovers and mergers that followed the Broadcasting Act are part of a longer-term break-up of ITV's federal system, a system no longer suited to the 'cut-throat commercialism' of the 1990s. Georgina Henry, writing in the *Guardian*, predicts:

> Already marginalised small ITV companies, like Ulster, Westcountry, Border, Grampian and Channel, will find their influence in ITV reduced still further, while the pressure will grow for the 15 region ITV 'map' to be redrawn into four or five mega-regions.

The Campaign for Press and Broadcasting Freedom goes further in predicting that two companies, possibly Carlton and Granada, will come to dominate the entire network. The 'commercial logic' of such a development in the face of giant international entertainment conglomerates appears irresistible to many within British broadcasting institutions.

The gradual abandonment of controls of ownership predicted by some critics following the 1990 Act seem to be partly borne out by subsequent amendments to the legislation. From 1 January 1994, for example, the government relaxed the ITV ownership rules to allow a company to hold any two regional licences (except in London), a 20 per cent stake in a third company and 5 per cent in any further licences.

The BBC, meanwhile, according to the National Viewers' and Listeners' Association, 'has cut and restructured itself far more radically than required by the Broadcasting Act' under Sir John Birt's marketing ethos. The obligation to find a minimum of 25 per cent of output from independent producers, 'contracting out' for cheaper services under 'producer choice' (1993) and a widescale 'rationalization' of BBC's production base has resulted in training cutbacks, job losses and short-term contracts for staff.

This has mirrored deskilling, deunionization, increased hours, wage cuts and widespread unemployment throughout the television industry. According to Williams (1994):

> A survey of employment and salaries in the trade magazine, *Broadcast*, summed it up for those working in the industry: 'For the senior elite, big bucks whether they won the franchises or were dismissed; for thousands, the sack whether the company won or lost; and for the majority who have

hung on to their jobs, more insecurity and the tightest squeeze on their wage packets for a long time.' The same issue of the magazine also has a news item that Carlton Communication's chairman, Michael Green, received bonuses on top of his £424,705 to push his income to £631,705 in 1993.

The consequence of Channel 4 becoming self-funding has been a continued move away from minority broadcasting towards more mainstream programming such as US sitcoms. The lifting of some of ITV's public service commitments has seen commercial pressures increasingly affecting certain types of programmes (news, documentaries and religious programming, in particular). These pressures may be responsible for the ever-growing popularity of US models and formats in, for instance, factual programming, daytime and chat shows, news, sports coverage and workplace dramas.

Murdoch's Sky TV (a non-UK satellite operation) was allowed to operate without the same technical, ownership and regulatory restrictions as BSB and thereby gained a vital advantage over its competitor which many critics regard as a major factor in BSB's failure and eventual takeover. In the view of Williams (1994) government inaction with regard to the threat from Murdoch's media empire was understandable: 'Sky was a more comfortable option for the Tories, rather than an organisation like BSB, founded on public service broadcasting principles.'

PUBLIC SERVICE V. COMMERCIAL BROADCASTING POST-1990

When you switch on your TV/PC in the year 2010, I fear BBC1 will not appear as it does now. In all probability, someone will pop up trying to sell you something (Birt, 1996).

The 1990 Broadcasting Act favours competition and limited regulation. It has split broadcasters between commercial television (ITV, cable and satellite) and public service broadcasting (BBC1, BBC2 and Channel 4). It can be seen as a partial, possibly temporary, compromise between public service broadcasting and commercial pressures, but has unleashed commercial pressures that make the long-term dismantling of public service broadcasting in Britain far more likely.

Barnett and Docherty (1986) identify eight basic principles and conditions for the existence of public service broadcasting. These principles are:

- geographic universality – broadcast programmes should be available to the whole population;
- universality of appeal – broadcast programmes should cater for all tastes and interests;

- universality of payment – at least one main broadcasting organization should be paid for equally by all users of television;
- broadcasting should be distanced from all vested interests, and in particular from those of the government of the day;
- broadcasters should recognize their special relationship to the sense of national identity and community;
- minorities, especially disadvantaged minorities, should receive special provision;
- broadcasting should be structured so as to encourage competition in good programming rather than competition in numbers;
- the public guidelines for broadcasting should be designed to liberate rather than restrict the programme makers.

Each of these features is under threat in one way or another in broadcasting's 'third age'. Broadcasting is increasingly falling into the hands of powerful commercial structures, multinationals and media corporations with vested political interests. Williams (1994) uses the graphic example of the Italian elections in March 1994 to illustrate this point:

> Silvio Berlusconi used his three TV stations, with 40% of the Italian audience, and other media interests, unremittingly to boost support for his Forza Italia and the wider right of the centre grouping – the Freedom alliance – that were virtually created from thin air. His media group, Finivest, is part of a new phenomenon abroad in Europe and globally – media conglomerates which can deploy awesome power to promote policies and political parties most favourable to their business interests.

In addition to the growing levels of information management by such groups in the pursuit of commercial objectives, previously critical voices in broadcasting have been silenced by business and political pressures. The political silencing has come in the form of 'conservative' appointments to the Board of Governors at the BBC, and the subsequent choice of Birt as director general, to the thinly veiled threats by a succession of governments to reduce or remove the licence fee if the BBC 'steps out of line' and appears too 'critical' on an issue such as government corruption or, indeed, any topic on the political agenda. As John Pilger, a journalist who has worked in broadcasting for many years, remarks:

> Today BBC current affairs is seldom controversial as it is secured within a pyramid of 'directorates' that have little to do with free journalism and are designed to control: to shore up assumptions, not to challenge them. In any case, silence is no longer optional in the increasingly centralised, undemocratic state that is the other side of the media society. As the market has been 'freed' from state controls (i.e. nineteenth century laissez-faire nostrums have been reimposed), so information has been subjected to draconian new controls (Pilger, 1992).

Before the 1990 Act broadcasting universally available throughout the country was pursued by the BBC and IBA with very little regard to commercial considerations. Scannell gives as an example the building of 65 new transmitting stations by the BBC in order to extend its service from 99 per cent of the population to 99.1 per cent. However, the new reality is likely to be, as Scannell (1990) suggests:

> Where commercial motives are primary broadcasters will go only for the most profitable markets – which lie in densely populated urban areas that can deliver large audiences without difficulty. The markets for cabled services are likely to prove even more selective: the affluent districts of major towns and cities will be wired up, while the poorer areas will be neglected. More sparsely populated, remoter areas will be ignored entirely.

The consequences for audiences, communities and cultures of the weakening of public service commitments are only now emerging. Stevenson suggests that the current importance of transnational media has accelerated the process of depoliticization and eroded allegiances to the national community:

> In Britain, national public service broadcasting has always been tied to notions of democracy, Englishness and nationhood. Reith's original conception of public service broadcasting was based on the principles of universality and equality of access, as well as the desire to educate the populace while binding them together in a nationally imagined community. The initial impact of commercial broadcasting was to undermine the cosy reverential disposition of the BBC towards the British state, but the end result seems to have been an enhancement of commercial forms of culture over the promotion of political identities. Current indications are that a relatively stable nationally articulated identity has been at least partially displaced by a more fluid, fragmented and shifting construction (Stevenson, 1995).

As for the pluralistic ideals championed by the Annan Committee – the public service broadcasting requirement to cater for a variety of cultures, tastes and minorities – these are also threatened by the commercial logic of the marketplace that values either mass audiences or wealthy niche audiences. In the place of mixed programming there is generic programming which fragments and atomizes audiences, destroying 'the principle of equality of access to all entertainment and informational resources in a common public domain' (Scannell, 1990).

Finally, the notion of a system run on guidelines which liberate without restricting programme makers – promoting competition in good programming, not audience figures – seems hopelessly idealistic in the post-1990 world. Williams picks out several examples of the changing values of broadcasters in the book *Britain's media*, but the example of documentary, and particularly the excellent and popular *World in Action*, is pertinent to this point and, in fact, reaches to the heart of the debate on public service broadcasting:

> Paul Jackson, Director of Programmes at Carlton, is clear about the value of challenging investigative current affairs programmes in the new, commercial ITV world where money means ratings. In an interview with the *Daily Telegraph* in May 1992 he said, 'If *World in Action* were in 1993 to uncover three more serious miscarriages of justice while delivering an audience of three, four or five million, I would cut it. It isn't part of the ITV system to get people out of prison.' He added, 'There is not going to be the latitude to find excuses for programmes which are not rating six, seven or eight million in primetime.' We should pause at this point to remind ourselves that an audience of five million is more than double the combined circulation of the *Telegraph*, *Guardian*, *Times* and *Independent* (Williams, 1994).

EXERCISES AND ESSAYS

Exercise

Write a brief manifesto for and/or against a broadcasting system determined by the free market.

Exercise

> The BBC had to compete to survive and has done so. Sometimes it has competed by formulaic programming, by copying, by buying from the competition programme-makers to whom it would not have given house room 30 years ago (Hoggart, 1995).

Look at the BBC's schedules for a week and find three examples of the type of programming described above by Richard Hoggart and three examples of programmes which you regard as meeting public service broadcasting ideals. Briefly outline your reasons for selecting these programmes in each case.

Essay

> Across Western Europe, these [public service broadcasting] institutions were perceived as paternalistic in their programme output, they tended to ignore the growing pluralistic and multicultural character of their own societies, and they were generally stagnant and in need of creative renewal (Dahlgren, 1995).

Changes to the British broadcasting system in the 1990s are a response to such criticisms. Do you agree?

Essay

What is public service broadcasting? To what extent have the principles of public service broadcasting come under threat in Britain in recent years?

Essay

A nation divided has the BBC on the rack.

Why? Is there any evidence for this view? (see also Chapter 9).

Exercise and Essay

What developments do you see in public service broadcasting in the next 10 years?

Essay

Public service broadcasting as envisaged by Lord Reith, if not dead, is in terminal decline.

How far do you think this is so?

Essay

How successful is contemporary British broadcasting (television and/or radio) in upholding the standards of public service broadcasting?

Essay

The basic choice is between a view of the organisation [the BBC] as a central guarantor of culture and information rights, addressing its viewers as citizens of a complex democracy, or as a quasi-commercial entity, relating to its audiences as customers and honorary shareholders (Murdock, 1991).

Which choice has the BBC made in recent years?

Sources

Barnett, S. and Docherty, D. (1986): *Public service broadcasting: crisis or crossroads?* Media Information Australia.

BBC (1992): *BBC 1991/1992 annual report.* BBC Publications.

Birt, J. (1996): Gateway to the BBC's Future. James MacTaggart Memorial Lecture, Edinburgh, August.

Branston, G. and Stafford, R. (1996): *The media student's book.* Routledge.

Central Office of Information (1993): *Broadcasting.* HMSO.

Dahlgren, P. (1995): *Television and the public sphere.* Sage.

Gration, G. (1992): *Communication and media studies.* W.W. Nelson.

Hoggart, R. (1995): Why treat us like dimwits? *Independent on Sunday* February.

Murdock, G. (1991): Whose television is it anyway? *Sight and Sound* October.

O'Sullivan, T., Dutton, B. and Rayner, P. (1994): *Studying the media – an introduction.* Arnold.

Peake, S. (1992): *The Media Guide 1993.* Fourth Estate.

Pilger, J. (1992): *Distant Voices.* Vintage.

Scannell, P. (1990): Public service broadcasting: the history of a concept. In Goodwin, A. and
    Whannel, G. (eds), *Understanding television.* Routledge.

Stevenson, N. (1995): *Understanding media cultures.* Sage.

Tunstall, J. (1993): *Television producers.* Routledge.

Williams, G. (1994): *Britain's media – how they are related.* Campaign for Press and
    Broadcasting Freedom (CPBF).

Life after television?

15

New Technology

TELEVISION

Televisions and video recorders both sold spectacularly well as they emerged as new consumer durables. They offered a perfect form of entertainment for societies with rising incomes, particularly as the nuclear family replaced the extended family as the norm.

Boom sales of televisions occurred in the USA and Britain throughout the 1950s, with a corresponding fall in cinema attendance. Relatively affluent families spent their disposable income on making the home more comfortable and on new leisure activities. Combining these desires, the television was status furniture and technology that brought entertainment into the living room, as the radio had done in the two preceding decades.

As television technology improved and became cheaper it gradually became available to millions of homes. *Colour* was introduced gradually in the USA through the 1950s but in Britain it did not arrive until 1969. Several competing television systems have been developed around the world. North, Central and parts of South America use the NTSC colour system on 525 lines whereas Britain, Central Europe, much of Africa and Asia use the German PAL standard on 625 lines UHV (ultra-high frequency).

High-definition and Digital Television

Various high-definition television (HDTV) systems offering better picture quality have been developed but, like all new technologies, they face high costs to introduce into the market. More than 60 European organizations are currently collaborating on the development of a 1250-line HDTV wide-screen system with the participation of 13 other countries. National Transcommunications Limited (NTL), the privatized body now responsible for transmitting ITV's services, is leading the development of satellite transmissions of HDTV and the BBC is leading the group responsible for developing the multichannel digital sound system that will be used (Central Office of Information, 1993).

In May 1996 Britain's two largest television operators, the BBC and BSkyB, announced that they were 'going digital'. BBC director general John Birt outlined a digital 'manifesto' that included 24-hour news, themed channels and wide-screen programming. Meanwhile, BSkyB chief executive Sam Chisholm promised a staggering 500 channels, with the first phase of digital satellite starting in the autumn of 1997. The reason for the BBC's and BSkyB's enthusiasm for such a costly enterprise is that the move from analogue to digital is accompanying a general European move towards pay-TV. Pay-TV, worth about US$6.2 billion in 1996, is due to expand in value to around US$15 billion by 2005 – around the same size as today's European television advertising market.

As Emily Bell (1996) notes, however, the real cost of pay-TV may be very high, with football matches, for example, costing US$6–US$8 to watch:

> Over the past five years, televisual sporting rights in Europe have been subject to something like 800 per cent inflation. Finding the cash to cover this investment means putting your hand deep into the consumer's pocket. Squeezing the paying public until the pips squeak is the price of investment in a digital infrastructure.

A ferocious struggle for control of the satellite space and decoder technology is already under way, with the Bertelsmann group reported to be investing more than US$1 billion in making and marketing its decoding 'box' against another German media conglomerate, Kirch, and its rival system:

> The vital gateway into the home in the digital age will be controlled by those who own means of delivery into the home: the navigation system which helps the consumer locate what is available; the encryption system which encodes and decodes the services; the subscriber or transaction management system which extracts payments for services used – probably all contained in a single set-top box. The battle for control and a share of the enormous economic value passing through that gateway will be one of the great business battles shaping the next century, to rival the 19th century battle for the railroad or the 20th century battle for office software systems (Birt, 1996).

In December 1996 the BBC admitted it was powerless to prevent BSkyB's effective monopoly of the set-top box decoders, subscription management technology and electronic programme guides needed to navigate viewers through the multichannel world. The Department of Trade and Industry insisted, despite the BBC's protest, that Mr Murdoch should be rewarded for his risk-taking. The BBC had argued for set-top boxes to contain a common interface for all broadcasters. Sir Christopher Bland, the BBC's chairman, said that the BBC had been unable to develop its own boxes because it could not spend licence income on risk ventures. Sir Christopher, arguing the abuse of power that Murdoch's monopoly posed, claimed: 'In the United States you would not be allowed to own the digital satellite technology when you are a substantial provider of programmes' (Culf, 1996).

VIDEO

The major technological development to accompany television in the past 40 years has been the introduction of video. Video recording technology was used from the 1950s by broadcasters and as domestic 'video cassette recorders' (VCRs) which sold in vast numbers throughout the 1980s. In the early 1970s as VCRs were being developed there were three rival systems: Philips V2000 (which was quickly scrapped), Sony Betamax and JVC VHS. Reliable domestic VCRs were being produced by 1978 using the VHS (Video Home System) and Betamax systems. Following a period of fierce competition in the early 1980s the VHS system emerged as the domestic market leader and Sony's Betamax, which captured only 10 per cent of the market, was finally bought out (despite Betamax's reputation for better picture quality) by the rival Japanese multi-national Matsushita (JVC/Panasonic). The suggestion that Betamax was a better system is given further credence by the fact that Sony's technology is still used by professional broadcasters.

Videos only emerged as a mass-consumer item when pre-recorded movies became available from the new video rental shops. In 1983, 18 per cent of households had a video, but by 1988 penetration had jumped to 50 per cent. In 1994 77 per cent of British households had a video machine. More than 520 million VCRs had been sold worldwide by 1996, but the development of digital videodisc players, or DVDs, may soon see the demise of this technology. DVDs play standard-size compact discs (CDs) containing high-resolution moving images and sound, and 'writable' (that is, recordable) discs are expected on the market in 1998. Computer manufacturers will build DVD-ROM drives into some of their computers, allowing far greater compatibility than was previously possible so that, for instance, DVD encyclopaedias could feature full-screen, full-motion videos instead of still images. According to Fumio Sato, the president of Toshiba, the Japanese computer company which along with Time Warner is developing the system: 'DVD technology will be a key to the expanding multimedia world.'

However, the video compression chips that make DVDs possible are also the key component in the direct-broadcast satellite business, and computer manufacturers are developing the capability for personal computers (PCs) to receive video programmes directly from satellites. Hence, manufacturers of DVD players may find the market for purchasing or hiring films greatly reduced by developments in 'pay-TV'.

TELETEXT

The BBC and IBA cooperated in the development of teletext – information broadcast on pages which can be read on their own or superimposed over a television programme. The BBC's Ceefax and ITV's Oracle services are teletext systems offering a variety of news, entertainment and information 'pages' on receivers equipped with the necessary decoders. These include a subtitling service for the hard of hearing, available for a limited number of programmes. Since April 1992 the BBC Ceefax television and radio pages have been produced by a private company, Intelfax. Over 40 per cent of households in Britain have teletext sets and over 7 million people turn to the service daily (more than the circulation figures for most daily newspapers). Teletext's major limitation is that it is a 'one-way' service, as no information can be fed into the system by those using it.

VIEWDATA

Viewdata differs from teletext in that it is not broadcast but transmitted by wire or cable. As a result viewdata systems such as British Telecom's 'Prestel' service are 'two-way' (interactive) technologies combining the television, computer and telephone. According to Hughes (1990) Prestel is a *public* viewdata system with access open to anyone willing to pay the running costs. He contrasts this to the various *private* viewdata systems available and used by wealthy individuals and organizations, such as the Stock Exchange (for financial information), travel agents (for holiday bookings) and retailers and manufacturers (communicating sales and deliveries required).

CABLE, SATELLITE AND THE INFORMATION SUPERHIGHWAY

Recent advances in television technology lie in the fields of satellite broadcasting, fibre optics and computerization. The replacement of the vacuum tube, initially with transistors and then by the microchip (with the capacity of millions of vacuum tubes on single slivers of silicon costing less than a dollar to make), has been perhaps the most significant technological step, allowing the development of video recorders, personal computers and most of the technology of the so-called 'information society'. As George Gilder explains, the vacuum tube necessitated the use of analogue systems requiring the television system's 'intelligence' – shaping sequencing, and storing picture signals – to be located at the broadcasting centre and not in the television receiver. Gilder describes this in electronic terms as a top-down or 'master–slave' architecture. Spectrum scarcity forced television to adopt a centralized system, limited to relatively few channels, with no two-way communication.

The development of the microchip, fibre-optics and digital transmission meant that:

Intelligence could move from the broadcast station into inexpensive home-based personal computers. The PC would eventually be able to manipulate video signals at the user's will, zooming in and out, performing replays, storing and even editing pictures. This video-processing power at the set would greatly reduce the need for complex and costly equipment at the event to be broadcast or at the broadcast station. A concert or sports event could be taped, for example, with just four video cameras, and then transmitted to give the viewer a 360-degree image that could be shaped at the PC. The choice now made by broadcasters at the event could be made at home through a viewer's mouse, handheld remote control, or even voice (Gilder, 1992).

Cable

The 1980s and 1990s witnessed an explosion in worldwide satellite and cable television broadcasting. Rupert Murdoch's Star TV satellite network alone reaches a global population of 300 million, and 5.3 million homes in Britain are now connected via cable or satellite dish to BSkyB (Bell, 1996). Fibre optics have revolutionized communications – not least in cable television. 'Cable' was first introduced over 40 years ago in areas that experienced poor radio and television reception. 'Fibre optic' cable, however, can carry potentially hundreds of television channels, telephone and computer services.

Until 1983 British cable companies could only relay broadcast television and radio material. However, the development of ultra-high-frequency (UHF) broadcasting and the public-service-motivated building of transmitters for remote areas made it easier to receive good quality broadcast transmissions around the country and by the early 1980s effectively left no role for cable systems within existing British legislation. The 1984 Cable and Broadcasting Act allowed cable companies to provide channels other than domestically broadcast stations and exposed the previously protected UK cable market to competition from powerful foreign (mainly US) media and communications corporations. Broadband cable franchises which permit cable companies to transmit up to 40 'acceptable' domestic or foreign channels to (mainly urban) areas are now awarded to the highest bidders by the ITC. That 'acceptable' should include the degrading spectacle of 'topless darts' (L!VE TV) is a measure of government disinterest in public service or even public interest regulatory policy.

Cable television has had a slow start in Britain, with only about 800,000 connected nationwide and 50 channels available in 1996, but growth is outstripping satellite and by 1998 it is expected that more homes will have cable than dishes. It is further estimated that 7 billion pounds will be spent on cable in Britain this century with around 5 million homes subscribing to cable television and telephone services by the year 2000. Interactive services such as home shopping, home banking, security and alarm services, electronic mail and remote meter readings will also be possible. Bizarrely, however, as British Telecom is specifically forbidden from offering broadcast entertainment down its telephone lines there is little incentive to lay down a national bidirectional fibre optic grid. Most of the franchises in the major conurbations have now been taken by US-based companies such as Nynex and Telewest (United Artists) who are using a patchwork of technologies including unidirectional cable suitable only for receiving broadcast material.

According to Williams these companies are using their marketing expertise developed in the USA to build a large number of subscribers to strengthen their negotiating hand over access to and the costs of programming:

> Cable Programming Partners One (CPPI), a consortium made up of Nynex, Comcast, Southwestern Bell, US West and TCI won exclusive rights for the 1996 Cricket World Cup for 7.5 million pounds – a massive leap from the 1 million pounds paid by BSkyB for the 1992 World Cup. The stations hope that showing the series will boost subscriptions to cable as happened with satellite – dish sales doubled at the last tournament. The deal negotiator, Bruce Smith, said, 'We are interested in "break-through events", employing the same marketing techniques Rupert Murdoch used to get Sky off the ground.'

Williams cautions that:

> Such hugely expensive deals threaten the ability of the BBC and even ITV companies to cover major national and international sporting events . . . Furthermore the insatiable demand for programming to fill the massive expansion of channels is likely to lead to a damaging price war, and accelerate the pace of mergers amongst ITV companies, or even alliances with cable companies, as they are forced to compete against cable channels as they pick up more and more subscribers in the mid to late 90s. It also, of course, threatens the BBC's ability to buy programmes if it doesn't have the funds to compete in this cut-throat battle (Williams, 1994).

Interactive Technology

Cable has already been extensively installed in the USA (64 per cent have access) and parts of Europe permitting a range of cable television services, telephone and, more recently, interactive computer communications. But this process is by no means confined to the Western world. It is estimated, for example, that 50 million people worldwide are logging on to computer networks at work, dialling on-line information services and chatting on electronic bulletin boards. The Internet, founded in 1969 to send data between two defence laboratories, is today only one amongst many loosely linked networks capable of sending information and moving images across the world.

As for the future, a range of communications technologies, including television, video, the telephone, CD music systems and the computer are rapidly merging to create new, more 'interactive' media. Examples of this include the US company Bell Atlantic's 'Stargazer' experiment with a video request service relayed via telephone to subscribers in Virginia and the so-called 'shopping channels' such as QVC which sell directly into the home to viewers linked by phone and credit card. More advanced systems being pioneered by Bell Atlantic, Viacom, SEGA and a variety of companies using bidirectional cable and digital compression systems include virtual shopping malls, educational links between remote communities, interactive games, video phones, digitally relayed music, on-line communications to doctors' surgeries, electronic newspapers and all the services of the so-called 'information superhighway'.

As George Gilder (1992) remarks in his essay *Life after television* in which he celebrates the new technology now available:

> No longer is there any justification for allowing television to hog the spectrum. No longer is there any reason for video to use a vulnerable, complex, inefficient, and unmanipulable signal. No longer is there any logic in leaving the brains of the system at the station. The age of television, for all intents and purposes, is over .... The new system will be the tele-computer, or 'teleputer', a personal computer adapted for video processing and connected by fiber-optic threads to other teleputers all around the world. Using a two-way system of signals like telephones do, rather than broadcasting one-way like TV, the teleputer will surpass the television in video communication just as the telephone surpassed the telegraph in verbal communication.

Evidence for this view emerges every month. In June 1997 Bill Gates's Microsoft made a US$1 billion investment in Comcast, a cable television company. This followed Microsoft's purchase of WebTV, which makes devices allowing television to access the Internet. Some critics portray the interactive future as either a battle to the death between the PC and TV or as one where the two devices merge. More likely, however, is a future in which different technologies coexist but share content, software and infrastructure. The whole notion of 'television' as the medium we understand it to be today is therefore likely to be radically challenged in the near future.

NEW TECHNOLOGY – ACCESS AND OWNERSHIP

> This is the multimedia era which we have long seen coming. Rupert Murdoch's News Corporation, moving from news to entertainment, and Michael Eisner's Walt Disney Company, moving from films into news and television ownership, are its harbingers. National regulation, because it allows one, sometimes two, of everything in each country, has probably reinforced the tendency to create international baronies linking newspapers,

publishers, film studios, record labels, and theme parks in many different places. The monopoly that is not available nationally is replaced by the oligopoly that can be constructed internationally.

Media that were once routinely critical, or even routinely malicious about the performance of others – newspapers of television, publishing of journalism, popular music of everything – are now linked. The competition between rival multimedia empires is not the same as that between different media. For one thing, today's rival may be tomorrow's ally or take-over partner. Empires conspire. They may compete, but they do not sit in judgement on one another (Woolacott, 1995).

There are several implications to the development of recent media technologies. Who will control them? Satellite broadcasting and computer services available on the international telephone network do not recognize national frontiers ... yet. Even the humble fax machine in the hands of a determined opposition can apparently undermine a nation's ideological security as the controversy surrounding Saudi dissident Mohammed Al-Mas'ari, who was threatened with deportation for faxing critical material from Britain, has proved. The Islamic fundamentalist Al Mas'ari was sending faxes from his flat in Willesden, a rundown area of north London; the faxes contained information about financial, sexual and political scandals which, he claimed, disgraced the House of Saud. The faxes were considered so offensive and destabilizing to the Saudi royal family that the Saudi authorities threatened to cancel £20 billion of military contracts with the British if Al Mas'ari was given political asylum in the United Kingdom and allowed to continue his activities. If a single man can cause such havoc with a fax machine, what chance, then, can countries hoping to retain and encourage their own cultures have against a barrage of foreign broadcasting and information?

How much real control do governments have, or even want, over developing technologies and the multinational companies that, on the whole, own them? Will megacorporations determine more and more what we see, hear and think? Has the notion of planning the development of new technology been surrendered entirely to the free market by most countries? Will the development of more interactive technology supplement democratic processes or further undermine public forms of discussion? Will there be proper debate as to the place of such technology in the cultural, social and political life of a nation-state, or will 'the technological rollercoaster' move unobstructed by political or social concerns?

A central paradox of recent media developments has been that while choices of what, how and when to consume have increased greatly, media *ownership*, profitability and control of information has been increasingly concentrated in the hands of a small elite. There are also related questions regarding *access* to these new technologies:

However much the range of choice available to consumers is increased, the ever-higher costs of hardware will inevitably produce greater inequalities in access to electronic information, between nations as well as individuals. At the same time, fewer organisations, subjected to fewer controls on their activities, will determine what choice is offered to consumers (Maltby, 1989).

Cable and satellite have already had an impact on terrestrial broadcasting – competing for advertising revenue with the commercial sector and threatening the long-term existence of public service broadcasting. The ethos of public service broadcasting with its emphasis on programming with wide appeal, information, education, cultural and minority programming is in various ways already in retreat. In its place, some fear, comes niche marketing and 'minority broadcasting' driven by the demands of advertisers. Stevenson (1995) argues that a negative consequence of the idea of 'Me TV' currently being developed in the USA, where the television set could 'select' programming on behalf of the viewer's known tastes and preferences, is that television watchers may become less tolerant of programmes they would not normally view, taking the elements of surprise and confrontation out of television culture. Stevenson also suggests, despite these reservations, that an opportunity exists to make available different kinds of programming for neglected sections of the audience:

> Just as newspaper and magazine production has been revolutionised by cheaper forms of technology (allowing the publication of feminist magazines, a black press and other radical publications) so the opening up of television will provide the same.

As audiences continue to 'fragment' and more channels chase limited funding the commercial logic is to reduce spending on programming. This loss of revenue will in many cases lead to reduced quality overall, with more repeats and greater reliance on programming from abroad, particularly from the USA. As director general of the BBC, John Birt, made clear in his lecture to the Edinburgh Television Festival in August 1996:

> the easy availability of programmes and services worldwide will encourage the emergence of a single global culture, and that huge increase in competition will result in a drop in programme standards. A single global culture will mean an Americanised world culture. Much of the distribution of new programmes and services will come via telecom wires and is therefore unstoppable by those who favour quotas or other means.

In news, one result of the global reach of satellite broadcasting has already been seen in unprecedented levels of self-censorship. This was demonstrated clearly by Rupert Murdoch's axing of the BBC from his Hong-Kong-based Star satellite for offending the Chinese government by covering human rights issues and similarly offending the Indian government over dissident groups and allegations of corruption. Murdoch's concern for his 'satellite interests' in the region was also dramatically underlined when he sold control of the *South China Morning Post* to a 'close friend of China' because of its anti-Beijing editorial stance and by his removal of the editor Andrew Neil at *The Times* for exposing corruption in the Malaysian government. Andrew Neil, in his recent autobiography, revealed how he was told by a British minister that the Malaysian prime minister Mahathir Mohamad had demanded Neil's head from Murdoch for exposing how British aid had gone to build the Pergau dam in return for a £1.3 billion contract to buy British arms. Clearly desperate to hold on to the huge audiences in these countries Rupert Murdoch has been prepared to ditch a newspaper, 'a trusted lieutenant' in the press and uncomfortable or embarrassing news from his satellite channels to secure continuing market dominance. And as Granville Williams (1994) asks, who precisely can stop Murdoch or any major media player from acting against the public interest?

> Murdoch is so powerful that no political group dare confront his interest and seek to reduce his power and influence for fear that media power will be directed against them. Murdoch shrugs off calls for tougher ownership restrictions, saying he feels no threat from a Conservative or future Labour government: 'A Labour government isn't going to do anything about it. They are not going to close Sky Television down.'

Is this the 'global democracy, warts and all' that the director general of the BBC referred to when describing the television of the future, or are the public about to be 'taken for a ride' by a small circle of private corporations? A study by the London Business School found that pre-1990 television institutions in Britain provided a very cost-effective national broadcasting system and that market-driven broadcasting options were more expensive. Furthermore, these options were not generally wanted by 'the market' (Stuart Hall, *Changing technology and TV*, broadcast by the Open University). For example, although some fans may welcome the chance to watch uninterrupted sports coverage on one of the new dedicated sports channels, many resent paying relatively high subscription rates to watch national events previously available at no extra cost on terrestrial channels.

This situation has been repeated in many countries. In Holland the premier football league recently signed a lucrative deal with a cable network to provide exclusive coverage of their matches. The negotiations were conducted in strict secrecy because of the furore such a decision was expected to cause with many football fans. The danger of such moves is that national events will no longer be available to all of the general public and will therefore cease to be 'national' events at all. Even from a purely commercial point of view such fragmentation of the viewing public can bring diminishing returns. More channels, therefore, will not necessarily mean more choice – it may in some cases mean less.

As to the 'interactive' developments already mentioned, the fact that such technology is largely in the hands of the private sector (and those who can afford its expensive price tag) has led to warnings that a technological *underclass* is emerging, cut off from the so-called 'communications revolution'). As more and more services and decisions come to be made electronically, including the possibility of voting at a local and national level, the ability to 'buy into' such new technology becomes more critical. According to Williams (1994) 80 per cent of revenue and nearly 100 per cent of telecommunications profits are generated from a few hundred major corporate customers and so there will be little incentive in an unregulated market to provide services to people and areas where profits are slim. The results, he argues, will be a reduction in information diversity for the average citizen with 'megamonopolies' emerging in telephone and television services with a 'frightening' degree of financial power and control of information, including information about our private consumer habits and lifestyle.

Even apparently philanthropic gestures by the communications industry, such as providing free televisions and news broadcasts to schools, mask commercial motives. Williams (1994) cites the example of Channel One, on which a 12-minute commercial news broadcast was provided by Whittle Communications to 40 per cent of US secondary schools:

> For each participating school WEN installs, insures and services a roof top satellite dish, two VCRs, ceiling mounted television monitors in classrooms and cable and wiring to the central receiving and broadcasting equipment. Controversy centres on the requirement for students to view two minutes of commercials per twelve minute broadcast. These commercials sell for $194,555 for each 30-second advertising spot for products like Reebok sneakers, Burger King fast food and Clearasil spot cream (Williams, 1994).

This violation of educational time by advertising promotes consumerism at a time when students are frequently assaulted for designer clothing, and encourages poor nutrition when teenage health disorders are sharply increasing. Furthermore, in a study by the University of Massachusetts, the highly fragmented and 'educationally unimportant' service offered by WEN was found to be most commonly adopted by underprivileged schools with the highest concentration of low-income and Afro-American students and found most infrequently in schools spending the most on education, and with the wealthiest students. Quoting from a study in *Intermedia* (February 1994), Williams concludes:

> The serious charge is that it marks the 'beginning of a new era in which public education is, de facto, privatised, and learning is stunted by the parameters of profit margins rather than expanded by the unbounded potential of young minds'.

What we are now witnessing is a *convergence* of formerly distinct activities and technologies associated with leisure, work, education and consumer spending. These 'information technology' (IT) systems are converging on the home, which has become both a 'multifunction workstation' and the location for the sale and consumption of goods and services. In his essay 'Today's television, tomorrow's world' Patrick Hughes suggests that restructuring the UK cable industry matches the government's long-term strategy of assisting private capital to weaken the distinction between home, work and commerce, and move towards an 'information society'. His conclusions are far-reaching and worth quoting at length:

> Since 1982, most public debate has accepted the assumption that 'cable' means 'cable TV'. Little attention has been paid to the implications of an electronic grid for the government's goal of an 'information society', and in particular the opportunities it offers to employers to create a new generation of white-collar homeworkers. Administrative and clerical work can already be done at home with a computer terminal (or a modified television) and a British Telecom telephone line to employers' premises. Companies such as ICL, Rank-Xerox, and F International have for some time operated such electronic white-collar homeworking. Electronics manufacturers such as Commodore and Rediffusion have produced computers ('work stations') which can be used at home and at work. However, the present high rents of telecommunications links make white-collar homeworking cost-effective only to employers of highly-paid professional and managerial staff. A cheap 'electronic grid' would enable employers to shift large areas of information processing work – such as secretarial/text processing, data entry, order processing, and even process control in manufacturing – from the office to the home.
>
> Working at home saves time and money on travel, and gives more flexibility in how and when to do the day's tasks. Hence its popularity with middle managers, and with women who have children but inadequate child-care facilities. However, it isolates workers thus reducing their ability to act collectively to protect their pay and conditions of work. It also means that individual workers, not the employer, pay the costs of lighting, heating, and maintaining their workplace.
>
> This may seem far removed from a discussion of today's television and of the 'cable revolution', until we remember that alongside the development of such an electronic grid would be the continuing trend towards monopoly in the provision of news, entertainment, and information across the whole of the culture and communications industries. For many people, the 'information society' could mean a future in which a few corporations dominate their working lives and their leisure lives via a video screen. For those corporations, and for those white-collar homeworkers, today's 'television' may well become tomorrow's world.

EXERCISES AND ESSAYS

Exercise

Trace your family's purchase and use of leisure technology: televisions, video recorders, stereos, and so on as far back as you can. How has it changed the way they spend their leisure time? Have the purchases meant an improvement in their quality of life? How?

Exercise and Essay

Utopia or Dystopia? What vision of the future is offered by new media technology?

Exercise and Essay

Digital video signals 'the beginning of the merger between PCs and home entertainment'. Why?

Essay

How might changes in access and ownership alter the future of our mass media?

Sources

Alvarado, M. (1987): *Television and video.* Wayland.

Bell, E. (1996): *Everyone wants a finger in the $6 billion digital pie. The Guardian Weekly* 19 May.

Birt, J. (1996): Gateway to the BBC's future. James MacTaggart Memorial Lecture, Edinburgh, August.

Central Office of Information (1993): *Broadcasting.* HMSO.

Culf, A. (1996): *Guardian Weekly* 8 December.

Ernsberger, R. (1996): Cinematic CDs. *Newsweek* 1 April.

Freedland, J. (1994): Cable revolution. *Guardian* 1 January.

Gilder, G. (1992): *Life after television.* W.W. Norton.

Hughes, P. (1990): Today's television, tomorrow's world. In Goodwin, A. and Whannel, G. (1990): *Understanding television.* Routledge.

Lewis, P. (1986): *Media and power: from Marconi to Murdoch.* Camden Press.

Maltby, R. (ed.) (1989): *Dreams for sale – popular culture in the 20th century.* Equinox.

Neil, A. (1996): *Full disclosure.* Macmillan.

O'Sullivan, T., Dutton, B. and Rayner, P. (1994): *Studying the media – an introduction.* Arnold.

Stevenson, N. (1995): *Understanding media cultures.* Sage.

Williams, G. (1994): *Britain's media – how they are related.* Campaign for Press and Broadcasting Freedom (CPBF).

Woolacott, M. (1995): The mouse that soared. *The Guardian* 19 August.

© Kobal

'Big Brother is watching you'

16

Ideology

INTRODUCTION

An ideology is a set of interlocking assumptions and expectations held by a person, a group or a culture – a set of ideas about how the world works, a system of values. As distinct from a philosophy, an ideology can readily become a programme for action. On the broadcast level, it so entirely infuses a culture that its members may not even be aware of sharing certain assumptions about the nature of people and the best way they can live together. An ideology can be so taken for granted that it comes to seem 'natural' the way the world works or ought to work (Kawin, 1992).

Ideology is a term which refers to the coherent set of beliefs and values which dominate in a culture, and which is particularly held by those who have power. Ideology is concerned with social and power relationships and with the means by which these are made apparent. The media communicate ideology to their audiences. This ideology can be found in the material by looking for covert messages (Burton, 1990).

The study of ideology can be usefully defined as 'the ways in which meaning (signification) serves to sustain relations of domination' (Thompson, 1984, quoted in Stevenson, 1995).

Ideology is a notoriously difficult concept to define. Napoleon Bonaparte used the term to attack democracy (regarded across Europe, in the early nineteenth century, as the philosophy of fanatics) blaming 'the doctrines of the ideologues' for all the ills of France. Bonaparte's emphasis (by 'ideology' he meant rigid and doctrinaire principles) is one still used today by the media. Len Masterman (1985) also notes a pejorative use of the term ideology by Marx and Engels to refer to 'false consciousness' or the misrecognition of material conditions and relationships. An example would be the case of feudal populations imagining that kings and lords ruled by divine right (the will of God), as the church and popular culture of the time led them to believe. The other sense of ideology used by Marx is as 'the set of ideas which arise from a given set of material interests'. Lenin uses the term in this sense when he refers to socialism as 'the ideology of the struggle of the working class':

Williams notes that there is here 'clearly no sense of illusion or false consciousness .... There is now "proletarian ideology" or "bourgeois ideology" and so on, and ideology in each case is the system of ideas appropriate to that class.' It also becomes possible now to speak of 'dominant ideology', and 'subordinate ideologies' (Masterman, 1985).

The sense here of competing ways of thinking (and behaving), or 'world-views', is the closest to the definitions of ideology generally agreed by contemporary critics. According to Burton (1990):

Ideology is a set of beliefs which add up to a particular view of the world and of power relations between people and groups. All sets of beliefs which have labels or titles are ideologies; Buddhism, Communism, Capitalism, Catholicism. These 'IMS' are often tied to particular cultures, but more than one may exist within a culture.

That is not to say that a person has to subscribe to an '-ism' to be subject to ideology. *Everyone* has some sort of ideology or view of the world – a notion of what, for them, is right and wrong, of how the world is and how it could be made a better place. This view of the world is affected by the country and culture we grow up in, our friends and family, the media, religion, educational institutions and other social forces. Much of what is regarded as 'common sense' is ideological, because ideology is so much a part of the way a person lives that it becomes *transparent*. A person travelling to a foreign country may experience a sense of the strangeness of that culture, of what is regarded as 'normal' or acceptable being quite different from what they are used to. Where the idea of having two, three or even four wives would be quite normal in much of the Arabic world, for instance, the idea of eating pork, or seeing a woman in a bikini would be shocking. The fact that 'norms' such as these are taken for granted in some cultures and yet are so 'strange' in others goes to show how vast populations are subject to the force of ideology.

The media plays a vital role in transmitting ideology. The arguments around how they transmit it, and its effects on a population are, in themselves, profoundly ideological. The two most influential frameworks for considering these arguments with regard to the media are *liberalism* and *Marxism*.

LIBERAL POLITICAL THEORY

Advances in the technology of tele-communications have proved an unambiguous threat to totalitarian regimes everywhere .... In short, the march of tele-communications technology has been a key factor in the enormous spread of freedom that is the major distinguishing feature of recent years (Rupert Murdoch).

Historically, liberalism has stressed the role of the mass media in promoting the free exchange of ideas. Critics writing from a liberal perspective have, since the nineteenth century, argued that privately-owned media organizations free from state control have been a major factor in promoting individual liberty. In *Culture and anarchy* Mathew Arnold (1932) writes 'A Liberal believes in liberty and liberty signifies the non-intervention of the state.'

Liberal media theory was further developed in the USA from the 1930s. In addition to providing a guarantee for individual liberty, the theory suggested, privately-owned and uncensored media promoted political and economic liberty. Liberal theorists claimed that democracies existed because of media freedom. Evidence for this claim could be found in Nazi Germany where the state's grip on the press, television and the cinema was a crucial element of the government's totalitarian control of society.

Classical liberal theory indicates that privately-owned media are a vital part of a pluralist state. The freedom to publish and broadcast in an unrestricted market ensures that a wide range of opinions and interests in society are expressed. If a viewpoint is not expressed it is only because it lacks a sufficient following to sustain it in the market-place. Some liberal theorists compare the operation of the market to processes of political representation. Media products, they contend, must submit to the equivalent of an election every time they go on sale, whereas politicians seek election only at infrequent intervals.

Liberal theorists argue that the media provide forums for public debate about issues of the day, articulating public opinion arising out of these debates, forcing governments to take account of what people think. The mass media play an important role in the wider education of citizens, enabling them to make informed judgements at election time. The various arms of the media, including television, provide a forum for discussion between different groups in society, allowing a natural consensus to emerge on issues of importance to the nation. Furthermore, because journalists, directors and programme makers are autonomous, they can effectively report on anything they want, including government mistakes or corruption. As such they are champions of the individual against the abuse of executive power and the misdeeds of the powerful.

Those writing within a determinist or Marxist tradition tend to qualify the 'freedom' granted by liberal theorists to the media by stressing the relationship of the media with the governing class:

> The importance and value of this freedom and opportunity of expression is not to be underestimated. Yet the notion of pluralist diversity and competitive equilibrium is, here, as in every other field, rather superficial and misleading. For the agencies of communication and notably the mass media are, in reality, and the expression of dissident views notwithstanding, a crucial element in the legitimation of capitalist society. Freedom of

expression is not thereby rendered meaningless. But that freedom has to be set in the real economic and political context of these societies; and in that context the free expression of ideas and opinions mainly means the free expression of ideas and opinions which are helpful to the prevailing system of power and privilege (Miliband, 1979).

Despite such criticism, the continuing widespread influence of liberal media theory can be seen, for instance, in Alan Peacock's 1986 Broadcasting White Paper and in the Conservative Government's 1990 Broadcasting Act which, although toned down, took on board many of Peacock's liberal assumptions.

MARXIST POLITICAL THEORY

Marxism has been concerned with examining the mass media as a form of social power in contemporary societies (see the reading at the end of this chapter). Marxist theory, unlike liberal theory, focuses on the media in terms of its patterns of ownership, its manipulation by powerful elites (as in public relations) and its ideological role in reproducing the *status quo*. Critics writing from a Marxist perspective have questioned how freedom of speech is possible without media institutions and cultural industries controlled largely by a tiny, unelected business class and driven by commercial imperatives. The following outlines of Marxist perspectives of ideology and its operation within the mass media are highly summarized versions of complex arguments and concepts outlined in more detail by Stevenson (1995), Strinati (1995) and others (refer to the Sources for further reading).

Karl Marx

According to Marx, 'The history of all human society, past and present, has been the history of class struggle' (*The Communist Manifesto*, 1996).

The obvious question posed by liberals and others against Marxists is why in conditions of free and open political competition the antisocialist parties have so regularly been voted into power with the popular mandate of the electorate, an electorate made up, on the whole, of the working classes socialists claim to be representing. The answer Marx gave to that question was, in a famous formulation, that:

the ideas of the ruling class are, in every age, the ruling ideas because ... the class, which is the ruling material force in society, is at the same time its ruling intellectual force. The class which has the means of material production at its disposal, has control at the same time over the means of mental production, so that thereby, generally speaking, the ideas of those who lack the means of mental production are subject to it (Marx, from *German ideology*, quoted in Miliband, 1979).

In the capitalist era the bourgeoisie control the means of intellectual production – publishing and all branches of the mass media, educational institutions, political parties and so on. In television this is illustrated by the close personal involvement of wealthy media moguls such as Ted Turner and Rupert Murdoch in their businesses, as well as the class composition of members of broadcasting company's executive boards, the majority share-holders and controlling interests of commercial television and even in the make-up of the BBC Board of Governors. As a result, this class – 'the ruling class' – effectively dominates the production, regulation and distribution of ideas. The bourgeoisie secure their position because their ideas are those most widely in circulation and therefore dominate the consciousness of subordinate groups. As a result class inequalities and the continued exploitation of the working class are maintained and justified.

Marx argues that the 'real foundation' or *base* of society – its relations of production (which could be primitive, feudal, capitalist or socialist – is what determines, or sets limits to, the *superstructure* of that society. By 'super-structure' Marx means 'the legal, political, religious, aesthetic or philo-sophical' – in short, the ideological forms of a society. Such ideological forms would include cultural manifestations such as the mass media.

Hence, according to those critics who would subscribe to Marx's analysis, the mass media in a capitalist society would generally promote a capitalist view of the world, or at least a view of the world that does not threaten capitalism and its exploitative rationale:

> There is nothing particularly surprising about the character and role of the mass media in advanced capitalist society. Given the economic and political context in which they function, they cannot fail to be, predominantly, agencies for the dissemination of ideas and values which affirm rather than challenge existing patterns of power and privilege, and thus to be weapons in the arsenal of class domination. The notion that they can, for the most part, be anything else is either a delusion or a mystification. They can and sometimes do, play a 'dysfunctional' role; and the fact that they are allowed to do so is not lightly to be dismissed, but that, quite emphatically, is not and indeed cannot, in the given context, be their main role. They are intended to fulfil a conservative function; and do so (Miliband, 1979).

Empirical research by Murdoch and Golding and the Campaign for Press and Broadcasting Freedom (amongst others) has shown, in support of Marx's thesis, that small groups of powerful economic and financial interests dominate the control of mass communication industries. The undisputed fact of increasing concentration of media ownership in recent years make Marx's analysis all the more relevant to contemporary history. As ownership and control of the media continues to pass to an elite, wealth-owning clique via multinational concerns and conglomerates critical perspectives and alternative viewpoints become further marginalized:

Those with most economic power will be able to improve their market position, and ensure that the media products least critical of the class structure will survive, and those most critical will not. This in turn, will make it more difficult for alternative viewpoints, politics and cultures to enter the market because they will lack the necessary economic resources. The pressure of rising costs means that all media have to try to reach as large an audience as possible. They can do this by aiming either at a large mass audience, or at smaller but affluent groups. Equally they cannot afford to lose audiences. It therefore becomes necessary to rely upon tried and tested formulae, rather than trying to be different and experimental (Strinati, 1995).

The Frankfurt School

Choose life. Choose a job. Choose a career. Choose a family. Choose a fucking big television, choose washing machines, cars, compact disc players and electrical tin openers (Renton, from the film *Trainspotting*; Hodge, 1996).

A logical extension to the Marxist view of the operation of ideology is the notion of *false needs*. According to this view people have 'real' needs of, for example, food, shelter, education, freedom and creativity. They need to be involved in the decision-making processes that affect their lives, their work and the society they are living in. In capitalism these 'true needs' are hidden by the 'false needs' of consumerism. Real freedom – to participate in a genuinely democratic society as a free-thinking, creative individual – is replaced by a series of choices between products and 'lifestyles' offered by the market and political parties all representing the interests of the dominant class.

Through the mass media, education and religion the capitalist order encourages conformity and acceptance of the *status quo*. According to the Frankfurt School for Social Research – founded by a group of left-wing academics in Germany shortly before the rise of the Nazi Party – the media as part of a wider 'culture industry' is highly destructive; for example,

the colour film demolishes the genial old tavern to a greater extent than bombs ever could . . . . No homeland can survive being processed by the films which celebrate it, and which thereby turn the unique character on which it thrives into an interchangeable sameness (Adorno, 1991, quoted by Strinati, 1995).

In addition to its economic function of promoting consumerism the culture industry is employed to infantalize its audience by developing their consciousness regressively:

It is no coincidence that cynical American film producers are heard to say that their pictures must take into consideration the level of eleven-year-olds.

In doing so they would very much like to make adults into eleven-year-olds (Adorno, 1991, quoted by Strinati, 1995).

The Frankfurt School suggested, in opposition to Marx, that capitalism was not in crisis but had, through wealth creation and the control of political institutions and the mass media, ensured its own survival. The working class were materially and ideologically bound to capitalism – secured by the success with which the system delivered financial prosperity and consumer goods. This radical break with Marx's identification of an ongoing class struggle is understandable in light of the period (the middle decades of the twentieth century) in which the School was writing. The rise of fascism, the fading or failure of revolutionary movements and the economic boom years of the West that followed the war, appeared to signify an end to working-class agitation that had previously characterized capitalism's short history.

Louis Althusser

Ideology, according to Althusser, 'represents the imaginary relationship of individuals to their real conditions of existence'.

French structuralist critic Althusser developed a more detailed interpretation of Marx's 'base–superstructure' account of ideology. Althusser, rejecting a crudely economic 'determinist' view of ideology, suggests that the economic base is the superstructural determinant 'in the last instant'. In other words, although the economy remains paramount in setting limits to the superstructure, it is not the only determinant. Althusser granted the superstructure and ideological forces operating within it a relative degree of autonomy from the economic infrastructure – going so far as to suggest the possibility of reciprocal action of the superstructure on the base.

In his essay 'Ideology and ideological state apparatuses' Althusser suggests that the superstructure secures labour's compliance with the (capitalist) mode of production via repressive and/or ideological means. Repressive state apparatuses (RSAs) are sanctioned to use force in defence of the system and include the police, the courts, prisons and the army. Ideological state apparatuses (ISAs), on the other hand, employing ideological means of subjection, include schools, the church, the family, popular culture and the mass media. The ISAs transmit ideological forms of misrecognition of the real relations of domination. Hence the mass media, in Althusser's view, perform an ideological role in securing the consent of the population for the continuation of capitalism.

Ideology attempts to smooth away all contradictions and consciousness of class conflicts. However, ideology, according to Althusser, is not simply something imposed on subordinate groups by a dominant class or even simply an illusory set of ideas in the mind of the people. Ideology is how people (mis)represent their relation to the real world, a relationship which although false and illusory has material forms which incorporate to a greater or lesser extent all members of society. An example would be the (material) practice of voting in an election. According to the perspective offered by Althusser such a practice would reflect an imaginary relation in the mind of the voter between himself or herself as a self-determining agent and the political realm. In these terms, the reality of an election is a stage-managed ritual: a selection between parties offering virtually identical policies for continuing the *status quo* (the preservation of capitalism). The idea in the voter's mind of participation in democratic decision-making is, therefore, an illusory one. Television, by concentrating on the 'fight' between the major political parties, it could be argued, plays an important role in reinforcing this 'illusion'.

The material force or practice of ideology can also be judged by how schools instil in children the 'know-how' required by the relations of production. Under capitalism this has necessitated at least basic numeracy and literacy in addition to an uncritical respect for authority. Without such an education there can be no effective workforce or profits for the owners of the means of production. All ideology works by recruiting or 'hailing' individuals and placing ('interpellating') them, as subjects within the framework of ideology, helping to shape their particular world-view:

> For example, a religion will place all individuals who participate in its material practices as subjects, or believers, who are subject to one subject. God. Similarly, the ideology of political democracy will place individuals as subjects in terms of their becoming citizens subject to the sovereignty of parliament. Patriarchal ideology will interpellate individuals as more powerful men or less powerful women. Popular culture in contemporary societies might be argued to function by taking individuals and placing them as workers or as members of social classes (Strinati, 1995).

Unlike the Frankfurt School, however, Althusser is careful to point out that such ideological functions as are performed by schools, religion, the mass media and popular culture will be confronted by and subject to conflict and class struggle.

Noam Chomsky

More recently, the Canadian critic Noam Chomsky has developed a view of the role of the media based on the Marxist perspectives outlined above. According to Chomsky's 'propaganda model' the media are used as a technique of control, creating the 'necessary illusions' which are in the interests of the ruling class. He divides the population into a political class which is the top 20 per cent 'relatively educated, reasonably articulate' group who have a role in decision-making, such as managers, writers, teachers. The political class has to be 'deeply indoctrinated' to fulfil their role effectively. The function of the remaining 80 per cent is, essentially, to follow orders. The media's function according to Chomsky's model is to reduce the subordinate population's ability to think, thereby reducing this group to apathy.

According to the 'propaganda model', there are elite medias such as the major television channels and the quality press. They set a general framework of news through selection of topics, distribution of concerns and the placing of emphasis, all of which serve the interests of the dominant elite groups in society. Chomsky was a leading figure in the anti-Vietnam-War movement in the 1960s, arguing that the possibility of a peaceful settlement to the conflict was consistently excluded by the US media who, he argued, bore a heavy responsibility for the continuation of the war.

Chomsky sets out to prove, using content analysis, how certain stories are underrepresented in the media because of powerful industrial interests. In one paired example he showed how atrocities committed by Indonesia in East Timor received only 70 column inches in the *New York Times* compared with 1175 column inches devoted to Khmer Rouge killings in Cambodia. Chomsky argues that although more people were actually slaughtered by the Indonesians in East Timor the fact that the weaponry was, and continues to be, supplied by the USA, Britain and Holland meant that it received low news priority.

Antonio Gramsci

The Marxist perspectives, as barely summarized above, tend to give the impression of a somewhat uniform culture doled out by the ruling class to a brainwashed population, somewhat akin to the world described by George Orwell in *1984*. The Italian political activist and critic Gramsci developed a more subtle elaboration of Marxist conceptions of ideology. Gramsci's concept of hegemony has come to take a crucial role in critical understanding of popular culture and the mass media. Hegemony is the ideological means whereby the bourgeois class maintain power by securing the 'spontaneous consent' of subordinate groups, including the working class, through the negotiated construction of a political and ideological consensus. The resulting hegemonic consensus, which comes to be regarded by large sections of the population as 'common sense', is built upon compromise and concessions both by the dominant and subordinate groups and acts as a kind of social cement. Subordinate groups accept the leadership of the ruling class while those leaders representing the interests of the bourgeoisie grant concessions and limited economic sacrifices (such as welfare provision or wage rises) in return for their support.

For Gramsci 'civil society' is the site where hegemonic control is negotiated and the state is responsible for the use of coercion. As the mass media are a part of civil society it follows that the media should be understood in terms of the concept of hegemony. Although hegemony may be regarded as a series of negotiated ideas and accepted values, these ideas and values, for Gramsci, ultimately serve the interests of the ruling class. Nevertheless, hegemonic consensus is something which emerges out of social and class struggle and therefore its hold over subordinate groups can never be guaranteed.

Stuart Hall

Ideology 'is what is most open, apparent, manifest', what 'takes place on the surface and in view of all men'. Though, 'what is hidden, repressed or inflected out of sight are its real foundations' (Hall, 1977, quoted in Masterman, 1985).

The work of Stuart Hall and the Birmingham Centre for Cultural Studies (of which he is a founding member) has continued the broadly Marxist analysis of society and the media as developed by Althusser and Gramsci. Hall argues that the mass media is the most important ideological apparatus of contemporary capitalism. Hall's specific contribution to mass communication research has been to examine both the ideological nature of 'encoding' of media messages and the work of audiences in 'decoding' these messages.

In *Policing the crisis* (1978) Hall and his colleagues gave an account of a press-led moral panic around mugging, drawing on the 'deviancy amplification' concept, and linked it to the breakdown of post-war consensus politics and the growth of an authoritarian state. Hall argues that the term 'mugging' had been introduced from the USA and was used to exaggerate fears of rising street crime in Britain and stigmatize black deviant behaviour at a time of economic and ideological crisis. The threat of the 'mugger' served to justify and legitimate increased police and court powers. 'Mugging' was a new term for a whole variety of age-old offences which was used to give the impression of a rising tide of street crime.

Hall uses the term 'primary definers' to refer to the work of the police, army, courts, the government and other powerful institutions to set an agenda for news reporting – the work of the media or 'secondary definers':

> Before the 'mugger' panic had appeared in the press there had been an intensification of police mobilisation against deviant blacks. The result of this strategy was the appearance of black offenders in court which, in turn, provided the setting for the spiralling of press attention . . . . The definitions of the police in the resulting moral panic are given extra ideological weight in that they are able to establish a high degree of cultural closure. This would not be the case in, say, media reporting of industrial relations where the primary definers would include trade unions as well as employers. As Hall points out, by 'virtue of being criminals, they have forfeited the right to take part in the negotiations of the consensus about crime' (Stevenson, 1995).

Hall suggests that 'muggers' were one useful scapegoat for wider social anxiety caused by the breakdown of the traditional political consensus in British politics and accompanying shifting social norms. The radicalization of marginal social groups such as young people, students, ethnic minorities and the limited progress made by trade unions, feminism and the gay and lesbian movement were just some of the threats posed to establishment values in the 1960s and 1970s. Hall suggests that the right, represented politically by Mrs Thatcher and the Conservative Party, offered radical, populist, authoritarian leadership – and set about the collossal task of hegemonically redefining the British people throughout the 1980s. Thatcherism appealed to 'commonsense' fears over street crime, the Soviet threat, union power, the privatization of state utilities and a whole range of 'Victorian values'. The entrepreneurial, deregulated but authoritarian state that Thatcherism offered, aided and abetted by an almost exclusively right-wing national press, successfully appealed to a range of identities across the class spectrum.

Hall does not suggest a monolithic ideological conformity either on the part of the mass media or the audience under Thatcherism or any other political system. Rather, he identifies dominant discursive strategies 'encoded' within the media texts and a variety of 'decoded' messages identified by the audience. Hall notes three reading strategies by audiences. First, he posited a 'dominant-hegemonic reading' which would accept the 'preferred reading' offered by the text. On the day following Robert Maxwell's death television and press reports of the press baron largely mourned his loss and were uncritical or obnoxiously sycophantic in the case of the paper he had owned, the *Mirror*. A dominant hegemonic reading would therefore support this view of Maxwell – a powerful, ambitious, charismatic, if slightly roguish, entrepreneur – 'The man who saved the Mirror' in the words of the *Mirror*'s headlines (see Chapter 12, pp. 168–9).

A 'negotiated reading' might accept the general thrust of the reports but consider them slightly generous and respectful in light of the accident and possible upset to the family. There may be an awareness of an outsized ego and dictatorial management style obliquely referred to in some of the reports. An 'oppositional reading' would reject the entire framework of the report – insisting against the text that Maxwell was a ruthless egomaniac who destroyed a campaigning tabloid, creating in its stead a feeble parody of a newspaper devoted to his personal aggrandizement. Such a reading, as was made public by the likes of *Private Eye*, would also argue that the man was a thief, a liar and a disgrace to Britain's public life (see also Chapter 12, pp. 168–9).

Roland Barthes

Ideology, according to Marxists, maintains an appearance of naturalness by effacing itself or 'disappearing' from view. Ideological assertions are scrubbed away without trace through what the French critic Roland Barthes identifies as 'myth'. Bourgeois ideology, according to Barthes, denies the existence of a bourgeois class. This 'vanishing act' by the owners of the means of production is seen most clearly in the mass media, where 'the bourgeoisie has obliterated its name in passing from reality to representation' (Barthes, 1973). The bourgeoisie do not, therefore, appear to exist in the mass media at all.

Myth for Barthes is a mode of representation, characterized most of all by its naturalness. 'Myth-consumers' take signification for a system of facts – they take myths at face value, as natural, 'what-goes-without-saying'. Television viewers, in this view, accept the world-view or 'ideology' of television as normal, 'the way things are'. In *Mythologies* – a collection of frequently tongue-in-cheek essays on ordinary objects and cultural practices such as wrestling, stripping, steak and chips, toys – Barthes rails against the confusion of 'Nature and History'. Barthes argues that 'ideological abuse' is hidden in the presentation of objects that are robbed of any sense of history or production. The question of how a thing is made, or who made it, is very rarely asked:

> Myth deprives the object of which it speaks of all History. In it history evaporates. It is a kind of ideal servant: it prepares all things, brings them, lays them out, the master arrives, it silently disappears: all that is left is for one to enjoy this beautiful object without wondering where it comes from (Barthes, 1973).

A Nike trainer, then, is just that. It is presented and advertised as such. The question of how and under what conditions this trainer was made is studiously avoided. In fact, this controversy has plagued the opening of Nike's multimillion-dollar showcase store in San Francisco. There are ongoing demonstrations outside San Francisco's Niketown against low wages paid to the company's employees in 'developing' countries. Protesters are particularly annoyed by Nike's saturation advertising and high price tag in 'Western' countries in light of these low wages. A parallel can be drawn between this protest and Barthes's challenge to the way products, beliefs, cultural or political practices and ways of living are presented as *natural*. They appear in such a way that denies politics and history. In one chapter of *Mythologies* entitled 'The new Citroën' Barthes wryly observes:

> It is obvious that the new Citroën has fallen from the sky in as much as it appears at first sight as a superlative *object*. We must not forget that an object is the best messenger of a world above that of nature: one can easily see in an object at once a perfection and an absence of origin, a closure and a brilliance, a transformation of life into matter (matter is much more magical than life), and in a word a *silence* which belongs to the world of fairy tales (emphasis in original).

Myth has erased the human activity, history, skill and effort of the car's production. And in this process of representation, which Barthes describes as a 'haemorrhage' or emptying of reality, nature, or 'what-goes-without-saying', floods in. To recover the ideological from the apparently natural requires methodical analysis at different levels: peeling back 'what is taken for granted' to discover the hidden values and assumptions that underpin all objects, texts and practices.

IDEOLOGICAL ANALYSIS

> Artefacts are cultural. Their existence is not accidental, any more than their particular qualities are. The shape, size, colour and every other quality of the objects which we see around us are so by design, and represent the result of conscious human choices. Because that chair, that glass or that home is *that* way rather than any other, it embodies meanings and reveals something of the values of the society in which it finds a place. The purpose of analysing objects if to unmask the choices implicit within them and most fundamentally to reveal them as the outcome of human rather than natural processes (Masterman, 1985, emphasis in original).

The relationship between the signified, the signifier and myth (see the previous chapter) can be more easily understood by applying three levels of analysis: denotative, connotative and ideological (for further explanation of these terms, see Chapter 17).

Denotative Analysis (Description)

Analysis at a denotative level requires a description of what can be seen or heard in a concrete sense. This may involve, in the case of a television sequence, describing in detail objects, people, clothes, speech, music, setting, camera angle, framing, focus, distortion (from the camera lens), colour, lighting, line, type of cut, pace of editing, movement, gesture and any other aspect of what appears or is heard in the sequence. In fact, as Masterman notes, hard and fast distinctions between denotation and connotation can never be absolute as the 'factual' inevitably involves particular ways of selecting, valuing and understanding experience.

Connotative Analysis (Related Associations)

Many, if not all, of the signs denoted in a text will have connotations. Connotative analysis is generally more ambiguous or open to interpretation than denotative analysis. We may agree at a literal level what we have seen or heard but argue over its meaning or associations. A black leather sofa may connote comfort and homeliness to one viewer, sophistication and luxury to another and crass machismo to a third. Low-key lighting (in which there will be shadows) is traditionally associated with mystery, suspense, horror. Tight framing may suggest intensity or entrapment. Rock music may connote youth, excitement, freedom, danger. Interpretation will be subject to historical context, nationality, culture, class, ethnicity, gender, sexual orientation, and personal and social experience.

Some signs or combination of signs may be more 'closed' or less 'polysemic' (open to interpretation) than others. An 'open' text, by contrast, will have no clear 'preferred reading'. It may invite a variety of readings and connotations may be ambiguous or multilayered. The Guinness television advertising campaign starring Rutger Hauer was to different audiences either sophisticated, entertaining, sexy, clever, perplexing, pretentious or nonsensical. Rutger Hauer himself connoted mystery, foreignness, star appeal, masculinity, ambiguity, smoothness, sexuality and, with his black coat and blond hair, a physical pint of Guinness! In fact, meaning is fairly clearly anchored in most advertising. Soap opera is a genre which is thought of as being more consistently open in its range of possible interpretations, owing to the competing perspectives and values offered within a serial and its more open narrative structure.

Ideological Analysis

> Ideological analysis – in the sense of analysis which is designed to uncover those more or less coherent sets of values and beliefs which are thought to underpin a text – consists of piecing together the text's connotative fragments (Masterman, 1985).

Stuart Hall, amongst others, has argued that media texts such as television programmes contain dominant ideological discourses:

> This is due to the fact that media producers' own professional routines and practice contain certain assumptions and ideas about how programmes should be made (the 'relations of production'). They draw agendas and meanings – 'definitions of the situation' – from the wider society, which are ideological in nature (the 'framework of knowledge'). Finally, television's own codes and conventions are employed to complete the encoding process, whose effect is to naturalise or make transparent the meaning of the programme for the audience (to deny its own ideological construction) (O'Sullivan *et al.*, 1994).

Ideological analysis will tease out the assumptions, myths and dominant discourses that lie behind a text. These might be only partly thought out or even wholly unconscious on the part of the producers. Gene Roddenberry, the creator of *Star Trek*, may not have deliberately created a Kennedy figure in Captain Kirk. However, Kirk's pleas for (racial) tolerance at a time of riots in the USA, or the frontier (imperialist) mission of the *USS Enterprise* have a fairly inescapable ideological resonance looking at the series in hindsight. Ideological analysis is, therefore, rarely concerned with an author's intentions but with the way the text is encoded and to a lesser extent how the audience decode them.

Len Masterman (1985) gives a brief but perceptive ideological analysis of *Mastermind*:

> So, in *Mastermind* (BBC), for example, the single chair, the pool of light, the clipped, impersonal tones of the questioner, the cutting to ever tighter close-ups of the contestants, all contribute to dominant and oppressive

associations of knowledge and learning with interrogation, humiliation and fear of failure. These associations are validated and legitimised by the formal university setting in which the show takes place, and by their connotative links with the importance of factual recall within the show, as well as with the frequently absurd specialisms, and predominantly middle-class backgrounds of the contestants (the odd cabbie or tube driver amongst them simply attesting to the opportunities for upward mobility which approved knowledge can bring with it). An examination of *Mastermind*'s connotative clusters, then, not only leads us directly to its major ideological themes and to its peculiarly de-humanised, hierarchical and oppressive construction of what counts as learning and intelligence. It also assures us, chillingly, that this construction has a great deal of purchase out there in the world of real and prestigious educational institutions.

John Fiske (1987) concludes an analysis of a scene from *Hart to Hart* by drawing the audience into the interpretative framework. The role of the viewer, he asserts, is also ideological:

If we adopt the same ideological practice in the decoding as the encoding we are drawn into the position of a white, male, middle-class American (or westerner) of conventional morality. The reading position is the social point at which the mix of televisual, social, and ideological codes comes together to make coherent, unified sense: in making sense of the program in this way we are indulging in an ideological practice ourselves, we are maintaining and legitimating the dominant ideology, and our reward for this is the easy pleasure of the recognition of the familiar and of its adequacy. We have already become a 'reading subject' constructed by the text, and, according to Althusser, the construction of subjects in ideology is the major ideological practice in capitalist societies.

MEDIA IMPERIALISM

Ninety per cent of international news published by the world's press comes from the 'big four' Western news agencies. They are United Press International (UPI), Associated Press (AP), Reuter and Agence France Presse (AFP). Two are American, one is British, one is French. Their output is supplemented by the transnational giants: from Murdoch to Times Warner to CNN. Almost all of these are American. The largest news agency, UPI, gets 80 per cent of its funding from US newspapers. A survey in the mid-1980s found that UPI devoted 71 per cent of its coverage to the United States, 9.6 per cent to Europe, 5.9 per cent to Asia, 3.2 per cent to Latin America, 3 per cent to the Middle East and 1.8 per cent to Africa.

'These figures', wrote the Canadian writer Don Rojas in *Third World Resurgence*, 'give a clear picture of the phenomenon called information imperialism. In the total volume of UPI's information, news about the United States took up more space than that devoted to the whole African continent, where more than 50 countries are situated.' Former Tanzanian president Julius Nyerere once noted sarcastically, wrote Rojas, that the inhabitants of developing countries should be allowed to take part in the presidential elections of the United States because they are bombarded with as much information about the candidates as are North American citizens (*Third World Resurgence*, issue 12, quoted in Pilger, 1992).

Media imperialism or monopolization is the transmission of a nation's ideology through the media. Monopolization of the media has been taking place since the 1920s when many nations complained of the influence of Hollywood over its culture. Since then governments, especially in the West, have seen the importance of the media in conveying their ideology to other nations. This was evident during the Cold War, as East and West battled over the radio airwaves to transmit their own ideological messages. By the late 1980s *The Voice of America*, the US world radio service, had an audience of around 120 million listeners transmitted from 66 superpower transmitters. The Soviet Union had 32 such transmitters, France 12 and Britain 8. External radio services were operated by 31 countries enabling them to spread their ideologies over their borders without too much expense.

The fear is that with satellite technology Western ideals are being reinforced throughout the Third World, leading to the loss of local cultural values. As Lewis (1986) notes, satellites are simply another example of how 'the free flow of communication' works to disadvantage 'Third World' countries. US satellites, for instance, which provide programmes for the domestic market, are casting their televisual shadow over many Caribbean nations. A statement from the Caribbean Broadcasting and Publishing Association, voices these concerns by stating:

> What is taking place quietly in the living rooms of thousands of Caribbean family units as they sit innocently before their television sets, frightens us. It is a process of deculturalization, which is painless, but also very thorough and long lasting.

Media imperialism continues to operate in the world today partly as a result of the high cost of broadcasting, especially as Western markets have large advertising revenues and can afford to dump their programmes and films at cut prices on developing nations. Furthermore, many Third World journalists and technicians are trained in Europe and the USA, which results in them adopting Western practices and media content. As it is, these locally-based media professionals rarely get a chance to develop the skills they have learned because there is often a chronic shortage of money to spend on even the most basic productions. Dowmunt (1993) illustrates this problem with the example of Zimbabwe's television company ZTV:

ZTV can only afford to produce about twelve hours of indigenous drama a year, albeit incredibly cheaply with the actors also doing day jobs and providing their own costumes. Drama series like *Ziva Kawakaba* (Know Your Roots) are very popular with the majority black audience, but the advertisers know they are going to get better value for money from imported programmes that appeal to the more affluent white or middle-class black audiences. And ZTV know they can acquire an episode of *Miami Vice*, say, for the special 'Third World' rate of $500 – a fraction of the already minimal budget of an episode of *Ziva Kawakaba*.

Television stations in developing countries, then, tend to cater to the status requirements of metropolitan middle-class groups whose tastes, aspirations, fashions and lifestyle are more 'Westernized' and consumerist. In this way, the development of global communication technologies has gone hand in hand with the growth of capitalism's requirements for new markets.

The threat to independence in the late twentieth century from the new electronics could be greater than was colonialism itself . . . . The new media have the power to penetrate more deeply into a 'receiving' culture than any other previous manifestation of Western technology. The results could be immense havoc, an intensification of the social contradictions within developing societies today (Smith, 1980).

In effect the concepts of 'media imperialism' and the 'globalization of culture' are inextricably linked. Global communications are owned and controlled, almost exclusively, by 'First World' (US, European, Australian and Japanese) corporate interests and largely by a handful of US transnational conglomerates. In this sense a worldwide 'McDonalds and Madonna' culture, as promoted by television and the mass media, is seen as powerful and threatening to local identity, creating economic dependence, social pacification and cultural displacement. However, as Stevenson (1995) notes, the charge that the media spearhead ideological and cultural dominance at a global level simply to create new needs and desires for consumer capitalism is an oversimplification. He suggests that 'public interest' programming, of the kind to be found particularly on public service broadcasting stations, as well as journalistic principles of truth, objectivity and balance and the work of more independent 'creative' artists are examples of resistance within the media to the 'colonizing influence' of money and power.

Resistance is also provided by audiences of Western forms of media production who frequently 'read' or interpret imported programming in unexpected ways. Fiske quotes a study by Katz and Liebes (1987) that looked at how Russian Jews, newly arrived in Israel, read *Dallas* as 'capitalism's self-criticism'. As O'Sullivan *et al.* (1994) remark, drawing together evidence from those few studies that have been conducted on the reception of foreign material by traditional and indigenous cultures:

Audiences on the 'receiving end' of American cultural products like *Dallas* emerge as active agents, more complex, critical or resistant and certainly less predictable in their cultural responses than has been assumed.

Furthermore, as Armand and Michelle Mattelart stress, it should not be assumed that because the 'media imperialists' are powerful we need to regard the ex-colonies as weak and suffering from many 'problems' with no solutions (Branston and Stafford, 1996). Nevertheless, the highly concentrated owner-ship of the means of producing and circulating images, news, and represen-tations remains a critical concern both nationally and internationally and it would be foolish to underestimate the effect global media systems have in consolidating Western imperial power. As Edward Said points out in his study *Culture and imperialism*, 'even Saddam Hussein seems to have relied on CNN for his news'.

CASE STUDY: THE SATELLITE AND ISLAM

There is an assumption that American TV imports do have an impact whenever and wherever they are shown, but actual investigation of this seldom occurs. Much of the evidence offered is merely anecdotal or circumstantial (Lealand, 1984).

The following interview is included to illustrate in concrete terms some of the issues discussed at a more abstract level in this chapter, notably the previous section dealing with media imperialism, and in Chapter 15.

This interview was conducted in December 1996 with three female teacher trainees studying in the desert town of Ibri in the Sultanate of Oman. Oman is a Muslim state which has, until recently, maintained a relatively successful policy of preserving its country's national and religious traditions. When at the women's teacher training college the students wear a headscarf, usually black, pinned around their head, and a long black cloak over their more colourful clothes. When they leave the college premises, under escort, many wear a thin veil over their heads to protect themselves from male eyes. They reveal themselves, in conversation and in their general demeanour, to be genuinely patriotic Omanis and devout Muslims, and prostrate themselves to pray five times per day. In the classroom, however, most of them are bright and forthcoming and are generally quite assertive within the bounds of acceptable Muslim behaviour.

Omanis are free to buy and install satellite dishes and can pick up over 40 different channels from around the world, beamed from three satellites: Arabsat, Asiasat and Panamsat. There are many Arabic channels broadcasting into Oman from the Gulf States and beyond. Omanis are keen followers of, for example, Syrian, Egyptian and Jordanian soap operas, camel racing from the United Arab Emirates and Arabic 'pop' videos. They are also able to receive

Asian and Western channels carrying material which many regard as explicit and offensive. Images of alcohol, cigarettes, and particularly 'underdressed' women found on these channels mean that many Omani families I talked to would not purchase a dish, despite being very keen to view the many Arabic stations available which are sensitive to Muslim mores.

The interview was conducted with two students whose families had a dish, and one – Maryam – who did not. At the beginning of the interview, not shown here, the reason Maryam gave for her family not buying a dish was that her brothers were still at school and her parents did not want them to be distracted from their studies. All three students were fond of several English and US programmes, either dubbed or subtitled, which they watched regularly, either on Omani television or on their dish. Programmes they mentioned included *The Cosby Show*, *Sesame Street*, *Mr Bean*, *Eye Witness Video* and *Rescue 999*. The interview continues as follows, with my comments shown in italics.

You said you like films. What kind of films do you like?

Aziza: Cowboy films. I love them, even the old ones in black and white.

Maisa: I like suspense movies and cowboy films, a little, and science fiction films. Many kinds.

Right, Maisa, is there anything you don't like about satellite programmes or channels?

Maisa: Sometimes, every twenty-four hours, only news, news, news. I want to see something different, something more exciting than this.

Aziza, what about you?

Aziza: Yes, sometimes they show some bad pictures . . . underdressed women: I don't like it, because my brother's always watching the dish. I don't want him to see this, and also I don't want to see this. What I love is watching a lot of news – I want to know everything about the world. CNN is very good news.

So, you're different from Maisa?

Aziza: Yes, very different.

If you have a family, will you have a dish?

Maisa: Of course.

But will you be worried?

Aziza: I will make times for my children, and for me [laughs] to see these channels, and not . . . I will choose the best programmes.

Right, how can you choose though. Is it in the newspapers?

Aziza: Yes, you can see all the films and programmes there. I will choose the time and I will tell them. They can see it then. I will lock the door [laughs].

So, how many hours will you let them watch?

Aziza: Maybe two. Two or three.

Why do you want to limit it? Why can't they watch more?

Aziza: It will not help. This will make them waste time. They will not use their time. I want them to study, I want them to learn, not just watch TV . . . . I want them to learn English and this is the only way because I learnt English this way.

Will you, Maryam, get a dish if you have a family?

Maryam: Yes.

Will you, like Aziza, say some time when your children can watch it, or . . . ?

Maryam: Yes, one or two hours.

Maisa: Me, there are some channels I would delete from the dish. I would not let them see them.

Which channels would you stop?

Maisa: Orbit, and also French channels.

Aziza: LBC from the Lebanon. It's a horrible channel.

Is it because you can see women with no clothes on, or for other reasons?

Maisa: It's very bad: not good for the children to see.

Is it because of violence . . . ?

Aziza: No.

Is it because of the way it shows women?

[They nod in agreement.]

What do you want to see more of on the satellite dish?

Maisa: I want to see more films, more children's programmes like . . . many, many things.

What would you like to see more of?

Maryam: Films, American films.

What about Arabic films?

Aziza, Maryam: No, I hate them.

Are there any Omani films?

Maisa: There are no Omani films.

I'm only asking, I don't know.

Maisa: There's only one, they made it last year.

What do you want to see more of on satellite?

Aziza: I want to see a lot of science films, American films.

Science fiction, like films about the future?

Aziza: Yes, and also programmes about science. And also more world news. I love watching world news.

You've got CNN, isn't that enough?

Aziza: No, it's not enough. You know, MBC sometimes has more . . . is looking for news more than CNN.

MBC or NBC?

Maisa: MBC. It's from London.

Aziza: Yes, but it's an Arabic channel. I was watching it and I saw a lot of, when Palestinians were fighting recently in Jerusalem – I saw it early on MBC and at night I saw it on CNN.

You saw it first on MBC?

Aziza: Yes, it was about 12 o'clock in the morning on MBC and about 10 o'clock or 11 o'clock in the evening on CNN.

Right. How many people in Oman have a dish? What percentage?

Aziza: 90 per cent.

90 per cent have a dish? Most families?

Aziza: Yes, some of them have two.

Maisa: Yes, we have two dishes in our house. One is Asiasat and the other is Arabsat.

That's interesting because I asked a class and maybe only six or seven out of forty said they had one.

Aziza: If you go to Muscat you'll see almost all the houses have a dish.

Yes, but we're not in Muscat, we're in Ibri, so . . .

Aziza: In Ibri also, and in my town Bahla I saw a lot . . . a lot. Now they are . . . everywhere.

Why do you think some families don't want a dish?

Aziza: Because they can't. My cousin, my uncle doesn't have a dish. He said to us: 'I can't bring it here.' So we said we could bring it and we will pay for it and do everything, but he said no. We asked him why and he said, 'There's a lot of bad things. They will make my son do bad things like smoking and some bad things. It's helping a lot to do these things.'

Um, what do you think, Maryam, are the dangers of the dish for Oman, or for Arab countries?

Maryam: Yes, because we have many channels, it's not normal.

Why is that?

Aziza: It's wasting time.

Anything else?

Maryam: And also our traditions. They're not the same.

Aziza: We are Muslim.

Maisa: It's very different, very different. We are Muslim. We are not allowed to see all of these pictures.

So, does that cause problems then?

Maisa: Yes, a lot of problems.

Maryam: For example, when people see the dish a lot of time – we have a time to pray – we are wasting this – and people don't pray.

You said 90 per cent of people have a dish, but also you said it caused big problems.

Maisa: Yes.

So is there a solution? What do families do?

Maisa: They take off some channels: such as the French channels. These are bad channels. On our dish we don't see the French channels.

Maryam: In my village we haven't a lot of money. I saw that we can't buy a dish. But some people have the money but they don't buy it.

Why?

Maryam: Because we are Muslim. We are not allowed to see these things. And also we are not allowed to waste our time just watching TV and listening to music. No.

This must be a problem for you, if you think on the one hand it's bad, but on the other you want to watch it, how do you balance it?

Aziza: When I go home I always watch TV, that's clear. But I don't watch these

American films or something like that. What I watch is CNN news, and I love it. I want to know everything about the world and I'm not wasting all my time. I watch it for two or three hours and then spend some time with my family and talk to them, that's all.

How many hours a day does your family have the TV on?

Aziza: The TV or the dish?

The dish.

Aziza: I don't think my father or my mother watch the dish, but only my little brother. Now he is 13 years old. Before the dish, his ideas were very different.

Really?

Aziza: Believe me. [speaks in Arabic to the others.] He changed a lot [laughs].

How?

[They speak in Arabic.]

Speak in English. Say what you think.

Maisa: Can we stop it [pointing to the tape recorder]?

No, don't stop.

Aziza: . . . The bad thing about dishes is that they bring a lot of people smoking and drinking. My brother is 13 years old. Before he wasn't making his hair like this [gestures a new hairstyle] and my cousin too.

What do you mean?

Aziza: Like Michael Jackson [laughs].

So he's changed his hair. Has he changed his clothes?

Aziza: No, not a lot . . . sometimes. And a lot of our neighbours changed – they have had bad haircuts and, oh my God [laughs], awful. That's because they're watching these channels. And some of them don't pray.

Any other changes from the dish?

Aziza: Some of them change their ideas about the world. Some of the channels make them know the world a lot. Not by changing their clothes, or changing their hair, but also by changing their ideas about everything, about other countries, about their countries, about politicians, about everything.

How do their ideas of other countries change?

Aziza: On our television, on Omani television, we don't see a lot of political things, but on CNN or MBC, or some of these channels we can see about your countries' politicians.

Right, so you can start to think about America and England . . .

Aziza: Yes, and about . . . everything.

Is that good or bad, or both?

Aziza: For me, it's good.

What about you, Maisa? Anything which has changed?

Maisa: I know that in our house . . . I have little sisters and brothers. 24 hours they are watching the dish. We want them to study – no, they don't want to study, they want to watch the dish. Why? Because, for example, in Dubai, there is cartoon television for them. It will finish in Dubai, it will then be from Abu Dhabi, then from Al 'Ayn, then Sharkia – like this. One channel finishes and another starts cartoons, so for 24 hours they are watching cartoons. They don't want to study . . . like this.

Any other last thoughts?

Maisa: Satellite is good and at the same time, it's bad. If we know how to use it, it will be good.

Maryam: The dish is very important to teach.

To teach? In schools, or in the home?

Aziza: At home.

Maryam: In schools.

Aziza: they don't use it in schools!

Maryam: The teaching programmes.

Do you mean documentaries? They can use documentaries and so on in schools?

Maryam: Yes.

Aziza: I want to say – what I want to say is that the dish is important – very important, especially because we are watching it every day. And what we want is to be like European countries – not like their behaviour, or something like that, but we want to improve in science . . . But the dish is very dangerous. And that will kill us – [laughs] one day it's going to kill us.

Thank you very much.

Questionnaire Results

A written questionnaire was conducted in which 100 Omani teacher trainee students were asked about their television viewing habits. As with any questionnaire, the answers they have given may be inaccurate for a variety of reasons – failure to understand the question properly, failure to estimate their answers correctly, peer pressure or embarrassment are just some of the factors that may have influenced these results. Nevertheless, they may give some indication of to what extent the opinions put forward in the interview with three students are typical of the wider population of young, female teacher trainees.

Question: Does your family have a television?

Answer: 100 per cent answered yes. The average number of hours of television that students said they watched per day was around 3.

Question: Does your family have a satellite dish?

Answer: 23 per cent answered 'yes', 77 per cent answered 'no'.

Question: Will you buy a satellite dish when you have your own home?

Answer: 27 per cent answered yes, 65 per cent no, and 8 per cent did not answer at all.

The channels most watched on the satellite dish were other Arabic stations broadcast from countries such as Egypt, Syria, the United Arab Emirates, the Lebanon, Iraq and Kuwait, although some non-Arabic channels were watched, particularly CNN. Reasons given for watching satellite channels varied, but included the following attractions: enjoyable programmes and films, news, information about the world and the opportunity to listen to the Koran. Students claimed that on average about 20 per cent of the programmes they watched were in English, usually with Arabic subtitles. These were popular because they said they helped them to learn English, were 'enjoyable' and 'interesting' and contained informative 'cultural information' about the ways other people live.

The ambivalent attitude to the dish seen in the interview was also evident in the questionnaire. Common phrases used to describe their opinion of satellite television included:

- dangerous
- it is against Islam
- it teaches children bad things
- it is against our traditions
- it is a waste of time
- it will destroy the countries who watch it
- it is important
- it is good for learning
- it is good for languages
- interesting
- it is good when you know how to use it

Many of the responses included both of these comments. The following sentences were typical:

> Television and the dish are good and bad at the same time. Their worth is limited by the person who sees them. I think they have bad ideas for children.

> Some programmes are good and some are very bad. We want to learn a lot of good things about other countries.

> Sometimes the television is a good thing because you can learn many things about history, science and you also can learn languages from it. But the dish is a very bad thing.

A total of 58 per cent of those questioned agreed with the statement 'I think the dish has a bad influence on people'.

A total of 48 per cent agreed with the statement 'I think we can learn a lot about the world through the dish and this will be a good thing for my country'.

A total of 47 per cent agreed with the statement 'I think the dish will have a bad effect on my country'.

Many of the respondents agreed with all the statements.

READING: THE POLITICAL INFLUENCE OF TELEVISION IN THE USA

The following is an extract from an article by Martin Walker (1997), a Washington political correspondent, which is interesting for the perspective it offers on some of the issues raised in this chapter and Chapter 14. According to the article, Bernie Sanders, a Democrat in the House of Congress representing Vermont, has put media ownership and control at the centre of the political debate for the Progressive Caucus. He claims that corporate control of the media, and in particular television, has become a decisive and, in his view, negative influence on US political decision-making, up to and including the policies of the President:

'I think Bill Clinton really tried in his first two years in office', Sanders said. 'His first budget, in 1993, was reasonably progressive. His tax reform was clearly progressive, cutting the taxes on the working poor, and only the richest 4 per cent saw their taxes increased. But nobody in America knew that. The Republicans were allowed by the media to portray it as the biggest tax increase in the history of the world. When I went speaking in my own district about the budget, people would tell me they didn't know the reality. I told President Clinton about this, and he just said yeah, he knew it, and they just couldn't get the news out. And then on health reform, when Clinton did the right thing, the media just ripped the shit out of him.'

Sanders identified four big issues for the Progressive Caucus to develop. The first is the continuing crisis of affordable healthcare. The second is the sharp and widening disparity in incomes, more marked now than it has been for more than 60 years, in which the richest 1 per cent own more than the bottom 90 per cent of Americans. The third is the 'crisis of our democracy', not just the falling turnout, but the way it is now financed and owned by corporate money and millionaires.

Sanders's fourth point, the one that seems most to ignite his outrage, is 'the corporate control over our media, which means most Americans just don't know that healthcare is free in places like Britain, that a college education is free or at least affordable, that most other advanced countries don't share out their wealth in this divisive way. The reason is pretty simple. Most Americans get their news from the four big TV networks. ABC is owned by Disney. NBC is owned by General Electric. CBS is owned by Westinghouse. Fox is owned by Rupert Murdoch. You just don't see those corporations reporting on trade unions, or the wealth gap, on the fact that over 90 per cent of the budget cuts the last Congress passed were taken from the poor.'

EXERCISES AND ESSAYS

Exercise

Produce an ideological analysis of a television programme of your choice.

Exercise

Find examples from television schedules of 'dominant–hegemonic', 'negotiated' and 'oppositional' texts (see also Chapter 12, pp. 166–8).

Exercise and Essay

What would the Frankfurt School make of contemporary television in Britain?

Exercise and Essay

What evidence is there, either for or against, liberal political notions of the role of television in promoting political and economic freedom?

Exercise and Essay

'Chomsky's "propaganda model" is a simplification of complex relations between the media and society': discuss.

Essay

> In general, then, the determining context for production is always that of the market. In seeking to maximise this market, products must draw on the most widely legitimating central core values while rejecting the dissenting voice or the incompatible objection to a ruling myth. The need for easily understood, popular, formulated, undisturbing, assimilable fictional material is at once a commercial imperative and an aesthetic recipe (Murdoch and Golding, quoted in Strinati, 1995).

Murdoch and Golding suggest that the ideology of television is the ideology of the market. Is this always the case?

Essay

> Murdoch's empire has always shared one thing with the Marxist enterprise. It turns ideas into social and economic experiments .... If BSkyB's swoop to seize control of televised soccer marks the climax of News Corporation's long-term plan for a self-reinforcing media system, it is also the culminating event in a social ... and even ideological ... transformation of Britain in the image of a radical philosophy: one which places the media corporation, as a

promoter of information to the ordinary consumer, in direct opposition to the established elites (Rothwell, 1992).

How far can a 'media system' bring about the ideological transformation of a country?

Essay

How might 'media imperialism' pose a threat to indigenous culture? Is there any evidence that it does?

Essay

We have seen in other countries that when commercial competition bites, choice narrows. The most effective means of countering the risks of the globalisation of culture, and declining standards will be by sustaining their publicly-funded broadcasters (Birt, 1996).

How, and to what extent, can public service broadcasting act as a check against media imperialism?

Sources

Adorno, T. (1991): *The culture industry.* Routledge.

Althusser, L. (1984): Ideology and ideological state apparatuses. In *Essays on ideology,* verso; quoted in Stevenson, N. (1995) *Understanding media cultures.* Sage.

Arnold, M. (1932): *Culture and anarchy.* Cambridge University Press.

Barthes, R. (1973): *Mythologies.* Paladin.

Birt, J. (1996): Gateway to the BBC's future. James Taggart Memorial Lecture, Edinburgh, August.

Branston, G. and Stafford, R. (1996): *The media student's book.* Routledge.

Burton, G. (1990): *More than meets the eye.* Arnold.

Chomsky, N. and Herman, E. S. (1988): *Manufacturing consent: the political economy of the mass media.* Pantheon Books.

Dowmunt, T. (ed.) (1993): *Channels of resistance.* British Film Institute/Channel 4.

Fiske, J. (1987): *Television culture.* Routledge.

Gramsci, A. (1971): *Selections from the Prison Notebooks.* Lawrence and Wishart.

Hall, S. (1977): Culture, the media and the 'ideological' effect. In Curran, J., Gurevitch, M. and Wollacott, J. (eds), *Mass communication and society.* Arnold.

Hall, S. (1978): *Policing the crisis.* Macmillan.

Hodge, J. (1996): *Trainspotting.* Film script. Faber and Faber.

Katz, E. and Liebes, T. (1987): *On the critical ability of television viewers.* Seminar paper presented at the University of Tübingen; quoted by Fiske, J. (1987): *Television culture.* Routledge.

Kawin, B. (1992): *How movies work.* University of California Press.

Lealand, G. (1984): *American Television Programmes on British Screen.* Broadcasting Research Unit; quoted in O'Sullivan *et al.* (1994): *Studying the Media.* Arnold.

Lewis, P. (1986): *Media and power.* Camden Press.

Maltby, R. (ed.) (1989): *Dreams for sale – popular culture in the 20th century.* Equinox.

Marx, K. (1996): *The Communist Manifesto.* Pluto Press. First published in 1848.

Marx, K. (1970): *German ideology: a students' edition.* Lawrence and Wishart.

Masterman, L. (1985): *Teaching the media.* Routledge.

Miliband, R. (1979): *The state in capitalist society.* Quartet.

Pilger, J. (1992): *Distant voices.* Vintage Books.

O'Sullivan, T., Dutton, B. and Rayner, P. (1994): *Studying the media.* Arnold.

Rothwell, N. (1992): Britain's class war in a satellite dish. *The Australian* 28 May; quoted in
Pilger, J. (1992): *Distant voices.* Vintage Books.

Said, E. (1993): *Culture and imperialism.* Chatto and Windus.

Smith, A. (1980): *The geopolitics of information: how Western culture dominates the world.*
Oxford University Press; quoted by Said, E. (1993): *Culture and imperialism.* Chatto and
Windus.

Stevenson, N. (1995): *Understanding media cultures.* Sage.

Strinati, D. (1995): *An introduction to theories of popular culture.* Routledge.

Thompson, J.B. (1984): *Studies in the theory of ideology.* Polity Press.

Walker, M. (1997): The political influence of television in the USA. *Guardian Weekly* 19
January.

Ceci n'est pas une pipe, 1929, by René Magritte (1898–1967)

17

Semiotics

> Our experience of the world is never pure or 'innocent' because systems of meaning make sure that it is intelligible. There is no such thing as a pure, uncoded, objective experience of a real and objective world. The latter exists but its intelligibility depends upon codes of meaning or systems of signs, like language (Strinati, 1995).

'Semiotics' (a science which is also known as 'semiology') is the study of 'signs' and their use within society. Semiotics is a relatively new, abstract and undeniably complex science, applicable to a whole range of disciplines (including media and communication studies). Semiotics is highly pertinent to the study of television because it concerns the way people generate meaning from a variety of sign systems available to them for communication purposes. Words, images and sounds are all regarded as 'signs' within semiotics, and as television makes use of all three types of signs, semiotics has a great contribution to make in our understanding of the medium.

Semiotics, however, is an area that is seemingly plagued by difficult terminology. Nevertheless, the terms are worth coming to grips with, if only either to challenge or to agree with those who claim that semiotics is probably the most important and far-reaching scientific discipline of this century. The following is a brief and by no means comprehensive attempt to explain semiotics and some of the terminology used.

SAUSSURE AND SIGN SYSTEMS

Semiotics emerged from linguistics – which is the study of one type of sign system: language. Linguists, such as Ferdinand de Saussure, observed that language is a system of signs that express ideas in much the same way as other 'sign systems' such as writing, morse code, smoke signals, war paint, etiquette, gestures, semaphore and so on. According to Saussure the *arbitrary* and *conventional* nature of the sign in language is especially clear. To take an example, the words *dog* (in English), *hund* (in German) or *kelp* (in Arabic) have no natural or intrinsic link to the concept of a four-legged, faithful domestic friend. They are sounds that have been agreed upon by those language speakers to mean the idea of that animal. The words could equally be *glak*, *jadj* or *sleez*. If enough English speakers agreed to use *jadj* instead of *dog* the word might enter the English language and even come to replace the word *dog* eventually. Interestingly, one television broadcast addressed to millions of viewers can, and has, done this. Jasper Carrott introduced the US slang term *zit* (meaning acne spot) to Britain overnight, following his explanation of the term on a live comedy broadcast in the early 1980s.

The notion that signs are on the whole arbitrary and conventional has profound consequences. As Jonathan Culler (1976) notes:

> If signs were natural, then there would really be nothing to analyse. One would say that opening a door for a woman simply is polite, and that's all there is to it. But if one starts out with the assumption that signs are likely to be conventional, then one will seriously seek out the conventions on which they are based and will discover the underlying system which makes these signs what they are.

SIGNS

Signs have a physical form: they are something we can perceive with our senses. They are recognized by people in society to refer to something other than themselves. For instance the word *snow*, either written or spoken in English, or transcribed in braille, or a photograph or a picture of snow or a character on a weather map such as ❄ conventionally refers to the concept of 'frozen water which falls as flakes'. Signs, then, are made up of a 'signifier' and 'signified'.

The *signifier* (or form) is the physical form such as letters, words, images, soundwaves. An example would be the word *cat* in English, *gato* in Spanish and *billi* in Hindi, or a photograph, cartoon, sketch, painting, video or audio recording of a cat. Some signifiers have many signifieds. *Snow*, for instance, has been used in particular drug cultures to refer to cocaine. The signifier *beauty*, interestingly, has an infinite number of signifieds.

The *signified* (or concept) is the mental concept attached to the signifier. The signifier *cat* refers to a 'furry, four-legged domestic animal'. The signified is not to be confused with the 'referent' – an actual, 'real' cat. As René Magritte's painting of a pipe declares, '*Ceci n'est pas une pipe*': This is not a pipe (it is, in fact, a painting, a representation of a pipe). Signifier and signified are divided only for analytical purposes and in practice are so tightly interwoven that the relation between them appears natural, normal and given.

The relationship between signifier and signified can change. For example, *bad* has come in some cultures and groups to mean *good*. A word such as *pious* was, for hundreds of years, used only as a term of praise, meaning '*devout*' or '*godly*'. The word today, however, is often used with sarcastic or negative connotations to mean self-righteous. *Gay* and *queer* are other terms which have undergone transformations in meaning and connotation. *Queer* in the sense of 'strange' or 'curious' came to be used as a term of abuse against homosexuals implying abnormality. However, in recent years, many homosexuals in the USA and Britain have used the term *queer* with pride, appropriating the term and thus, hopefully, robbing the word of its power to hurt and insult.

Signifieds, as Hartley (1982) points out, are not natural, given entities corresponding to distinct parts of the world 'out there', 'Signifieds are just as much a part of language as signifiers – they perform the function of dividing up the natural and perceived continuum of sense-impressions into organised categories.' Hence *snow* is the one word English speakers use to refer to 'frozen water that falls like flakes'. It is distinct from *sleet* or *hail* or *slush* or *rain*. The Inuit (Eskimos), however, have over 200 words which refer to different types of 'snow'. Hence a single-sense impression or concept in English has over 200 equivalents in Inuit.

Saussure argued that signs were defined 'not by their positive content but negatively by their relations with the other terms in the system. Their most precise characteristic is in being what other are not' (quoted by Hartley, 1982). Hence *snow*, in the English language, is simply 'frozen water that falls like flakes', but not 'frozen water' (ice) or 'frozen pellets of ice' (hail). Similarly, ❋ or ❊ might be used as signifiers of snow, but not ✓ or ♅. Accordingly, then, as Hartley suggests:

> The value of signs is determined wholly by their relationships with others in a system. Hence it follows that these values are social. Language is a 'social fact' and meaning is a product of socially recognized (conventional) differences.

Three Classes of Signs

The US philosopher Pierce was interested in how signs relate to objects in the world. He proposed three ways that signs relate to their 'referent' (the 'real' object rather than the mental concept):

- An *icon* is where the sign resembles the object; for example a photo, map, and so on. Onomatopoeic words such as *bang*, *hiss* and *buzz* are also iconical.
- An *index* is connected to the object causally or sequentially. Smoke would be an index of fire. Tracks are signs of the type of animal likely to have produced them. A pipe might be an index of Sherlock Holmes. The crown is sometimes used to indicate the institution of monarchy. A part is used to stand in for the whole, as the crown is only a part of the royal regalia.
- A *symbol* (or *sign proper*) does not resemble or have a causal relationship to the object. The object is signified according to convention. The word *cat*, in

English, is conventionally agreed upon to refer to a species of furry domestic animal. Male and female signs, ♂ and ♀, similarly, do not resemble, and have no causal relationship to, their referents 'male' and 'female' or to their other referents the planets Mars and Venus. All spoken and written language is symbolic.

Television uses icons, indexes and symbols.

Signs are organized into *codes* or *sign systems*. Semiotics is less concerned with individual signs than how they operate together as a system. It is the primacy which Saussure accorded to 'systems of relations' that links semiotics to a whole series of disciplines, including physics, and is most clearly articulated in the shift from nineteenth-century 'materialism' to a twentieth-century 'theory of relativity' in its broadest sense. According to the philosopher of science, Alfred North Whitehead:

> The misconception which has haunted philosophic literature throughout the centuries is the notion of 'independent existence'. There is no such mode of existence; every entity is to be understood in terms of the way it is interwoven with the rest of the universe (quoted in Culler, 1976).

According to Hartley (1982) the sequence of signs that makes up any act of communication involves relations in 'two dimensions'. These sequences are selected according to syntagmatic and paradigmatic choices. A *syntagm* (which we may conceive of as the 'horizontal' axis of choice) describes the relationship between elements in a sequence, as in words in a sentence. A *paradigm* – a class of objects or concepts – (the 'vertical' axis of choice) describes the relationship between items that might replace each other in a sequence thereby altering its meaning, as in:

demonstrators ...
peaceful protesters ...
students and workers ...
union activists ...
protesting strikers ...   took to the streets again today ...
violent protesters ...
rioters ...
anti-government forces ...
criminal elements ...

As Strinati (1995) suggests, 'it is the relational character of the structure which enables the item, unit or sign to acquire meaning'. Hence 'terrorists liberated', although grammatically correct, is unlikely, because the sign 'terrorist' and the sign 'liberated' belong to two opposing discourses in social use (Hartley, 1982). We learn to read and employ signs in different combinations or codes. A bride is unlikely to attend her wedding dressed in black, you are unlikely to eat baked beans and jelly on the same plate, and a television news report is unlikely to be read in extreme close-up. Some codes, however, are more rigid than others. Whereas many conventions of news broadcasts are strictly adhered to, in other genres the conventions are more flexible. *Hill Street Blues* borrowed certain documentary 'codes' and was considered 'groundbreaking' for having inter-connecting storylines. *NYPD Blue* also broke several conventions of police series, using jump cuts and deliberately 'jerky' camera movements. The legal drama *Murder One* dealt with only one storyline over 23 hours' worth of episodes – and was 'unconventional' in this sense. The success of all three series produced by Steven Bochko, may, in part, be attributed to the way they 'broke the rules' in a highly controlled manner, pushing forward the boundaries of highly conservative or 'codified' US television series.

Signification is the connection between signs. According to Roland Barthes signification is how signs (for example languages) work within a culture, how they create meanings. Barthes talks about 'readers' and 'readings'. These readings will be at two levels of signification (see Chapter 16 for further explanation of these terms): denotation and connotation.

Denotation describes the relationship between signifier and signified at the *first* order of signification. This is a seemingly objective and value-free level which refers to the literal, obvious 'surface' meaning of a word. A photograph of a street denotes that particular street; the word *street* denotes an urban road lined with buildings. The denoted meaning is thus, basically, *what* is represented.

The *second order* of signification includes connotation and myth. *Connotation* refers to the more unconscious meanings which we associate with that which is denoted. For example, the word *alley* has the denoted meaning of 'narrow street', but it also has connotations for people from our culture, since we associate alleys, particularly at night, with darkness, risk, danger, crime and illicit activity. In another context, however, alleys have quite different associations. In a cathedral city, for instance, alleys might be associated with antiques, expensive tourist and craft shops, pubs and restaurants, and be considered pleasant to wander around. Connotation occurs when the denotative meaning of a sign is placed within a culture. This interpretation will be specific to the culture in which the sign is placed. A reader belongs to a culture and will therefore bring certain associations, interpretations and judgements to the reading of signs. Connotation is both subjective and inter-subjective (shared in a culture). Shared connoted meaning makes up cultural identity.

Connotation is a value-laden interpretation and evaluation of meaning. The connoted meaning is thus, basically, the context or background which, in some sense, lies behind a word, an image, an object. It is what we *imply*, *infer* or *associate* rather than what is there for all to see.

Myth – not, in the more common sense of ideas we do not believe in but rather ideas that we *do* believe in – is a chain of concepts that are accepted and recognized in a culture. Myth is used to make sense of the world. For example *countryside* is recognized generally as a place of peace, leisure, recuperation, beauty and spiritual refreshment; whereas *city* is thought of as an unnatural, tense and stressful place. These myths, however, are not fixed or unchanging. In Britain in the eighteenth century, for example, and in other cultures today, these myths are quite the reverse. The countryside, according to these perspectives, is considered rude, poor, uncivilized and primitive whereas the city is urbane, wealthy, polite and civilized.

Myths, then, are not eternal, universal or natural. They are *cultural constructions*. The naturalization of myths, however, make them seem so obvious that they no longer seem like constructions. Myths obscure their origins, they appear given because they are shared by a culture. They are the result of intersubjectivity. However, myths are never in unanimous consensus. There is a *hierarchy* of myths. Some reach dominance: these are the most widely circulated. However, a range of countermyths also exist. For example, television always shows family quiz shows, soaps, comedy, interviews, and so on. 'The family' is a pervasive sign on television. We can attack the myth of security, truthfulness, caring, sharing. It is a sickly myth that we are, at least at times, able to recognize because the status of the family in Western society is currently in transition. Occasionally we see the family 'myth' challenged on television. In the US situation comedy *Grace Under Fire* the heroine is a single-parent mother who 'jokes' about her abusive, drunken husband from whom she is separated. Despite massive numbers of single-parent families in Britain and the USA, situation comedy is one of the few genres where the conventional representation or myth of nuclear families is occasionally challenged. Television generally *reproduces* dominant myths. It is rare, in television, to represent countermyths because broadcasting appeals to mass audiences and invites consensus.

Multiaccentuality

Signs do not have fixed meanings, they are capable of signifying different values. The 'multiaccentuality' of signs can be easily illustrated. The phrase 'I'm sorry', for instance, contains various meaning potentials which may be 'accented' according to the speaker, the social context, the 'voice' or tone, and so on. In the sentence, 'I'm sorry, I didn't know you were sleeping', the phrase is likely to be apologetic. In the phrase 'I'm sorry, we were not told that information', however, the meaning of 'I'm sorry' is less likely to be apologetic than confrontational. Nevertheless, in both examples – with a certain tone of stress – the meaning potentials could be reversed.

With more subjective words such as *happy* and *ugly* or ideologically loaded terms such as *intelligent*, *liberal* or *racist* there is scope for radical disagreement over the signifieds. Ideologically, charged signs are the sites of struggle reflecting wider tensions and confrontations in society. Jean Marie Le Pen, the leader of the National Front in France, denies he is a racist. His understanding of the term – that 'signified' by the signifier 'racist' – is likely to be very different from a French Jew or Arab's understanding of the word.

An example of how a signifier's generally accepted meaning (or signified) can 'shift' and change ideologically can be seen in the US political establishment where 'liberal' has, in recent years, become a term of abuse. Under the rise of the New Right, particularly in the Republican Party, liberalism is now regarded by the political 'mainstream' in the USA as an 'extremist' political ideology. President Clinton publicly denied he was a liberal, or a 'closet-liberal' in much the same way that actors and screenwriters denied being communists in the McCarthy trials of the 1950s. The dominant meaning or connotation of 'liberal' in the USA is now quite different from a European understanding of the term – where 'liberal' as a political label is still regarded by most countries as mildly progressive, with associations of compromise and a 'middle way' between socialism and conservatism.

SEMIOTICS AND TELEVISION

The notion of multiaccentuality suggests that signs do not have a fixed (dictionary) meaning. They are negotiated in the public arena between speaker and listener, painter and viewer, reader and writer, musician and audience, broadcaster and viewer. (Hartley (1982) suggests that

> meaning is never 'there' in the sign or in the text. Meaning is the product of the dialogic interaction that occurs between speaker (or text) and hearer (or reader/viewer). Therefore every utterance or text is incomplete – it is a 'moment' in the continuous generative process of language.

In the case of television, messages in the form of combinations of signs are 'encoded' by the programme makers and broadcasters (the 'senders') and 'decoded' by the viewers (the 'receivers'). Without the receivers these messages would remain meaningless transmissions broadcast into the earth's atmosphere. Television programmes or texts are orientated towards different audiences, just as we change what we say, and how we say it, depending on who we are talking to. The BBC's *The Money Programme* or the satellite channel Asia Business News are orientated towards a wealthy niche audience of investors who are extremely attractive to advertisers and programme makers, thereby justifying the cost of reaching such a numerically small number of viewers. *The National Lottery*, on the other hand, will be orientated towards, or 'aimed at', a mass audience, and this fact is reflected in every aspect of the presentation of the programme from music and set design to choice of presenters. Audience targeting is the planned orientation of programmes and schedules towards particular ages, nationalities, socio-economic or ethnic groups.

Television produces meaning visually and verbally, employing a wide range of signs combined in complex codes and conventions. Unlike spoken language, morse code or semaphore which are transmitted in a linear fashion (one word or sign after another), television presents signifiers such as speech, music, sound effects, colours, gestures, facial expressions and movement simultaneously. The complexity and diversity of signs and codes employed on television means that it is a highly *polysemic* medium, or open to a variety of readings and interpretations. Because the meaning of any television sequence is, therefore, potentially diverse and multilayered, a number of strategies are applied, some more successfully than others, to *anchor* the meaning. Anchorage is an attempt to control and focus the meaning potential of the signs employed – to *prefer* a particular reading over others and signal this reading clearly for the audience. If other meaning potentials are heavily suppressed by programme makers the programme may be described as a *closed text*. News reports are, on the whole, 'closed texts'. 'Authority' is signified via a number of codes (including music, lighting, shot types, accent, dress, tone, and so on) and is exercised continuously, particularly through the newsreader, to impose a single interpretation of the images offered. An *open text*, by contrast, does not prefer any single reading. This strategy sometimes occurs in music videos (which often revel in the instability and abundance of signifiers employed).

For those working in television who wish to prefer a particular meaning, television has one major advantage over other media: so many of the signs used are *iconic*. A moving image of a politician giving a speech at a conference will closely resemble its signified (a property also known as *motivation*). Whereas the word 'politician' has an arbitrary relationship to the signified and can be easily replaced in a sentence (or 'defining sequence') by the terms *statesman*, *orator*, *charismatic leader*, *crook*, *dictator*, *hawk*, *extremist*, *rabble-rouser*, *fraud* or *windbag*, a moving television image cannot be so easily transformed. Nevertheless, a television picture of a politician is only that: a picture. This picture is made up of signals converted electronically into coloured light, fired in a series of lines in a vacuum-sealed tube at a screen. There is a 'planned resemblance' to the real – modified over the years by technological developments and standards. Furthermore, the codes and conventions which allow us to recognize the broadcast as a political speech have only been established in the relatively recent history of broadcasting and yet are highly manipulated by the dominant political parties. Camera angle, framing, lighting, sound, music, background, gesture, body language, facial expression, phrasing, timing, in fact a very long list of variables are carefully modified and juxtaposed for maximum impact on the television audience. The *constructed* nature of this television event, like all television events, can all too easily be forgotten.

EXERCISES AND ESSAYS

Read the following account by Roland Barthes from his book *Mythologies* (1973):

I am at the barber's, and a copy of *Paris-Match* is offered to me. On the cover, a young Negro in a French uniform is saluting, with eyes uplifted, probably fixed on a fold of the tricolour. All this is the meaning of the picture. But ... I see very well what it signifies to me: that France is a great Empire, that all her sons, without any colour discrimination, faithfully serve under her flag, and that there is no better answer to the detractors of an alleged colonialism than the zeal shown by this Negro in serving his so-called oppressors. I am therefore ... faced with a greater semiological system: there is a signifier, itself already formed within a previous system (a black soldier is giving the French salute); there is a signified (it is here a purposeful mixture of Frenchness and militariness); finally, there is the presence of the signified through the signifier ... French imperiality.

For Barthes the photograph distorts the historical fact of French colonial exploitation and asserts a myth: 'The French Empire? It's just a fact: look at this good Negro who salutes just like one of our boys' (quoted by Strinati, 1995).

Exercise and Essay

Look at how any national event is represented on television: for example the National Lottery, Last Night of the Proms, A War Documentary, The Queen's Speech, the closing transmission (the National Anthem), and so on. What 'myths' are offered about Britain and its people or history?

Exercise and Essay

Watch the opening 30 seconds of a title sequence for any two programmes in the same genre (for example two competing breakfast-time shows). What does a semiotic analysis of these sequences reveal? You may wish to structure your description as denotative, connotative and ideological 'levels' of analysis. What myths, if any, are revealed by such an analysis?

Sources

Barthes, R. (1973): *Mythologies*. Paladin.
Branston, G. and Stafford, R. (1996): *The media student's book*. Routledge.
Culler, J. (1976): *Saussure*. Fontana.
Eco, U. (1979): *The role of the reader*. Indiana University Press.
Fiske, J. (1987): *Television culture*. Routledge.
Fiske, J. and Hartley, J. (1978): *Reading television*. Methuen.
Hartley, J. (1982): *Understanding news*. Methuen.
O'Sullivan, T. Dutton, B. and Rayner, P. (1994): *Studying the media – an introduction*. Arnold.
Strinati, D. (1995): *Popular culture*. Routledge.

Interviews

Steven Bochko (1996): broadcast on BBC World Service.
Steven Bochko (1996): *Guardian*, at National Film Theatre, October/November.

Suggested Reading

Allaun, F. (1988): *Spreading the news*. Spokesman.

Alvarado, M. (1987): *Television and video*. Wayland.

Baehr, H. and Dyer, G. (eds) (1987): *Boxed in: women and television*. Pandora.

Barratt, D. (1986): *Media sociology*. Routledge.

Bazalgette, C. *et al.* (1933): *Teaching Coronation Street*. British Film Institute Education.

Braham, P. (1987): *Media effects*. Open University Press.

Branston, G. and Stafford, R. (1996): *The media student's book*. Routledge.

Burton, G. (1990): *More than meets the eye*. Arnold.

Buxton, D. (1990): *From The Avengers to Miami Vice: form and ideology in television series*. Manchester University Press.

Chomsky, N. and Herman, E. S. (1988): *Manufacturing consent: the political economy of the mass media*. Pantheon Books.

Corner, J. (1995): *Television form and public address*. Arnold.

Dowmunt, T. (ed.) (1993): *Channels of resistance*. British Film Institute/Channel 4.

Eldridge, J. (ed.) (1993): *Getting the message*. Routledge.

Ellis, J. (1982): *Visible fictions – cinema: television: video*. Routledge.

Fiske, J. (1987): *Television culture*. Routledge.

Fiske, J. and Hartley, J. (1978): *Reading television*. Methuen.

Giannetti, L. (1988): *Understanding movies*. Prentice Hall.

Gill, D. and Adams, B. (1988): *ABC of communication studies*. Macmillan Education.

Goodwin, A. and Whannel, G. (eds) (1990): *Understanding television*. Routledge.

Hartley, J. (1982): *Understanding news*. Methuen.

Hartley, J. *et al.* (eds) (1994): *Key concepts in communication and cultural studies*. Routledge.

Lewis, P. (1986): *Media and power: from Marconi to Murdoch*. Camden Press.

Lusted, D. (ed.) (1991): *The media studies book*. Routledge.

Maltby, R. (ed.) (1989): *Dreams for sale – popular culture in the 20th century*. Equinox.

Mason, D. (1991): *Gameshow handbook*. Random Century.

Masterman, L. (1980): *Teaching about television*. Macmillan.

Masterman, L. (1985): *Teaching the media*. Routledge.

Neale, S. and Krutnik, F. (1990): *Popular film and television comedy*. Routledge.

Negrine, R. (1989): *Politics and the mass media in Britain*. Routledge.

O'Malley, T. and Treharne, J. (1993): *Selling the Beeb*. Campaign for Press and Broadcasting Freedom (CPBF).

O'Sullivan, T., Dutton, B. and Rayner, P. (1994): *Studying the media – an introduction*. Arnold.

O'Sullivan, T. and Jewkes, Y. (1997): *The media studies reader*. Arnold.

Root, J. (1984): *Open the box*. Comedia.

Schlesinger, P. (1987): *Putting reality together – BBC news*. Methuen.

Stevenson, N. (1995): *Understanding media cultures*. Sage.

Strinati, D. (1995): *An introduction to theories of popular culture*. Routledge.

Tunstall, J. (1993): *Television producers*. Routledge.

Wheen, F. (1985): *Television – a history*. Guild Publishing.

Williams, G. (1994): *Britain's media – how they are related*. Campaign for Press and Broadcasting Freedom (CPBF).

Index